WRITTEN OFF

Written Off tells the story of how mental health stigma comes to have a profound impact on the lives of people diagnosed with mental illnesses. It reviews theory, research, and history – illustrated with a multitude of personal stories – in four major areas. These areas are the prevalence and predictors of negative attitudes and behaviors toward mental illness; the impact of community attitudes and behaviors on the self-perceptions of people diagnosed with mental illnesses; the impact of self-perceptions on the community participation of people diagnosed with mental illness; and how to change self-perceptions through a variety of approaches.

PHILIP T. YANOS, Ph.D., is Professor of Psychology at John Jay College, City University of New York. He is Associate Editor for the journal *Stigma and Health*, and the interim Director of Clinical Training for the clinical psychology Ph.D. program at John Jay College. Yanos is the co-developer of "Narrative Enhancement and Cognitive Therapy," a group-based treatment that addresses the effects of self-stigma among people with mental illnesses. This treatment approach has been translated into five languages. He is the author of more than ninety articles and book chapters, and is the principal investigator on two recent large, federally funded projects.

WRITTEN OFF

Mental Health Stigma and the Loss of Human Potential

PHILIP T. YANOS

City University of New York

CAMBRIDGE
UNIVERSITY PRESS

CAMBRIDGE
UNIVERSITY PRESS

University Printing House, Cambridge CB2 8BS, United Kingdom

One Liberty Plaza, 20th Floor, New York, NY 10006, USA

477 Williamstown Road, Port Melbourne, VIC 3207, Australia

314–321, 3rd Floor, Plot 3, Splendor Forum, Jasola District Centre, New Delhi – 110025, India

79 Anson Road, #06–04/06, Singapore 079906

Cambridge University Press is part of the University of Cambridge.

It furthers the University's mission by disseminating knowledge in the pursuit of education, learning, and research at the highest international levels of excellence.

www.cambridge.org
Information on this title: www.cambridge.org/9781107196957
DOI: 10.1017/9781108165006

© Cambridge University Press 2018

First published 2018

Printed in the United States of America by Sheridan Books, Inc.

A catalogue record for this publication is available from the British Library.

Library of Congress Cataloging-in-Publication Data
NAMES: Yanos, Philip T., 1968- author.
TITLE: Written off : mental health stigma and the loss of human potential / Philip T. Yanos.
DESCRIPTION: New York, NY : Cambridge University Press, 2018. | Includes bibliographical references and index.
IDENTIFIERS: LCCN 2017027455 | ISBN 9781107196957 (Hardback : alk. paper)
SUBJECTS: | MESH: Social Stigma | Mental Disorders–psychology | Stereotyping | Mentally Ill Persons–psychology | Case Reports
CLASSIFICATION: LCC RC455 | NLM HM 1106 | DDC 616.89–dc23 LC record available at https://lccn.loc.gov/2017027455

ISBN 978-1-107-19695-7 Hardback

For my father, and my children

Contents

Figures

Tables

Foreword

I was introduced to Philip Yanos by his dissertation director, Lou Primavera, Ph.D. Lou was one of the professionals in New York State who believed in and supported the early recovery movement. Lou said Philip was very perceptive. He asked me to help Philip with his dissertation. I agreed.

In 1997, Phil and I drove from Albany South to Poughkeepsie where the drop-in center he wanted to study was located. It was one I had helped start. I was CEO of the Mental Health Empowerment Project. We started about 600 mutual support groups for people with serious diagnoses from the public mental health system. Out of those groups about 60 small consumer-operated services emerged. This whole effort took about 12 years. About eight years into the effort Philip showed up wanting to do a study. I realized the importance of research if the self-help movement was to be established and maintained. I had been doing some research myself to this end.

Phil told me he experienced anxiety. I suffered from panic attacks and generalized anxiety myself. We formed a connection around our having been labeled. We both knew stigma from the inside. We had "spoiled identities." Spoiled in the eyes of others but not our own. Hence our resilience. Erving Goffman had used the terminology of "spoiled identity" in his seminal work on stigma.

In New York several years before, the MHEP had hosted about 11 Stigma Forums all over the state. These forums were open to labeled people and those related to them. We reached an important conclusion in those forums. The most stigmatizing group of people were mental health professionals. In this regard Lou was an important figure in establishing recovery as a reality. That we can and do recover counters one of the main stereotypes of mental health clients, that we are sick without hope forever. Lou agreed with us at meetings in Albany and he had a grad student (Philip) he was supporting to do research which would help build a scientific basis for recovery.

During the Stigma Forums an important issue arose. Many of the long-time advocates such as George Ebert and Laura Ziegler made the point that "stigma" was a special word reserved for those with mental health labels. Other groups like Blacks or women would find similar realities described as prejudice, stereotyping, and discrimination. If you are labeled with a mental label, the word "stigma" is used instead. At MHEP we were aware of this critique before we did the forums. We decided to use the term because it was an established word in mental health systems. If we did not use the term "stigma," would anyone know what we were talking about? This book faces the same dilemma in naming. There are many studies of various sorts on stigma but not on stereotyping, prejudice, and discrimination. It is a difficult practical matter.

We decided to do a follow-up to the Stigma Forums. We focused on the finding of stigma among professionals and decided to do Recovery Dialogues and Hope Dialogues. They were similar. The focus question for the Recovery Dialogues was: What blocks recovery for people with a mental health diagnosis? The follow-up question was: What can be done to support recovery? The focus question for the Hope Dialogues was: What blocks hope for people with mental health diagnoses? The follow-up question was: What supports hope for people with a mental health diagnosis?

The dialogues brought together professionals and psychiatric survivors and consumers around these questions. The dialogues created an atmosphere that allowed state mental health funds to flow to consumer and psychiatric survivor projects. This was a step forward for those suffering from stigma. Professionals saw, many for the first time, that psychiatrically labeled people could be very articulate about their plights. Both sides had a heightened sense of hope for psychiatrically labeled people. The dialogues helped create a social atmosphere in the mental health community that allowed psychiatrically labeled people to receive funding for delivering support services and even more. The psychiatrically labeled community in New York received funding eventually for running housing, advocacy, education, and job services. These were serious steps forward against the denigrating forces of stigma.

There is a long-standing argument among psychiatrically labeled people about what we should be called. Some, emphasizing our segregation, call themselves psychiatric survivors. Others, wishing to point out marketplace choice, choose the word "consumer." Psychiatric survivors often point out that they feel consumed but do not feel they have marketplace choice, so "consumer" is not a good word to use. In New York the fighting over these labels was fast and furious. At MHEP we came up with an attempt to be neutral and began using the term "mental health recipient." Many times, meetings were held captive to arguments about consumer versus survivor. The term "recipient" allowed the meetings to proceed without long arguments about what we should call ourselves. Both terms, in their own ways, revolve around stigma. Survivors are arguing the stigma is so strong that we have no choice. Consumers are holding out an ideal to strive for. Market choice. Both terms attempt to address stigma in different ways.

On the research front, Phil did an important study at the drop-in center. He showed that peer support improved functioning and socializing. This study became an important part of the evidence used by SAMHSA to recognize consumer-operated services as an evidence-based practice. The SAMHSA website has a toolkit on peer-run services as an evidence-based practice. This body of evidence, of which Phil's study is an important part, has strong anti-stigma effects. It counters well the notions that mental health clients are helpless and hopeless. Although I moved to Colorado when Phil was doing his dissertation in 1997, I have continued to stay in touch and collaborated on a number of projects and papers. I've been pleased to see him grow and develop as a researcher and move the field forward.

Phil's book is true to my experience and what we learned in New York. It is an important statement of evidence-based theory on stigma. He has brought order to an amazingly diverse body of studies. He lays out in a clear logical way the many studies that have been done, forming from them an excellent theoretical statement. Phil grounds each chapter in an experiential example and the relevant evidence to the point the chapter is making. Although some in the field of mental health have embraced the concept of recovery since the late 1990s, this book makes it clear why stigma is still a major issue that the field needs to contend with, and points the way toward some possible solutions. It will serve as a basis for a continued dialogue between professionals and those people who are psychiatrically labeled.

Edward L. Knight, Ph.D.

Acknowledgments

There are many people who have made it possible for me to write this book. First, I must thank my mother and father. You gave me education, unconditional love, support, encouragement, examples of hard work and duty, and moral grounding. Thank you for everything that you have given me. I would not be able to do the work that I do without it.

There are many good friends, including my brother Alexander, who encouraged me to believe in myself when I was growing up and helped give me the confidence to believe that I could do something like write a book. I am grateful to all of you for your support. The late Kip Haris was an especially important friend, and I probably would not be doing this without the encouragement that he showed me many years ago. Kip was a special person, and having him as a friend and bandmate opened up new worlds for me. Thank you always for being my friend, Kip. There is hardly a day that I don't think about you in some way.

Professionally, my journey would not have been possible without the support and encouragement of several key individuals. Louis Primavera introduced me to the concept of recovery and supported me in conducting my dissertation on a topic that was well outside of the mainstream of what was done at my Ph.D. program. Ed Knight taught me about the complex nature of recovery and empowerment many years ago, and continues to inspire me. Bruce Link, whose work has been so important to the field, showed interest in my work and helped give me my "big break." I would probably not have been able to pursue a research career without it. David Mechanic, Alan Horwitz, and Jamie Walkup gave me excellent guidance and mentoring during my postdoctoral fellowship. Kim Mueser and Kim Hopper have been key role models in my professional journey.

I also thank all of the clients who have given me the privilege of working with them as a therapist over the years. Thank you for teaching me about bravery and resourcefulness in the face of adversity. I hope that this book helps in the fight against stigma.

Research collaborations, with peers and doctoral students, have also been essential to the work described in this book. David Roe and Paul Lysaker have been my most important research partners and helped me move into new areas of research. Other key collaborators have been Sam Tsemberis, Barbara Felton, Mary Jane Alexander, Ana Stefancic, Christina Pratt, Josh Koerner, Isaac Brown, Weili Lu, and Steven Silverstein. Thank you all. My collaboration with doctoral students in clinical psychology at John Jay College, including Stephen Smith, Michelle West, Sarah Kopelovich, Lauren Gonzales, Ginny Chan, Beth Vayshenker, Joseph DeLuca, and Lauren O'Connor, has also been very important to my career development. Much of the work described here was made possible by their initiative and dedication, and I hope that I have credited it adequately. I thank all of you for working with me, and I especially thank Joe and Beth for reading early drafts of chapters and providing me with helpful feedback on them.

Within John Jay College, I am grateful to the department chair who hired me, Maureen O'Connor, as well as my current department chair, Angela Crossman, for their support and validation of my work. My colleague Kevin Nadal also gave me helpful feedback during the early part of the book proposal process. I am also grateful for funding support provided by the Office for the Advancement of Research at John Jay College. The National Institute of Mental Health has also supported much of the research discussed in this book and I am grateful for their support. I also thank Matt Bennett at Cambridge University Press for believing in this project and for encouraging me to "go big" in my vision for the book. The colleagues who anonymously reviewed the proposal as well as the first draft of the book also provided very helpful feedback.

I thank my father-in-law, Bill, and my mother-in-law, Sandy, whose support and encouragement have also been extremely helpful.

Last, I must thank Victoria "Tory" Frye (my wife and partner for more than 20 years) and my children. Tory, an accomplished researcher, has provided unwavering support to me throughout this journey, going back to before graduate school. You're always there for me, and I love you. Our children, Theo and Lexy, are my ultimate inspiration. We talk about stigma and prejudice often, and I hope that this book can contribute to making the world a better place for them.

CHAPTER I

Why Stigma Matters

In the late 1970s and early 1980s, Margot Kidder was one of the world's most popular actresses, having played the female lead in the box office smash *Superman*, as well as a series of other popular and critically acclaimed films. In April 1996, however, Kidder's life and career were in a totally different place, as she wandered and slept in the streets of downtown Los Angeles in terror, believing that her ex-husband was trying to kill her. Though Kidder had the financial means to sleep elsewhere, she was led to the street through a series of apparently irrational actions. *People* magazine reported:

> In the early hours of April 21, she tried to take a taxi but didn't have enough money for the trip. She tried to use her ATM card outside the airport but thought the cash machine was about to explode. "I took off running," Kidder recalls. "I slept in yards and on porches in a state of fear."[1]

After four days of wandering and being out of touch with her family, Kidder eventually sought help from a stranger, who contacted the police. After a brief hospitalization, she was reunited with her family and her life began to return to normal. Since this widely publicized incident, Kidder has spoken about having bipolar disorder, which is consistent with the characterization of her behavior as being the result of a manic episode with psychotic features.

By 2012, Kidder was still in the public eye and had continued to work as an actor (though with less frequency than before); however, she stated that in many ways the general public had not been able to get past the 1996 incident. Railing against the view that people often have about the words "mental illness" and the perception that it is a permanent and irrevocable condition, she stated: "[I]f I were a cancer patient, I would today be considered cured – I haven't had an episode in 14 years."[2]

While Margot Kidder's apparent psychotic episode was reported in the news, it occurred prior to the age of social media, which allows celebrities to directly communicate with their fans and others. Actress Amanda Bynes, who rose to celebrity as the teenaged star of shows on the TV channel *Nickelodeon*, came into contact with the implications of this type of communication in 2014, when she used her Twitter account (which reached more than 3 million followers) to accuse her father of sexual abuse, before retracting the statement with the post: "My dad never did any of those things/ The microchip in my brain made me say those things but he's the one that ordered them to microchip me."[3] This statement and a series of odd public incidents were widely reported. Public comments to internet-based articles indicated that while some members of the general public were concerned, others were delighted. Examples of comments to one article included: "She's cute for a nutjob," and "another vapid, clueless, selfish, insane celebrity demonstrating what happens when she doesn't take her medications."[4] After an involuntary hospitalization, Bynes withdrew from the public eye, although she subsequently announced, via Twitter, that she had bipolar disorder and was receiving treatment for it. At the time of this writing, she is enrolled as a student at the University of Southern California, and is described by Wikipedia as a "former actress."[5] It remains to be seen what direction her young life will take, and the impact that her apparent public demonstration of the symptoms of mental illness will have on its direction.

Although the two presented examples concern famous actors, most people who experience episodes of what is usually called mental illness live far from the world of Hollywood celebrity. Jose (actual name and other identifying information have been changed) is a thoughtful man in his early thirties with a college degree. He is well read and a talented writer of prose and poetry who has also experienced a number of episodes where he acted bizarrely (e.g., walking the streets of New York City at night singing loudly) and reported having visions he interpreted as coming from God. These episodes invariably led to hospitalization, and he has been diagnosed with schizoaffective disorder. Not having experienced any such symptoms for more than a year, Jose desperately wants to work, engage in a spiritual community, and have a romantic relationship, but is terrified of entering social situations where he might be asked questions about his life that could lead others to find out about his psychiatric history. As a result, he avoids entering new social situations (including going to religious services) that could provide him with the opportunity to meet new people. Although he regularly looks for work, he often does not apply for jobs that look interesting or are in his area of expertise because he is overcome by thoughts that he is not capable of doing more than a service-sector job as a result of his history of mental illness. He also struggles with the belief that he is a failure and intermittently has thoughts of suicide.

From Labeling Behavior to Labeling People

What do the examples in the preceding section have in common? Although they all concern situations in which individuals with other talents and attributes have engaged in behavior that was explained as being the result of a mental illness, they also concern the long-standing implications of others' judgments of these behavioral instances. If we pay close attention, a series of processes are occurring. First, the instance of unusual behavior leads to labeling (e.g., Amanda Bynes goes from being a starlet to a "nutjob" or "insane"). The label, which is linked to certain assumptions, then sticks and affects people's impressions of the individuals' behavior, even when they are not demonstrating any signs of unusual behavior (e.g., Margot Kidder's experiencing that she was still thought of as mentally ill when she had not had an episode in more than 14 years). Furthermore, we see the individuals' social behavior and self-image being affected by their awareness of others' labeling (e.g., Jose's belief that he is a failure and his related avoidance of social situations that he is interested and capable of engaging in).

All of these processes are tied to an idea that is most often called *stigma*. Although other terms capture aspects of what is going on (stereotyping, discrimination, social rejection, shame, etc.), stigma has served as a useful umbrella term for the overall process. The word has origins in ancient Greek (referring to the practice of branding or otherwise mutilating an individual to show that he or she is a member of a morally discredited group), but modern usage[a, 6] of the term is usually linked to sociologist Erving Goffman's 1963 book *Stigma: Notes on the Management of a Spoiled Identity*.[7] In this influential work, Goffman described how stigma impacts people from a number of social categories, but paid repeated attention to the experience of people who have been diagnosed with mental illness, whom he referred to as "ex-mental patients." Goffman specifically discussed how stigma impacts ex-mental patients by making them not just "discredited,"

---

[a] The Oxford English Dictionary offers the following as the second definition of stigma: *Figurative*. "A mark of disgrace or infamy; a sign of severe censure or condemnation, regarded as impressed on a person or thing; a 'brand'." The OED notes that the first recorded use of the word in this figurative connotation was in 1620. Bruce Link and Heather Stuart have also documented that there was "pre-Goffman" use of the term stigma in relation to mental illness in the 1950s.

but "discreditable" in their social interactions. Discredited interactions are ones where others are aware of the person's psychiatric history and are therefore biased by this awareness (we may think of overt discrimination or social rejection as instances of this). However, discreditable interactions can be even more pernicious. In this case, the ex-mental patient interacts with others who have no knowledge of his or her history (and therefore do not prejudge him or her) but lives in fear of them finding out, and therefore "discrediting" whatever positive impressions he or she is able to make. As Goffman stated: "By intention or in effect the ex-mental patient conceals information about his real social identity, receiving and accepting treatment [from others] based on false suppositions concerning himself."[7]

A key part of the stigma process, which was implied by Goffman but that is not always made clear, is that members of society go from labeling a specific instance of behavior (e.g., acting oddly = psychotic episode) to labeling a *person* (person who has ever acted oddly = "a mentally ill person"). That label is then attached to a series of assumptions, or "negative stereotypes," about what a person with that label is like and will continue to be like. As we'll see, the most commonly endorsed negative stereotypes about mental illness include beliefs that the person is dangerous, unpredictable, incompetent, and unable to function in society.[8] As Goffman indicated, this means that future actions that the individual takes, regardless of how reasonable they are, can be viewed through the lens of this label, and therefore discredited, or "written off."[b] Thus, there is a movement from discrediting *actions* performed by people to discrediting the *people* themselves. The experience of being aware that one has been discredited then has a profound impact on the person's social behavior and self-image.

In this book, I will explain in detail what we know about this process from more than five decades of research. First, however, I will clarify what types of psychiatric experiences are most likely to result in stigma and provide some general information about these experiences.

What Are We Talking about When We Say "Mental Illness"?

Not all constellations of behavior and internal experiences that can be categorized as psychiatric disorders are necessarily linked to significant stigma. The diagnostic manual of the American Psychiatric Association (the current edition is called the *DSM-5*) catalogues a number of constellations of experiences that are considered "mental disorders," including

---

[b] Merriam-Webster defines to "write off" as "to regard or concede to be lost."

relatively minor conditions such as specific phobias (e.g., fears of snakes or spiders) and short-lived mood disturbances called adjustment disorders. Based on the best estimates from population surveys in the United States, roughly 25% of the US population meets criteria for a DSM disorder at any given time, while roughly 45–50% of the population experiences a disorder at some point in life.[9] The most common mental disorders in the United States include specific phobia, social anxiety disorder, and alcohol use disorder. The reader may intuitively recognize that, given how common mental disorders are, it is not plausible for all constellations of experiences meeting technical criteria for "mental illness" to be subject to equal amounts of stigma. In fact, this is supported by research findings, which indicate that it is a subset of mental disorders, often called "severe mental illnesses," which are most subject to stigma.[10] "Severe mental illnesses" are usually defined as consisting of mental disorders that have a substantial impact on functioning (employment, relationships, etc.) and/or lead to hospitalization.[11] Research is fairly consistent in finding that roughly 5–7% of the US population meet criteria for a severe mental illness. Although not a diagnostic category, the concept of severe mental illness has been found to be useful among policymakers in determining who to prioritize for funding and high intensity services.

What characteristics do the disorders that can be classified as "severe" have? Although there are no definitive diagnostic criteria, a frequent element is the experience of "psychotic" symptoms that often lead to psychiatric hospitalization. Psychotic symptoms include experiences such as delusions, hallucinations, and disorganized (or illogical) thinking, and involve, as a common theme, a disruption in one's perception of reality. A person who is experiencing psychotic symptoms may not be sure about what is and is not real, and, like Margot Kidder in the prior example, may act in ways that do not make sense to others. In another age, these were the experiences that were most likely to lead to the characterization that one was "mad" or "insane." Although psychotic symptoms can occur in a number of disorders, they are most often associated with two conditions: schizophrenia (and other disorders in its "spectrum" such as schizoaffective disorder), which is defined by the presence of psychotic symptoms, and bipolar 1 disorder, which is commonly characterized by psychotic symptoms during "manic" episodes. Both of these disorders are relatively rare, occurring in roughly 1–2% of the population each.[12]

It is important to note that, while both schizophrenia and bipolar 1 disorder are "persistent" disorders (meaning that they tend to be a recurring part of one's life for a long time after symptoms are first experienced), it is also clear that they are typically "episodic" (meaning that intense symptoms come and go in waves that vary in length, from just a few days to many months).[13] It has been estimated that people with severe mental illnesses typically spend only 5% of their lives in states of "acute" distress (where intense symptoms are being experienced), meaning that the vast majority of the time they are not likely to be demonstrating overt symptoms.[14] It is also important to note that, while these disorders, by definition, have a substantial impact on functioning (including work and social relationships), evidence supports that, when followed-up 20 or more years after the initial experience of symptoms, roughly one-half to two-thirds of them show minimal impairment in their life functioning.[15] Thus, people tend to improve in their life functioning over time, although the process of improvement sometimes takes decades.

Psychotic Symptoms: Part of the Human Experience?

As indicated above, diagnosable disorders that feature psychotic symptoms are rare, and there is an inherent assumption that they lie outside of the everyday range of human experience. However, although disorders that require that one experience psychotic symptoms that interfere with functioning are rare, psychotic experiences themselves are considerably less so. Community surveys have investigated the prevalence of psychotic experiences (e.g., transitory experiences of auditory hallucinations or beliefs that one is being persecuted) in the general population around the world and have consistently found that close to 10% of the general population reports having had psychotic experiences, with some large studies reporting estimates as high as roughly 20%.[16] Clearly, the majority of these individuals did not develop a psychotic disorder (meaning that the experiences were not frequent enough and/or never interfered with functioning), although it is plausible to think that they might be at a higher "risk" for developing such a disorder under the right conditions. However, in most cases the experiences lead to nothing further.[c, 17] An example of the experience of psychotic symptoms not interfering with functioning is provided by Sigmund Freud, the "father" of psychoanalysis and modern psychotherapy, who revealed that he had hallucinatory experiences as a young man:

---

[c] It should be noted that longitudinal research with people with "subclinical psychotic experiences" has found that people who continuously have these experiences at a high level, over the course of several years, are at greater risk of adverse outcomes, such as job loss, than people who experience them at a lower level or less continuously.

During the days when I was living alone in a foreign city – I was a young man at the time – I *quite often* [emphasis added] heard my name suddenly called by an unmistakable and beloved voice; I then noted down the exact moment of the hallucination and made anxious enquiries of those at home about what had happened at that time. Nothing had happened.[18]

Mahatma Gandhi, who discussed hearing the "voice of God" at key instances in his life, provides another example of hallucinations not interfering with functioning. Describing the "voice," he stated:

Could I give any further evidence that it was truly the Voice that I heard and that it was not an echo of my own heated imagination? I have no further evidence to convince the skeptic. He is free to say that it was all self-delusion or hallucination. It may well have been so. I can offer no proof to the contrary. But I can say this, that not the unanimous verdict of the whole world against me could shake me from the belief that what I heard was the true Voice of God.[19]

In addition to the extent to which psychotic experiences are relatively common, it has also been asserted that some of the cognitive processes involved in developing delusions reflect exaggerations of basic human cognitive processes. In his book *The Storytelling Animal*, writer Jonathan Gottschall compellingly argues that the cognitive process involved in developing delusions is related to the fundamental, and usually healthy, human tendency to "make a coherent story" out of the chaos of information that the universe provides us with. This has been confirmed in experimental studies where people are presented with a list of unrelated events and are found to seek to connect them with a narrative thread that has its own internal logic. The human mind abhors coincidences. Sometimes, however, this leads people to want to make a coherent story out of a confusing situation, even when the resulting tale has no basis in fact. As an example, Gottschall points to the popularity of conspiracy theories that lack any evidence, but that help people make sense of confusing or distressing events since they explain them in such a tidy manner. Notably, poll research found that at one time roughly a third of the US population endorsed the view that the US government was involved in a conspiracy that caused the September 11, 2001 attacks.[20] Readers will likely also be familiar with other, more recent, examples of the widespread belief in conspiracy theories propagated by "fake news" internet sources.

A related line of thought has concerned the tendency for many people to "jump to conclusions," or draw hasty conclusions from incomplete information. A "jumping to conclusions" tendency has been found to be very common among people who develop delusions (occurring in about 50% of such individuals), but to also be common in the general population (occurring in about 20% of nonclinical samples).[21] Research has found that individuals who show the "jumping to conclusions" bias are more likely to show evidence of subclinical paranoid ideation (i.e., general suspiciousness) and have odd perceptual experiences, despite not meeting the criteria for any psychotic disorder.

Given this evidence, it has been hypothesized that anyone, under the right circumstances (especially if we include the use of mind-altering substances), might have the capacity to develop psychotic symptoms, though some people certainly seem to have a greater propensity to develop them than others. This hypothesis is impossible to ethically test, but there is no reason to dismiss it out of hand, given evidence that psychotic experiences are related to imbalances in neurotransmitters that all humans possess. The theory that "anyone can experience psychosis" became real to my family when my father, a psychiatrist who had spent much of his career treating psychotic symptoms, began to experience visual hallucinations late in life after experiencing a cerebral stroke.

One might think that, given the degree to which psychotic experiences and other forms of irrationality are a potentially common part of the human experience, people would react to them with empathy rather than judgment or aversion. This certainly makes superficial sense, but, as is the case with other stigmatized attributes in human society, things do not always work that way. For example, given evidence that attraction to members of the same sex is to some degree normative in human society,[22] one might think that homosexuality would not be stigmatized, but this has been far from the truth for much of human history. Or, consider how being significantly overweight is stigmatized even though concern about weight and struggles with weight-control are so common.

Does Stigma Really Make a Difference?

Even if they acknowledge that mental health stigma exists (which I will demonstrate in the next chapter), many readers will certainly question whether it really makes that much of a difference in the lives of people who have been diagnosed with a severe mental illness, given that mental illness symptoms have a great impact themselves. It was not stigma, they may reason, that led Margot Kidder to the streets of Los Angeles, but the symptoms of an untreated mental disorder. This is a valid consideration, and, in large part, it will be the task of this book to persuade readers that

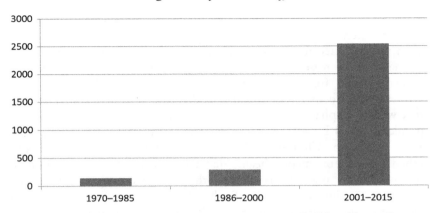

Figure 1   Articles in peer-reviewed journals on "mental illness" and "stigma" or "labeling," by 15-year period

the balance of the evidence indicates that stigma has a measurable impact on the lives of people diagnosed with severe mental illness *above and beyond* the direct impact of symptoms themselves. However, this does not mean that the impact of stigma cannot be overstated.

In the 1960s, this occurred when some researchers had become adherents of "labeling theory," which argued that most or all of the behavior that is associated with what is called mental illness is the result of the person having been so labeled.[23] The actual behavior that led to the label being applied was largely beside the point, according to this view. Although, as we'll see, some aspects of labeling theory *are* supported by research evidence, the more extreme version of this theory did not hold up to empirical tests. As a result, there was a backlash against any assertions that stigma mattered in the 1970s and early 1980s. In 1982, Walter Gove declared labeling theory dead and stated "in the vast majority of cases the stigma [of mental illness] appears to be transitory and does not appear to pose a severe problem."[23] Guido Crocetti and colleagues went further and argued that, in addition to there being very little evidence for stigmatizing attitudes or behavior in the general public, it was, rather, "the *belief* [emphasis added] that stigma is attached to mental hospitalization" that was "potentially harmful and dangerous," because it led people to avoid treatment out of fear of becoming stigmatized.[24]

These views were influential, and scientific interest in stigma was minimal between 1970 and 1985 (see Figure 1). This changed with the publication of articles by researcher Bruce Link in the late 1980s, which revived interest in the topic (we will learn more about the implications of his research in Chapter 5).

In the most recent period, as Figure 1 makes clear, there has been a dramatically increased interest in stigma. This has been reflected in official interest from institutions affiliated with the US government. However, the focus is not usually on the aspects of the stigma process that will be emphasized in this book. Rather, the typical focus is on the problems posed by stigma as a barrier to seeking help. For example, in 1999, during the Clinton administration, the US Surgeon General published a report on mental health that paid a great deal of attention to stigma, but its main focus was on the impact of stigma on seeking treatment.[25] Similarly, in the Bush administration's 2003 *President's New Freedom Commission on Mental Health* report, stigma was prominently discussed, but with an emphasis on how it interferes with seeking treatment (one of the report's main recommendations was "advance and implement a national campaign to reduce the stigma of seeking care").[26] President Obama was no different, convening a National Conference on Mental Health in 2013, and issuing the following statement on the importance of stigma:

> We've got to get rid of that embarrassment; we've got to get rid of that stigma. Too many Americans who struggle with mental health illnesses are still suffering in silence rather than seeking help, and we need to see it that men and women who would never hesitate to go see a doctor if they had a broken arm or came down with the flu, that they have that same attitude when it comes to their mental health.[27]

People avoid seeking treatment because of concern about stigma, the logic goes; if stigma were reduced, they would seek treatment. A corollary of this view is the contention that, if people can only seek treatment, symptoms will decrease and stigma will go away.[28]

This emphasis is well-intentioned, but although the association between stigma and help-seeking is certainly important, it is not, I will demonstrate, the main reason why stigma is a major issue. Rather, the main reason why stigma is important is because it diminishes people's participation in community life, and inhibits them from achieving their full potential as people. As a result, *all* of society suffers from the loss of these individuals' potential contributions to their communities. Stigma, I will show, would persist even if everyone with a diagnosable mental disorder received treatment, and, in some respects, treatment can make stigma worse if it is not implemented properly.

Mental Health Stigma: A Social Justice Issue

Therefore, instead of viewing mental health stigma as a help-seeking issue, we should view it as a *social justice* issue. As this book will demonstrate, mental health stigma is linked to substantially diminished opportunities for full community participation among people diagnosed with severe mental illnesses. As Patrick Corrigan and others have argued,[29] viewing stigma from a social justice perspective requires that we move away from just focusing on eradicating symptoms, and instead focus on the negative social reaction to them. In this manner, the effort to overcome the effects of stigma can be linked to other social movements that have sought (with some success) to reduce the social marginalization of people from a number of backgrounds, such as lesbian, gay, bisexual, and transgender persons, physically disabled persons, and members of derogated racial and ethnic groups.

Taking a step further, when we think of the importance of mental health stigma, it is helpful to break out of the mindset that we are thinking about something that relates to a small but important subgroup in human society, and replace it with the view that we are thinking about something that relates to a small but important part of *ourselves as humans.* This makes sense when we adopt the mindset that psychotic and related experiences associated with mental illness can happen to anyone, meaning that stigma is a potential problem for all of members of society. In fact, although most people develop them as young adults, a substantial proportion (roughly 20% according to most estimates) of persons who develop schizophrenia and bipolar disorder develop these disorders *after age 40.*[30] Thus, though most choose not to acknowledge it, even if one has no mental illness at present, few can be certain of whether or not they will have a severe mental illness sometime *in the future.* As Judi Chamberlain stated in her 1978 classic *On Our Own,* because of the stigma attached to the label of mental illness, "we are all rendered a little less human." Going further, she stated: "This is a problem not just for patients and ex-patients but for everyone, because anyone can become a mental patient."[31]

In *A Theory of Justice,* political philosopher John Rawls argued that, in order to determine what is just, we should do so from the perspective of the "Original Position," in which none of us knows in advance which position we will occupy in society.[32] None of us would choose to live in a society in which being born a woman, African-American, or gay leads to systematic social exclusion or diminished opportunity, if we knew that it was possible that we might inhabit one of those categories ourselves.

Figure 2   A newspaper headline in New York City in 1999, following a random violent incident that was committed by a man subsequently found to have no evidence of mental illness. Photo by NY Daily News Archive via Getty Image.

This perspective makes it clear that inequities based on inherited statuses such as gender, race, and sexual orientation would be universally agreed-upon to be unjust if all were able to view them from the Original Position. If we extend this perspective to the experience of a severe mental illness (which most would agree is a status that is largely the result of forces beyond an individual's control), it becomes clear that stigma and its related effects on full community participation are a social justice issue. Theoretically, no one would choose to live in a society in which having a severe mental illness leads to de facto marginalization, if it was known that they might have a mental illness themselves.

This perspective rings especially true if we are able to put ourselves in the position of people who have been diagnosed with mental illnesses and imagine how we might feel when confronted with a newspaper headline like the one shown above (see Figure 2). Can we imagine an equivalent derogatory term for another group appearing in such a manner on the front page of a major US newspaper, with no measurable outcry as a result? As noted psychologist (who has also spoken about her experience with bipolar disorder) Kay Jamison has stated: "Newspapers and television stations can print and broadcast statements about those with mental illness that would simply not be tolerated if they were said about any other minority group."[33] Indeed, we are all rendered less human when these types of headlines not only appear but are *tolerated*. And this is indicative of only the loudest and most public expressions of stigma; there are many more person-to-person expressions of stigma that do not make it to the "headline" level but that can be even more hurtful to those that hear them, as we will learn in subsequent chapters.

The sometimes frightening experiences that we call mental illness are not just a social construction – they are very real. However, stigma makes a difficult and challenging part of the human experience much worse, as we move from discrediting actions to discrediting people, and as the discrediting views of others come to be internalized by those who have been diagnosed with a mental illness. In this book, we will learn how this occurs, and will also begin to look toward ways to imagine a future where experiencing mental illness no longer leads to this process.

References

1 Reed, J. D. (1996). Starting over. *People, 46*. Accessed online August 16, 2017: www.people.com/people/archive/article/0,,20142326,00.html.

2 Accessed online November 18, 2015: www.canada.com/story.html?id= 2113d53b-8e22-4c5e-9686-936fd85f5b44.

3 McNiece, M. (2014). Amanda Bynes checks into California treatment center. *People*. Accessed online August 16, 2017: http://people.com/celebrity/amanda-bynes-and-her-heartbreaking-family-feud/.

4 The *New York Daily News* Comments section. Accessed online August 16, 32017: www.nydailynews.com/entertainment/gossip/chippy-amanda-bynes-sue-celeb-mags-lies-article-1.1968390.

5 Accessed online November 18, 2015: https://en.wikipedia.org/wiki/Amanda_ Bynes.

6 Link, B. G., & Stuart, H. (2017). On revisiting some of the origins of the stigma concept as it applies to mental illness. In W. Gaebel, W. Rossler, & N. Sartorius (Eds.), *The stigma of mental illness – end of the story?* (pp. 3–28). Basel: Springer International.

7 Goffman, E. (1963). *Stigma: Notes on the management of a spoiled identity*. New York: Prentice Hall.

8 Corrigan, P. W., & Penn, D. L. (2015). Lessons from social psychology on discrediting psychiatric stigma. *Stigma and Health, 1*, 2–17.

9 Kessler et al. (2005a). Lifetime prevalence and age of onset distributions of DSM-IV disorders in the National Comorbidity Survey Replication. *Archives of General Psychiatry, 62*, 593–602; Kessler et al. (2005b). Prevalence, severity

and comorbidity of 12-month DSM-IV disorders in the National Comorbidity Survey Replication. *Archives of General Psychiatry, 62,* 617–627.

10 Wood, L. et al. (2014). Public perceptions of stigma towards people with schizophrenia, depression, and anxiety. *Psychiatry Research, 220,* 604–608.

11 Ruggeri, M., Leese, M., Thornicroft, G., Bisoffi, G., & Tansella, M. (2000). Definition and prevalence of severe and persistent mental illness. *British Journal of Psychiatry, 177,* 149–155; Kessler et al. (1998). A methodology for estimating the 12-month prevalence of serious mental illness. In R. W. Manderscheid and M. J. Henderson (Eds.), *Mental Health, United States, 1998* (pp. 99–109). Rockville, MD: US Department of Health and Human Services. .

12 Kessler et al. (2005b). Prevalence, severity and comorbidity of 12-month DSM-IV disorders in the National Comorbidity Survey Replication. *Archives of General Psychiatry, 62,* 617–627; Kessler et al. (2005c). The prevalence and correlates of nonaffective psychosis in the National Comorbidity Survey Replication (NCS-R). *Biological Psychiatry, 58,* 668–676.

13 Judd, L. I. et al. (2005). Psychosocial disability in the course of Bipolar I and II Disorders. *Archives of General Psychiatry, 62,* 1322–1330; Jobe, T. H., & Harrow, M. (2010). Schizophrenia course, long-term outcome, recovery, and prognosis. *Current Directions in Psychological Science, 19,* 220–225.

14 Davidson, L., Rakfeldt, J., & Strauss, J. (2010). *The roots of the recovery movement in psychiatry: Lessons learned.* Chichester, West Sussex, UK: Wiley-Blackwell.

15 Calabrese, J. D., & Corrigan, P. W. (2005). Beyond dementia praecox: Findings from long-term follow-up studies of schizophrenia. In R. O. Ralph and P. W. Corrigan (Eds.), *Recovery in mental illness: Broadening our understanding of wellness* (pp. 63–81). Washington, DC: American Psychological Association.

16 Van Os, J., Linscott, R. J., Myin-Germeys, I., Delespual, P., & Krabbendam, M. (2009). A systematic review and meta-analysis of the psychosis continuum: Evidence for a psychosis proneness–persistence–impairment model of psychotic disorder. *Psychological Medicine, 39,* 179–195.

17 Rossler, W., Riecher-Rossler, A., Angst, J., Murray, R., Gamma, A., Eich, D., Van Os, J., & Gross, V. A. (2007). Psychotic experiences in the general population: A twenty-year prospective community study. *Schizophrenia Research, 92,* 1–14.

18 Quoted in: Sacks, O. (2012). *Hallucinations.* New York: Alfred Knopf.

19 Quoted on the Mahatma Gandhi Research Foundation website. Accessed online August 16, 2017: www.mkgandhi.org/momgandhi/chap05.htm.

20 Gottschall, J. (2013). *The storytelling animal: How stories make us human.* New York: Mariner Books.

21 Freeman, D., Pugh, K., & Garety, P. (2008). Jumping to conclusions and paranoid ideation in the general population. *Schizophrenia Research, 102,* 254–260; Freeman, D., & Freeman, J. (2008). *Paranoia: The 21st century fear.* New York: Oxford University Press.

22 Dickson, N., Paul, C., & Herbison, P. (2003). Same-sex attraction in a birth cohort: Prevalence and persistence in early adulthood. *Social Science & Medicine, 56,* 1607–1615.

23 Gove, W. R. (1982). The current status of the labelling theory of mental illness. In W. R. Gove (Ed). *Deviance and mental illness.* Beverly Hills, CA: Sage.

24 Crocetti, G. M., Spiro, H. R., & Siassi, I. (1972). *Contemporary attitudes toward mental illness.* Pittsburgh: University of Pittsburgh Press.

25 US Surgeon General's Office (1999). *Mental health: A Report of the Surgeon General.* Accessed online August 16, 2017: http://profiles.nlm.nih.gov/ps/retrieve/ResourceMetadata/NNBBHS.

26 President's New Freedom Commission on Mental Health. (2003). *Executive Summary.* Accessed online August 16, 2017: http://govinfo.library.unt.edu/mentalhealthcommission/reports/FinalReport/FullReport-1.htm.

27 Accessed online August 16, 2017: https://obamawhitehouse.archives.gov/blog/2013/06/03/national-conference-mental-health.

28 Lillienfield, S. O., Smith, S. F., & Watts, A. L. (2013). Issues in diagnosis: Conceptual issues and controversies. In W. E. Craighead, D. J. Miklowitz, & L. W. Craighead (Eds.), *Psychopathology* (2nd Edn.) (pp. 1–35). Hoboken, NJ: Wiley.

29 Corrigan, P. W. (2005). Mental illness stigma as social injustice: Yet another dream to be achieved. In P. Corrigan (Ed.) *On the stigma of mental illness* (pp. 315–320). Washington, DC: American Psychological Association.

30 Pearman, A., & Batra, A. (2012). Late-onset schizophrenia: A review for clinicians. *Clinical Gerontologist, 35,* 126–147

31 Chamberlain, J. (1978). *On our own: Patient-controlled alternatives to the mental health system.* New York: McGraw-Hill.

32 Rawls, J. (1972). *A Theory of Justice.* Cambridge, MA: Belknap.

33 Jamison, K. R. (2006). The many stigmas of mental illness. *Lancet, 367,* 533–534.

CHAPTER 2

Does Mental Health Stigma Really Exist?

"There is no problem with stigma- these are inferior persons."
–Unidentified psychiatrist speaking at a professional meeting in 2015.

"Scumbag, trash . . . this is what happens when you let people breed like rabbits or rats and do not enforce birth control rules."
-Research participant in 2015 giving impression of a person stated to have a mental illness who had allegedly committed a violent crime.

In the fall of 1939, Adolf Hitler, with the support of the German medical community, authorized a secret, and now largely forgotten, initiative called the "T-4" program, named after the Berlin address of the program's coordinating center (Tiergartenstrasse 4). The plan was to perform "euthanasia," or mercy killings, of persons that the Nazi party considered to be *Lebensunwertes Leben,* which translates as "life unworthy of life" (another commonly used term was *Unnütze Esser* or "useless eater.") These persons were residents of public and private hospitals, psychiatric institutions, and nursing homes who met certain criteria, including persons who had been diagnosed with schizophrenia, dementia or other psychiatric and neurological disorders that were considered incurable, people who had been committed on criminal grounds, and anyone who had been at the institution for more than five years. People identified by physicians were then moved to special centers, where they were killed using newly developed poison gas procedures, and their remains disposed of using mass cremation.[1] Although the T-4 program was not limited exclusively to people that we would now consider to have severe mental illnesses, it is clear that such individuals made up the bulk of those targeted. Estimates for the total number of persons killed under the T-4 program vary, and range from roughly 80,000 to 250,000.[2] It is estimated that roughly three-quarters of Germans with a diagnosis of schizophrenia were killed under the T-4 program.[3]

The T-4 program is historically significant because it predated by roughly two years the much larger Nazi effort to kill derogated ethnic groups, including Jews, Gypsies and others, and it is regarded by many to have been a "dress rehearsal" for this campaign (which we now know of as the Holocaust), since it used essentially the same methods of killing and cremating. In the context of mental health stigma, however, the T-4 program is very important because it can be seen as definitive evidence that negative stereotypes about severe mental illnesses can have powerful social effects when taken to their logical conclusion. The T-4 program was an extreme action, but it stemmed from many of the same negative stereotypes that were widely held at the time and that (to some extent) persist to this day (see quotes at the beginning of this chapter). In fact, as we shall see, the actions of the Nazi state were greatly influenced by ideas that were widely supported in the United States and the United Kingdom prior to World War II.[4]

The role of negative stereotypes leading to the T-4 program is evidenced by the logic that the Nazis used to justify their widespread extermination of people with mental illnesses. These were individuals who were believed to be "without hope" of recovery (see Figure 3), hence the belief that the killings met the criteria for euthanasia or "mercy killing." They represented a "burden" on public resources, and their tainted genes threatened the genetic integrity of the German people.

How did humanity arrive at the point where attitudes toward people diagnosed with mental illness had become so negative that they were considered unworthy of life, and how far have we come since then? This chapter will review what we know about the extent to which mental health stigma has always been a part of human society, how it has changed over time, and what its current status is. It will then discuss some theories about why mental health stigma exists and persists.

Mental Illness and Mental Health Stigma through History

Has severe mental illness existed throughout human history and does it exist in all human societies? A number of historians and cultural anthropologists have been concerned with answering this question. Many of these investigations also provide information on a related question: Are people that exhibit severe mental illnesses always responded to with negative stereotypes and social exclusion/discrimination, and are they responded to in the same way in all human societies? Although sifting through these examinations is a complicated process, I will try to draw

Figure 3   Photos from a Nazi propaganda film intended to provide support for the
T-4 Euthanasia program. The photos show residents of an insane asylum, and
the captions translate as "life without hope" and "life only as a burden."
Source: United States Holocaust Memorial Museum Archives.

some conclusions from an examination of this literature. I will then discuss
what we know about *why* stigma occurs, when it does.

With regard to whether mental illness has always existed, findings from
the historical and anthropological literature are clear: As best we can tell,
mental illness appears to have existed throughout human history, and it
manifests itself in all human societies, regardless of level of industrialization
or development. As historian Andrew Scull summarized in his comprehensive review of the history of "madness" in human society (*Madness in
Civilization*), there are descriptions of behavior consistent with mental
illness going back to some of the earliest human writings in ancient Israel,

Greece, and China. More importantly, as sociologist Allan Horwitz summarized in *Social Control of Mental Illness*, behaviors that are seen as "incomprehensible" (i.e., that cannot be explained as motivated in some coherent way) are almost always *labeled* in some way as "mad" or "crazy."[5] Moreover, twentieth-century cultural anthropologists who have studied contemporary tribal societies (including aboriginal societies in New Guinea, tribal groups in Nigeria, and native arctic tribes) have consistently found that such groups all have conceptions of, and labels for, behavior that is consistent with the Western idea of mental illness.[6] It should be noted, however, that, in most cases, the labeled behavior is not explained as being the result of a psychological or biological process, but is explained using supernatural conceptions (e.g., that it is the result of magic, a curse, or demon/spirit possession).

Tribal Societies

Although evidence is fairly clear that mental illness exists in all human societies, there is considerably more controversy regarding whether people who exhibit severe mental illnesses are always responded to with negative stereotypes and social exclusion. Beginning with research on tribal societies, anthropological studies of these groups suggest that they tend to take a very supportive and caring stance toward persons demonstrating behavior likely to be related to mental illness. However, for the purpose of this book, the more important question is whether the *person* is "discredited" as a result of having demonstrated such behavior. Some anthropological studies suggest that, at least in some tribal contexts, people are not discredited when they demonstrate "incomprehensible" behavior. For example, studies of arctic Inuit societies have found that these communities use the word *pibloktoq* to describe episodes of wild and odd behavior (similar to episodes of mania or psychosis). A study of how people who have exhibited *pibloktoq* are subsequently treated, however, found that:

> an attack of *pibloktoq* is not automatically taken as a sign of the individual's general incompetency ... The attack may be the subject of good-humored joking later but it is not used to justify restriction of the victim's social participation. There is, in other words, little or no stigma; the attack is treated as an isolated event rather than as a symptom of deeper illness.[7]

Similarly, in a study of the Bena tribe in New Guinea, an anthropologist found that, in response to people who experienced *negi negi*, or episodes of wild and odd behavior: "There is no stigma attached to having such an episode – no public censure – and the occasion is soon forgotten."[8]

Despite these examples, there is disagreement regarding whether people who have experienced episodes consistent with mental illness are *never* discredited in tribal societies. Horwitz concluded that the literature suggests that there is minimal social exclusion of people with mental illnesses in such societies, however, in a review of the literature on this topic, anthropologist Horacio Fabrega[9] found mixed evidence for this conclusion, and determined that the extent of stigma depends on both the specific society being studied and the specific types of mental illness behavior being demonstrated. Perhaps one way of making sense of this is to consider that if supernatural explanations are used to explain "incomprehensible" behavior, the extent to which people will be stigmatized depends on the meanings that are attached to the supernatural forces at play. For example, if black magic or spirit possession is invoked, is this the result of mere chance or the fault of some other person who cast a spell, or is it the result of a blameworthy action assumed to have been performed by the possessed person? We can easily imagine how the first explanation could be shrugged off as "bad luck" and have no long-term impact on the possessed person's reputation, while the second might lead to assumptions that the possessed person is in some way "tainted" for having upset local spirits or dabbled in black magic.

The Ancient World

There is similar controversy when examining evidence for the existence of stigma throughout the history of the major civilizations of Europe, Asia, and Africa (information on the Americas is largely missing). Indeed, there seems to have been some variability in how mental illness was responded to, depending on how its causes were understood. In ancient Greek writings, there is ample discussion of behavior consistent with mental illness, and many of the terms that we use currently to describe psychiatric symptoms (such as *mania*, *melancholia*, and *phobia*) were first used in ancient Greece. The ancient Greeks introduced biological explanations developed by Hippocrates (specifically, that madness resulted from an imbalance of body fluids or "humors"), but primarily saw mad behaviors as resulting from supernatural factors (being cursed by the gods, for example). Although we might expect that demonstrations of madness resulting from the actions of the gods might be seen as temporary and not the fault of the affected person, it appears that the Greeks usually regarded madness to be evidence that the person had done something to deserve being cursed.[10] As a result, the response often consisted of many of the reactions that we would now see as consistent with stigma, including ridicule, condemnation, avoidance, and the ritual of spitting upon the sight of the mad person.[11] For example, an incident that was recorded as occurring in Alexandria indicated that a "lunatic named Carabas . . . whose madness . . . was of the easy-going gentler style" was "made game of by the children" and publicly mocked.[12] Similar responses seem to have predominated in ancient Rome.

In ancient Israel, despite the belief in only one God, madness (represented by the still-familiar word *meshugga*) was also often seen to be the result of a divine curse. And, since the actions of God were believed to always be correct, this meant that the curse was justified because the person had done something to incur God's punishment. As a result, people who demonstrated "mad" behavior were often mocked and publicly scorned. In addition, Israelite law officially limited the rights of people who were mad, and invalidated marriages where one member was found to be insane.[13] On the other hand, there appear to have been some mixed feelings about apparently mad behavior, as the "prophets," important figures in Israeli society, sometimes behaved in a manner that was consistent with madness (the Hebrew word for "to rave" translates as "to behave like a prophet"), but were revered instead of scorned.[14]

In ancient China, historians indicate that there was much less discussion of what we now call mental illness and less differentiation of it from physical illness, making our understanding of the extent to which stigma was demonstrated more difficult. Officially, behavior that was incomprehensible was explained as being the result of disequilibrium of internal forces. Nevertheless, historians have concluded that even given these explanations, there is evidence for a high degree of shame regarding madness throughout Chinese history, exacerbated by a belief that a family's reputation was tainted when it was known that a family member had exhibited mad behavior.[15] The reasons for the shame are not fully clear, but a plausible explanation is that while the Chinese did not employ the concept of genetics per se, they believed that one's "lineage" or ancestry was a major contributor to one's behavior and social value, and the demonstration of madness by a family member could taint the reputation of one's lineage, as well as pose a specific threat to the marriage prospects of family members.[16]

The Medieval European and Islamic Worlds

After the fall of the Roman Empire, Christianity dominated European society, but supernatural explanations of what we now call mental illness persisted. Most typically, madness was seen to be the result of demonic possession. However, contrary to what was usually believed by the ancients, possession was not necessarily thought to be the fault of the person who had become possessed. Furthermore, there was a belief that practices such as exorcism could lead to healing or "cure." As a result, there were a number of saints' shrines that were believed to be places where madness could be cured. Notably, the shrine of St. Dymphna in Gheel (present day Belgium) became a major pilgrimage destination for families seeking the cure of a "mad" family member, and as a result became a place where the behavior of people considered to be mad was greatly tolerated by the general community.[17] Despite the case of Gheel, whether or not what we now call mental illness was widely tolerated in Medieval European society is the subject of debate among historians. French philosopher Michel Foucault, in his book *Madness and Civilization*,[18] put forth the view that there was widespread tolerance and acceptance of madness in Medieval Europe, but others have disputed this conclusion.[19] Although it is hard to determine what the true situation was, it might be safe to say that the Medieval Christian perspective at least allowed for the *possibility* that a person who had demonstrated "mad" behavior could return to a normal social role and therefore not be permanently discredited.

The Medieval Islamic world (which comprised the Middle East, North Africa, and parts of Europe) presents an interesting contrast with Christian Europe because physiological interpretations of the causes of mental illness, drawn from the writings of ancient Greek and Roman scholars, became widely accepted. In addition, the teachings of Islam placed a strong emphasis on charity and communal responsibility, and it has been stated that the Quran specifically mandates charity toward the mentally "incompetent."[a, 20] As a result, there is evidence that the Medieval Islamic world was quite "progressive" in its response to mental illness in the sense that people were not blamed for exhibiting signs of madness, there was a belief that families bore a responsibility to patiently care for relatives experiencing episodes, and, in some cases, people were offered treatment in specialized hospital units (the first of their kind in the world). Although it was also

---

[a] "Do not give to the incompetent their property that God has assigned to you to manage; provide for them and clothe them out of it, and speak to them honourable words."

believed that demons (or *jinn*) could cause mental illness, there was not a corollary belief in the value of supernatural healing or exorcism, so this did not factor into the "treatment" that was offered. In an assessment of the degree to which mental illness was stigmatized in the Medieval Islamic world, Fabrega determined that there is evidence that stigma was less of a factor in these than in other societies.[21]

The Early Modern World

A number of important changes in the conceptualization of and treatment toward what we now call mental illness began to take place in the late 1700s, as European and North American society became more secular and government power became more centralized. With regard to conceptualization, the first major factor was that supernatural explanations were no longer favored and biological conceptualizations became preferred. Specifically, the brain and the nervous system began to be seen as the center of thought and emotion, and madness was increasingly seen as a "nervous disorder." Another major factor was that as society became more urbanized, the poor were increasingly believed to be responsible for their plight, and the publicly "mad," along with others, were lumped into the category of "subhuman brutes."[22] With regard to treatment, the major change was that there was a move toward greater *confinement*, such that it was believed to be less and less acceptable for the poor and others (including the publicly mad) to "roam freely." The process of confinement proceeded in a series of stages, beginning with confinement in general poorhouses, jails, and a small number of "madhouses," and eventually asylums (for a more thorough review of this process, the reader is referred to Scull's *Madness in Civilization*).

The "asylum movement" describes the rapid and massive process of confining people deemed to be "insane" in specialized treatment institutions (called asylums) that occurred in the early 1800s throughout the Western world. Asylums were initially developed around the humanistic belief that allowing people who were "insane" to live in an environment that was protected from the stresses of the home and urban, industrialized society would facilitate a recovery from madness.[23] Treatment was supposed to be strict but humane (the use of shackles and beatings, which had been used in the earlier "madhouses," was prohibited). In fact, the early asylums reported high "cure" rates of 70% and higher, and "cured" individuals were allowed to return to the community. This suggests that, despite high rates of confinement, the early period of the asylum movement represented a time of greater optimism regarding the potential for people with what we now call mental illness to recover, and therefore less of a complete discrediting of the person.

Nevertheless, the early optimism of the asylum movement deteriorated within a few decades and, by the mid-1800s, asylums were becoming overcrowded and considerably less humane in their treatment approach. Reported cure rates declined and it became increasingly less likely that persons admitted to asylums would be able to return to the community. For example, of the roughly 8,000 people admitted to a large asylum in New York State between 1869 and 1900, less than 20% were ever discharged, with the remainder spending the rest of their lives in the asylum.[24]

Were people who were confined to asylums "discredited"? Evidence from the writings of people who lived in them certainly suggests so. For example, John Clare, a poet who spent 27 years in British asylums in the early 1800s, poignantly wrote:

> I AM: yet what I am none cares or knows,
> My friends forsake me like a memory lost . . .
> And e'en the dearest – that I loved the best –
> Are strange – nay rather stranger than the rest[25]

A later account of the experience of living in an asylum that communicates the "discredited" nature of living in one of these settings is provided in the memoir of Dr. Perry Baird (recovered and transcribed by his daughter), a prominent dermatologist who experienced periodic manic/psychotic episodes. Dr. Baird wrote: "once one has crossed the line from the normal walks of life into a psychopathic hospital, one is separated from friends and relatives by walls thicker than stone; walls of prejudice and superstition . . . The brutalities that one encounters in state and city psychopathic hospitals must be the by-product of the fear and superstition with which mentally ill patients are regarded."[26]

The Rise of Eugenics

Attitudes toward people deemed to be insane took a particularly negative turn in the late 1800s as the idea of "moral degeneracy" (popularized in the work of French psychiatrist Benedict-Augustin Morel) became part of the conventional wisdom in Europe and North America. Essentially, this perspective viewed social ills, including insanity, to be signs of the decay of civilization. New ideas about heritability combined with this view to lead to the belief that insanity was biologically determined, immutable, and a sign of "inferiority." Although charged with caring for people with mental illness, psychiatrists (or alienists, as they were also called) could be among the most virulent believers that these persons were "tainted" and "defective." For example, prominent British psychiatrist Henry Maudsley, after whom a major London psychiatric hospital is named, wrote repeatedly about the incurability of insanity and equated it with moral degeneracy and criminality.[27]

The term "eugenics" was coined by British aristocrat (and cousin of Charles Darwin) Francis Galton in 1883 to describe a moral philosophy to improve human society. Influenced by his cousin's writings and the belief that human traits were genetically inherited, he proposed that it would be to the betterment of society if people with the "healthiest" traits were encouraged to have more children with each other. The types of traits that most interested Galton were "genius," "beauty," "talent," and "character"; he did not put much of an emphasis on insanity, and experienced at least two "nervous breakdowns" himself (descriptions of them are consistent with the interpretation that he experienced manic episodes).[28] However, his colleague Karl Pearson, after whom a major statistical analytic technique is named, linked "insanity" to degeneracy and bad character, and others were quick to agree.[29]

Galton's ideas soon enjoyed wide support in Britain and especially took off in the United States, where their popularity was probably linked to their appeal in providing "scientific" justification for racist and anti-immigrant sentiment. Rather than just focusing on increasing positive traits, American eugenicists (Charles Davenport and John Harvey Kellogg, of the breakfast cereal company, were two major adherents) also focused on the need to eliminate "defective" inherited traits, including "insanity," "feeble-mindedness," and "criminality" (see Figure 4). The American eugenicists also introduced a new idea for reducing the degree to which "defective" traits existed in the human gene-pool: forced sterilization.

Lest the reader question how popular these views actually were in the United States in the early twentieth century, the evidence should speak for itself: 40 of 48 states enacted forced sterilization laws (groups that could be sterilized included the "feeble-minded" and "insane"), and roughly 21,000 persons were sterilized by 1935. These laws were upheld by the US Supreme Court in an infamous 1935 decision that has never been officially overturned. Furthermore, America's forced sterilization laws directly inspired Germany's new Nazi regime, which created its own sterilization law in 1933 and honored American eugenicist Harry Laughlin at a

Figure 4　American eugenics display used with exhibits and "fitter family" contests, circa 1926. Top sign reads "Every 15 seconds $100 of your money goes for the care of people with bad heredity such as the insane, feeble-minded, criminals & other defectives."
Source: Image Archive of the Eugenics Movement.

Heidelberg University ceremony in that year for his pioneering work in the area.[30] Germany's forced sterilization laws were the precursor to the "euthanasia" effort described in the beginning of this chapter.

After World War II

As should be well-known to readers, the end of World War II exposed the horrors of the Holocaust to the world, and it became far less acceptable to espouse eugenic ideas in this period (despite this, forced sterilization continued in some US states until the 1970s, when the last forced sterilization laws were struck down). The 1950s and early 1960s were a time of great change and optimism with regard to the treatment of people with severe mental illnesses, as new medications that might successfully manage symptoms became available (beginning with the discovery of chlorpromazine, commercial name Thorazine, in 1952), and as a gradual reversal of the practice of mass long-term hospitalization began ("deinstitutionalization").

The extent to which deinstitutionalization was an overall success or failure has been discussed amply by others[31] and is not the focus here; rather, the question is, did the "discrediting" of people who had been diagnosed with a mental illness persist during this transitional period? Two major studies of the American public were conducted in the 1950s that provided some answers to this question. The first, which included more than 3,000 participants, was conducted by Shirley Star at the National

Opinion Research Center and was discussed in two presentations given in the 1950s (unfortunately, an official summary of findings was never published).[32] The second was conducted by Jum Nunnally and used a method called the "semantic differential scale" to gauge the favorability of the public's opinions toward various groups, including "mental patients."[33] Summarizing her findings, Star concluded that attitudes toward people with psychotic disorders were generally pessimistic and that the general public largely believed that such individuals were dangerous and/or unpredictable. For example, Star stated that "only a fifth of the American population believes that most psychotics can *and* do get better again, while two-fifths feel that most can, but don't."[34] She also indicated that roughly two-thirds of the American public "viewed the typical psychotic patient as dangerous" and "feel that all psychotics should be institutionalized." Furthermore, a summary of Star's findings in 1961 stated that they indicated that 60% of the American public endorsed that they would "not feel or act normally toward an ex-mental patient."[35] Nunnally's research was of a smaller scale and only included persons living in Illinois; however, his findings also supported that the public's perception of "mental patients" was unfavorable, and that the public endorsed the association of such individuals with undesirable characteristics, including unpredictability, weakness, and dangerousness.

These studies led many at the time to conclude that the general public had unfavorable attitudes that needed to be addressed through public education. This fueled several large efforts to educate the public about mental illness and the need for treatment. Many of these efforts were focused on emphasizing that mental illnesses are "diseases like any others" and are not the fault of the people who have them. The 1990s were a period of particular emphasis on educating the general public about the presumed biological origins of mental illness, and were dubbed "the Decade of the Brain" in a 1990 proclamation by President George H. W. Bush. In the proclamation, President Bush expressed a desire "to enhance public awareness of the benefits to be derived from brain research."[36]

Where Are We Now?

As a result of public education campaigns, and the "decade of the brain," the US general public is now much more likely to be exposed to information offering a professional perspective on mental illnesses and their treatment than in the 1950s. For example, in the 2000s, people watching late night television or perusing a general interest magazine might have casually come across an advertisement for Abilify, an antipsychotic medication promoted for its effectiveness in the treatment of depression and bipolar disorder. Are negative stereotypes really that prevalent if advertisements for antipsychotic medications are so commonplace?

Unfortunately, evidence suggests that negative stereotypes about people with severe mental illnesses do persist to a large extent. Focusing on the United States specifically, two studies conducted by researchers Bernice Pescosolido, Bruce Link, Jo Phelan, and others, used data from national US surveys to examine if attitudes had changed over time. The first analysis used a subsample of survey responses from Star's 1950s survey (described in the previous section) and compared them to 1996 survey findings. Analyses suggested that while the public's perception of what constituted a mental illness had broadened since the 1950s (and included more nonpsychotic disorders), public perceptions of the dangerousness of people with psychotic disorders had *increased*.[37] Separate analyses revealed that in 1996, 61% of the American public believed that a hypothetical person with schizophrenia was likely to be violent, and that 63% reported a desire for social distance from this individual.[38] In a later analysis of change from 1996 to 2006 (after many of the "decade of the brain" public education efforts), the authors found that while the public showed a significant increase in its attribution of the causes of mental illness to neurobiological factors and a belief that treatment was necessary, there was no resultant decrease in expectations of dangerousness or desire for social distance.[39]

Things do not look much different if we broaden our perspective beyond the United States. The Stigma in a Global Context – Mental Health Study, which included more than 6,000 participants in 16 countries across six continents, found that in response to a vignette of a person with schizophrenia, there were a core of attitudes that were endorsed at a high level across the countries, including: "likely to be violent to others" (endorsed by 53% on average), "not likely to be productive" (endorsed by 51% on average), "unpredictable" (endorsed by 70% on average), and "shouldn't care for children" (endorsed by 84% on average).[40] These findings varied by country, with Iceland showing the lowest endorsement and Cyprus the highest, and with the United States falling somewhere in the middle. Another article reviewed more than 100 studies conducted around the globe regarding attitudes toward people with mental illness and found that while "the majority of the public show pro-social reactions, i.e., they feel sorry for persons with mental illness," several negative stereotypes were widely held, including the view that people with schizophrenia are unpredictable (endorsement ranged from 54 to 85% depending on the country) and dangerous (endorsement ranged from 18–71% depending on the country).[41] There was also an examination of international trends in change with regard to negative stereotypes between the 1990s and 2000s, which confirmed that while "the public's literacy about mental disorders clearly has increased … at the same time, attitudes towards persons with mental illness have not changed for the better, and have even deteriorated towards persons with schizophrenia."[42]

Why have attitudes been resistant to change in the face of the widespread dissemination of information that severe mental illnesses are "diseases like any other"? One interpretation of this finding is that the emphasis on genetics and biology that the "decade of the brain" pushed, partly in an effort to reduce stigma, has backfired. Specifically, analyses from the US surveys suggested that holding the view that mental illnesses are genetically caused "brain diseases" tended to *increase* the odds that stigmatizing attitudes would be endorsed.[43] The authors interpreted this finding to mean that while the general public feels that persons with "brain diseases" are not to blame for their conditions, they are less likely to believe that such persons can get better. Further support for the view that connecting mental illness to "genetics" can increase stigma was found in a separate study conducted by Jo Phelan, which experimentally manipulated whether people were told that the cause of a hypothetical person's mental illness was genetic or not.[44] This study found that people who were told that the cause of a mental illness was genetic were more likely to think that it was serious and unlikely to change. Another study, employing a similar methodology, found that assigning people to a description linking schizophrenia to genetic explanations was related to both greater desire for social distance and belief in dangerousness, relative to a description of schizophrenia that did not provide a genetic explanation.[45] A review of 25 studies on the relationship between the endorsement of "biogenetic" beliefs and stigma also found a similar overall pattern.[46]

There is also evidence that diagnostic labels such as "schizophrenia," which, as a result of public education efforts, are now strongly linked with notions of genetic causes in the public's view, may serve as a particular trigger for negative stereotypes. This was supported by an experimental study conducted by German researcher Roland Imhoff, who presented more than 2,000 community members with identical descriptions of an individual experiencing symptoms that met the diagnostic criteria for schizophrenia, except that a random half of participants were also told that the individual had a diagnosis of schizophrenia, while the others were given no such label.[47] Imhoff found that participants assigned to the "label" condition were significantly more likely to describe the individual as "dangerous" and less likely to describe him as "competent." This research challenges the view, which some have articulated, that stigma is only triggered by behavior and not affected by diagnostic labels.[48]

The conclusion that emphasizing genetics, biology, and diagnostic labels in an effort to combat stigma is problematic makes particular sense when we consider the history of these concepts in the public discourse about mental illness. As we saw earlier in this chapter (and as articulated in Siddhartha Mukherjee's best-selling book *The Gene*), historically, notions of traits being related to genetics have been frequently linked to the idea of *essentialism*; that is, that certain aspects of a person are inherent and cannot be changed.[49] Although scientists know that "the brain" and "genetics" are complicated concepts that do not mean that something is unchangeable, the general public may lack this nuanced understanding. This suggests that different aspects of what we know about mental illness may need to be emphasized in order to reduce stigma.

Where Does Stigma Come from?

We can see from the previous sections that, although the endorsement of negative stereotypes has fluctuated over time and varies by location in the present day, there is evidence that stigma has existed to some extent for a large part of human history and exists currently in almost all human societies. This raises the question of why mental health stigma exists in the first place and why it is so resistant to change.

Origins of Stigma

Mental illness is, of course, not the only social category that is linked to negative stereotypes. In fact, there are a myriad of other human characteristics that are or have been linked to prejudicial notions and associated behavior in various locations, such as racial/ethnic heritage (e.g., African American, Arab-American), religious affiliation (e.g., Catholicism, Judaism, or Islam), sexual orientation, physical characteristics (e.g., deformities or physical disability), and other health conditions (e.g., HIV/AIDS).[50]

Why do people so commonly develop negative assumptions about others that they do not personally know? Social psychologists have proposed that the origins of stigma lie in cognitive processes that are intrinsic to being human. Specifically, in the mid-1950s social psychologist Gordon Allport proposed that stereotyping derives from the cognitive process of *categorization,* or the tendency for humans to group pieces of information into chunks or categories.[51] Categorization facilitates memory and simplifies the task of dealing with the world and other people. When categorizing other people into groups, we are provided with a general framework for interacting with them that can guide our interactions. To give a relatively innocuous example, if we're babysitting middle school children, we might rely on stereotypes about what such children tend to like, to guide what interests we might try to engage them in (e.g., middle schoolers probably like computer games like *Minecraft*). Of course, we might be wrong, but we might still want to use these stereotypes for our initial plan of interaction, since there are potentially an unlimited number of interests that middle school children can have, and it would be impractical to try to prepare for all of them.

Certainly, the process of labeling a group and linking certain assumptions to that label is related to categorization, but that does not explain why some human characteristics are stigmatized (meaning that distinctly negative stereotypes are attached to them) while others are not. To address this, Jo Phelan, Bruce Link, and John Dovidio proposed that there are three essential reasons *why* certain characteristics are stigmatized: (1) exploitation/domination ("keeping people down"), (2) enforcement of social norms ("keeping people in"), and (3) avoidance of disease ("keeping people away").[52] According to this typology, characteristics become selected for stigma either because they facilitate the maintenance of a power hierarchy, facilitate conformity, or reduce exposure to possibly contagious disease.

Origins of Mental Health Stigma

How does this logic apply to attitudes toward severe mental illnesses? In a further discussion of their typology, Link and Phelan suggested that the initial impetus for mental health stigma is probably a desire to "keep people in."[53] Specifically, they explained that people with mental illness may often violate social norms when they are actively experiencing symptoms (e.g., think of my description of Jose in Chapter 1, who would wander the streets late at night singing loudly). People react negatively as they try to get the person to conform to how one "should" act (e.g., only singing loudly when it's culturally sanctioned, such as at concerts, parties, or religious events). Furthermore, in instances where individuals are not responsive to initial efforts to get them to conform, there may be further efforts to keep them "away," by forcing them to stay in settings (e.g., hospitals or segregated housing sites) where their nonconforming behavior will not disrupt the "normal" social order.

Although Link and Phelan's typology is a helpful start to understanding where stigma comes from, it does not account for a number of aspects of the mental health stigma process. For example, if the main purpose of stigma is to get people to conform to social norms, why is it that people with severe mental illnesses are "discredited" or "discreditable" even when they are not demonstrating any symptoms that might lead them to violate social norms (recall from Chapter 1 that a key part of the stigma process is that a label that is initially linked to behavior comes to be attached to the person)? Furthermore, why do the negative stereotypes about mental illness center on "dangerous," "incompetent," and "unable to recover" rather than "nonconformist" or "weird"?

Another perspective suggests that these specific stereotypes have developed because they have grown from a "grain of truth"; that is, although they may not accurately describe the reality of all or most people with mental illnesses, they are essentially exaggerations of reality.[54] This view is consistent with Allport's initial thinking about why specific stereotypes develop about particular ethnic groups.[55] Is there evidence that there is a "grain of truth" to these stereotypes of dangerousness, incompetence, and inability to recover? Many have argued that there is, given that (to focus on the dangerousness stereotype), although research confirms that the great majority (roughly 90%) of people with severe mental illnesses do not engage in violent behavior,[56] there is adequate evidence to support the idea that certain symptoms of mental illness increase the *risk* for violent or aggressive behavior.[57, b]

However, while the "grain of truth" perspective might explain where a given stereotype originates, it does not explain why it is maintained in the face of disconfirming evidence, and why it is held when there is ample evidence that other groups (e.g., in the case of dangerousness, young men[58, c]) are much more likely to demonstrate the characteristic, yet are not similarly

---

[b] The relationship between severe mental illness and violence is a complicated one and has been the subject of a number of different types of research, too numerous to review here. The best summary that can be provided is that, although evidence supports that experiencing specific symptoms, such as persecutory delusions and command hallucinations, increases risk for engaging in violent behavior relative to people who do not have such symptoms, evidence also supports that the great majority (roughly 90%) of people with schizophrenia and bipolar disorder do not engage in violent behavior.

[c] Research consistently supports that the intersection of youth and male gender is one of the largest predictors of violence among people. For example, the National Comorbidity Survey (a survey of the US population) found that roughly 33% of men between ages 25 and 34 had recently engaged in violence, in contrast with roughly 1% of both men and women over 45.

stigmatized. This suggests that there are other factors at play that lead to the maintenance of the stereotype. For this reason, Patrick Corrigan and Amy Watson proposed that a different approach to understanding stigma, called "system-justification," should be considered.[59] This approach suggests that we should understand negative stereotypes as coming about in an effort to *justify* inequities that have arisen for historical reasons. For example, women might be stereotyped as weak and incapable of complex thought to justify their being barred from leadership positions in society (an arrangement that benefits men), while African Americans may have been stereotyped as intellectually inferior to justify slavery and other oppressive institutions. Applying the system-justification perspective to the case of mental health stigma makes some sense when we consider that while the discrediting of people with mental illnesses has existed for a long time, the stereotypes that support it have varied depending on local and historical context. For example, while the current driving-force for stigma is concerns about dangerousness ("Get the Violent Crazies off Our Streets"), the eugenicist and Nazi justifications for stigma made little mention of this, instead focusing on the insane being a "hopeless burden" to society. In this regard, it is plausible that the "second-class citizen" status of people with mental illness, which potentially benefits others in society, is the outcome that these different stereotypes seek to justify. In Chapter 4, we'll consider further whether and how a focus on negative stereotypes about mental illness might benefit particular groups in society.

Nevertheless, the system-justification perspective runs into problems when we try to use it to explain every aspect of stigma. For example, it seems to be a bit too much of a coincidence for the "system" that stigma supports to have existed in so many different human societies over the course of history. Furthermore, there undeniably *are* aspects of the behavior that many people with mental illness sometimes engage in when they are actively symptomatic that are genuinely disquieting and frightening to others. Of course, our concern here is why people continue to be "discredited" during the 95%[60] of their lives when they are not demonstrating any symptoms, but it is plausible that societies have developed some of the negative stereotypes that exist about mental illness as a method of self-protection.[61] The fluctuating and episodic nature of mental illnesses may be confusing to others seeking to predict future behavior, so societies may have developed a tendency to apply blanket labels to people with any history of symptomatic behavior as a means of increasing their sense of security. For example, although people with severe mental illnesses are less likely to engage in violent behavior than many other groups in society that are not negatively stereotyped, many community members may feel that they can predict when these other groups are likely to be violent (since it's more likely to be driven by "comprehensible" motives), and therefore protect themselves from harm. However, an inability to understand the internal motives of people with mental illnesses and therefore predict their behavior may lead community members to be more frightened of them, even though the risk that they pose is actually lower than other groups.

No part of the discussion of the reasons for stigma is intended to excuse people for holding on to stigmatizing attitudes. We do not excuse people for endorsing racist, sexist, or homophobic views even though those prejudices arose for a reason as well. However, it is helpful to form an understanding of the origins of stigma in order to develop a directed plan for combating it. Perhaps there is no single satisfactory explanation for why stigma persists because stigma, like many other issues in human society, is determined by a number of factors. This suggests that efforts to overcome stigma will require a combination of strategies. We will further explore explanations for stigma in Chapter 4 when we consider some of the demographic and personal characteristics that are associated with a greater likelihood that a given individual will endorse stigmatizing attitudes and behavior, and theoretical explanations for those associations, while our focus in the next chapter will be the ways that negative stereotypes impact community members' behavior toward people with mental illness.

References

1 United States Holocaust Memorial Museum. Accessed online August 21, 2017: www.ushmm.org/wlc/en/article.php?ModuleId=10005200; Scull, A. (2015). *Madness in civilization*. Princeton, NJ: Princeton University Press.
2 Jewish Virtual Library. Accessed online August 21, 2017: www.jewishvirtuallibrary.org/jsource/Holocaust/t4.html.
3 Read, J. & Masson, J. (2013). Genetics, eugenics and the mass murder of "schizophrenics." In J. Read and J. Dillon (Eds.), *Models of madness* (2nd Edn., pp. 34–45). New York: Routledge.
4 Scull, A. (2015). *Madness in civilization*. Princeton, NJ: Princeton University Press.
5 Horwitz, A. V. (1982). *The social control of mental illness*. New York: Academic Press.
6 Murphy, J. M. (1976). Psychiatric labeling in a cross-cultural perspective. *Science, 191*, 1019–1028.
7 Wallace, A. F. C. (1972). Mental illness, biology and culture. In F. Hsu (Ed.), *Psychological anthropology* (pp. 363–4020). Cambridge, MA: Schenkman. Cited in Horwitz (1982).

8 Langness, L. L. (1965). Hysterical psychosis in the New Guinea highlands: A bena bena example. *Psychiatry, 28,* 258–277. Cited in Fabrega (1991a).

9 Fabrega, H. (1991a). Psychiatric stigma in non-Western societies. *Comprehensive Psychiatry, 32,* 534–551.

10 Scull, A. (2015). *Madness in civilization.* Princeton, NJ: Princeton University Press.

11 Fabrega, H. (1990). Psychiatric stigma in the classical and medieval period: A review of the literature. *Comprehensive Psychiatry, 31,* 289–306.

12 Rosen, G. (1968). *Madness in society.* New York: Harper Torchbooks.

13 Fabrega, H. (1990). Psychiatric stigma in the classical and medieval period: A review of the literature. *Comprehensive Psychiatry, 31,* 289–306.

14 Rosen, G. (1968). *Madness in society.* New York: Harper Torchbooks.

15 Fabrega, H. (1991a). Psychiatric stigma in non-Western societies. *Comprehensive Psychiatry, 32,* 534–551.

16 Yang, L. H., Purdie-Vaughans, V., Kotabe, H., Link, B. G., Saw, A., Wong, G., & Phelan, J. (2013). Culture, threat and mental illness stigma: Identifying culture-specific threat among Chinese American groups. *Social Science & Medicine, 88,* 56–67.

17 Scull, A. (2015). *Madness in civilization.* Princeton, NJ: Princeton University Press.

18 Foucault, M. (1965). *Madness and civilization: A history of insanity in the age of reason.* New York: Random House.

19 Fabrega, H. (1990). Psychiatric stigma in the classical and medieval period: A review of the literature. *Comprehensive Psychiatry, 31,* 289–306.

20 Youssef, H. A., & Youssef, F. A. (1996). Evidence for the existence of schizophrenia in medieval Islamic society. *History of Psychiatry, 7,* 55–62.

21 Fabrega, H. (1991a). Psychiatric stigma in non-Western societies. *Comprehensive Psychiatry, 32,* 534–551.

22 Fabrega, H. (1991b). The culture and history of psychiatric stigma in early modern and modern Western societies: A review of recent literature. *Comprehensive Psychiatry, 32,* 97–119.

23 Davidson, L., Rakfeldt, J., & Strauss, J. (2010). *The roots of the recovery movement in psychiatry.* Hoboken, NJ: Wiley-Blackwell.

24 Penney, D., & Stastny, P. (2008). *The lives they left behind: Suitcases from a state hospital attic.* New York: Bellevue Literary Press.

25 Cited in Scull (2015). *Madness in civilization.* Princeton, NJ: Princeton University Press.

26 Baird, M. (2015). *He wanted the moon: The madness and medical genius of Dr. Perry Baird, and his daughter's quest to know him.* New York: Broadway Books.

27 Scull, A. (2015). *Madness in civilization.* Princeton, NJ: Princeton University Press.

28 Gillham, N. W. (2001). *Life of Sir Francis Galton: From African exploration to the birth of eugenics.* Cary, NC: Oxford University Press.

29 Painter, N. I. (2010). *The history of white people.* New York: Norton.

30 Image Archive of the American Eugenics Movement. Accessed online August 21, 2017: www.eugenicsarchive.org/eugenics/list2.pl.

31 Lamb, H. R., & Weinberger, L. E. (2001). *Deinstitutionalization: Promise and problems*. San Francisco: Jossey-Bass.

32 Star, S. A. (1952). *What the public thinks about mental health and mental illness*. Chicago: National Opinion Research Center. Accessed online August 21, 2017: www.norc.org/PDFs/publications/StarS_What_Public_Thinks_1952.pdf.; Star, S. A. (1955). *The public's ideas about mental illness*. Chicago: National Opinion Research Center. Accessed online August 21, 2017: www.norc.org/PDFs/publications/StarS_Publics_Ideas_1955.pdf.

33 Nunnally, J., & Kittross, J. M. (1958). Public attitudes toward mental health professions. *American Psychologist, 13*, 589–594.

34 Star, S. A. (1955). *The public's ideas about mental illness*. Chicago: National Opinion Research Center. Accessed online August 21, 2017: www.norc.org/PDFs/publications/StarS_Publics_Ideas_1955.pdf.

35 Joint Commission on Mental Illness and Health. (1961). *Action for mental health*. New York: Basic Books.

36 Accessed online August 21, 2017: www.loc.gov/loc/brain/proclaim.html.

37 Phelan, J. C., Link, B. G., Stueve, A., & Pescosolido, B. A. (2000). Public conceptions of mental illness in 1950 and 1996: What is mental illness and is it to be feared? *Journal of Health and Social Behavior, 41*, 188–207.

38 Link, B. G., Phelan, J. C., Bresnahan, M., Stueve, A., & Pescosolido, B. A. (1999). Public conceptions of mental illness: Labels, causes, dangerousness, and social distance. *American Journal of Public Health, 89*, 1328–1333.

39 Pescosolido, B. A., Martin, J. K., Long, J. S., Medina, T. R., Phelan, J. C., & Link, B. G. (2010). A "disease like any other"? A decade of change in public reactions to schizophrenia, depression, and alcohol dependence. *American Journal of Psychiatry, 167*, 1321–1330.

40 Pescosolido, B. A., Medina, T. R., Martin, J. K., & Long, J. S. (2013). The "backbone" of stigma: Identifying the global core of public prejudice associated with mental illness. *American Journal of Public Health, 103*, 853–860.

41 Angermeyer, M. C., & Dietrich, S. (2006). Public beliefs and attitudes toward people with mental illness: A review of population studies. *Acta Psychiatrica Scandinavica, 113*, 163–179.

42 Schomerus, G., Schwahn, C., Holzinger, A., Corrigan, P. W., Grabe, H. J., Carta, M. G., & Angermeyer, M. C. (2012). Evolution of public attitudes about mental illness: a systematic review and meta-analysis. *Acta Psychiatric Scandinavica, 125*, 440–452.

43 Pescosolido et al. (2010). A "disease like any other"? A decade of change in public reactions to schizophrenia, depression, and alcohol dependence. *American Journal of Psychiatry, 167*, 1321–1330.

44 Phelan, J. C. (2005). Geneticization of deviant behavior and its consequences for stigma: The case of mental illness. *Journal of Health and Social Behavior, 46*, 307–322.

45 Lee, A. A., et al. (2014). Genetic attributions and mental illness diagnosis: Effects on perceptions of danger, social distance, and real helping decisions. *Social Psychiatry and Psychiatric Epidemiology, 49*, 781–789.

46 Kvaale, E. P., Gottdiener, W. H., & Haslam, N. (2013). Biogenetic explanations and stigma: A meta-analytic review of associations among laypeople. *Social Science & Medicine, 96*, 95–103.

47 Imhoff, R. (2016). Zeroing in on the effect of the schizophrenia label on stigmatizing attitudes: A large-scale study. *Schizophrenia Bulletin, 42*, 456–463.

48 Lillienfield, S. O., Smith, S. F., & Watts, A. L. (2013). Issues in diagnosis: Conceptual issues and controversies. In W. E. Craighead, D. J. Miklowitz and L. W. Craighead (Eds.), *Psychopathology* (2nd Edn.). Hoboken, NJ: Wiley.

49 Mukherjee, S. (2016). *The gene: An intimate history.* New York: Scribner.

50 Major, B., & O'Brien, L. T. (2005). The social psychology of stigma. *Annual Review of Psychology, 56*, 393–421.

51 Allport, G. W. (1979). *The nature of prejudice* (25th anniversary edition). Reading, MA: Addison-Wesley.

52 Phelan, J. C., Link, B. G., & Dovidio, J. F. (2008). Stigma and prejudice: One animal or two? *Social Science and Medicine, 67*, 358–367.

53 Link, B. G., & Phelan, J. (2014). Stigma power. *Social Science and Medicine, 103*, 24–32.

54 Treatment Advocacy Center (2014). What is the main cause of stigma against people with serious mental illness? Accessed online August 16, 2017: www .treatmentadvocacycenter.org/storage/documents/backgrounders/what%20is %20the%20main%20cause%20of%20stigma%20against%20individuals% 20with%20serious%20mental%20illness%20final.pdf.

55 Allport, G. W. (1979). *The nature of prejudice* (25th anniversary edition). Reading, MA: Addison-Wesley.

56 Elbogen, E. B., & Johnson, S. C. (2009). The intricate link between violence and mental disorder: Results from the National Epidemiologic Survey on alcohol and related conditions. *Archives of General Psychiatry, 66*, 152–161.

57 Link, B. G., Andrews, H., & Cullen, F. T. (1992). The violent and illegal behavior of mental patients reconsidered. *American Sociological Review*, 275–292.

58 Corrigan, P. W., & Watson, A. C. (2005). Findings from the National Comorbidity Survey on the frequency of violent behavior in individuals with psychiatric disorders. *Psychiatry Research, 136*, 153–162.

59 Corrigan, P. W., Watson, A. C., & Ottati, V. (2003). From whence comes mental illness stigma? *International Journal of Social Psychiatry, 49*, 142–157.

60 Davidson, L., Rakfeldt, J., & Strauss, J. (2010). *The roots of the recovery movement in psychiatry: Lessons learned.* Chichester, West Sussex, UK: Wiley-Blackwell.

61 Kurzban, R., & Leary, M. R. (2001). Evolutionary origins of stigmatization: The functions of social exclusion. *Psychological Bulletin, 127*, 187–208.

CHAPTER 3

What Does Stigma Look Like?

In 2009, Mindi, a single-parent residing in De Soto, Kansas, experienced a psychotic episode shortly after the birth of her first child. The psychotic episode led Mindi to believe that her infant daughter had been raped by someone, and, while attempting to convince staff at a pediatric hospital in Missouri of her certainty that this had occurred, her daughter was taken into custody by child welfare authorities (this occurred even though there had been no evidence that she had abused or neglected her daughter while symptomatic). Following this incident, Mindi received psychiatric treatment and, according to her psychiatrist, soon no longer experienced psychotic symptoms. She quickly petitioned to regain custody of the child but was denied it, based on a Missouri law stating that parental rights can be terminated if the parent has a mental illness. In making the decision, despite evidence that Mindi was no longer experiencing symptoms, the Judge stated that she had "a mental condition which is shown by competent evidence either to be permanent or such that there is no reasonable likelihood that the condition can be reversed." In 2011, Mindi gave birth to another child whom she has retained custody of, and was found by a family therapist to be providing a "nurturing, loving environment and had met all of [the child's] needs." Nevertheless, in 2014 she was ultimately denied custody of her first child, who was legally adopted by her foster parents.[1] As we shall learn, in many locations it is common for parents with psychiatric histories to be denied custody of their biological children, based on the assumption that mental illness makes one unqualified to parent.

In another life context, many people with mental illnesses report being harassed by community members who are aware of their diagnosis. For example, an individual living in England participating in a survey about discrimination experiences reported: "Various gangs in the district call me 'nutter' and spit at me. The gangs on the estate got to know I was a psychiatric outpatient so I am teased and harassed."[2] An individual living in New York City who participated in one of my research studies similarly reported that neighbors who were aware that he had a mental illness put garbage in front of his door as a form of harassment. In both cases, participants reported being frightened as a result of these experiences.

The common theme to the above examples is that negative stereotypes about severe mental illnesses (that people with mental illness never improve, that they are incapable of being responsible, and that they represent a danger to the community) can become reflected in the actions of community members, including a society's legal institutions. These actions can then have a significant impact on the life opportunities of diagnosed individuals. In this chapter, we will learn about the myriad ways that stigma impacts how community members interact with and treat people diagnosed with severe mental illness.

How Do Attitudes Impact Behavior?

In the previous chapter, we reviewed how stigma is reflected in community members' endorsement of *negative stereotypes* about a labeled group. However, such beliefs do not necessarily have a meaningful impact unless they influence *behavior* toward the labeled group. In *The Nature of Prejudice*, Gordon Allport proposed that there were five ways that such biases (or prejudice) can impact behavior toward members of a targeted group: (1) antilocution (or verbal rejection), (2) avoidance, (3) discrimination, (4) physical attack, and (5) extermination.[3] In this chapter, we will use a related typology to explore ways that negative stereotypes about mental illness impact community members' behaviors. Figure 5 demonstrates a conceptual breakdown of the components of community stigma. As the figure shows, the larger concept of "Community Stigma" has three components: community member attitudes (discussed in the previous chapter), community member behavior, and "structural" stigma. Community member behaviors and structural stigma each represent real-life results of attitudes in ways that can have a tangible impact on the lives of people with severe mental illness. Below, I will discuss the various forms of each in greater detail.

Community Member Behaviors

Community member behavioral expressions of stigma can take a variety of forms across a range of severity. I will focus on five types of behavior, ordered roughly by severity: microaggressions (or subtle discriminatory

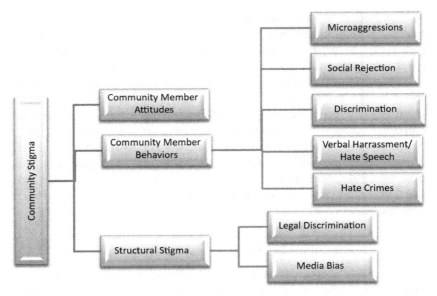

Figure 5 Forms of community stigma

behaviors), social rejection (including the avoidance of social contact), discrimination, verbal harrassment/hate speech, and hate crimes.

How do we know whether and how often community members engage in each of these types of behaviors? There is no "gold standard" for assessing them, but information comes from a number of sources, each with its own strengths and weaknesses. Potential sources include self-reports from surveys with community members about past or intended future behavior, self-reports from people with mental illnesses about behaviors they have experienced, experimental studies examining the likelihood that community members will treat a hypothetical person with a mental illness label differently than an identical person without the label, observations of actual behavior, and official reports from legal sources. These research approaches each tell us different things, and nothing tells the full story. For example, while self-reports from people with mental illnesses tell us whether and how often someone has *perceived* that they experienced a type of discriminatory behavior from a community member, they do not tell us what proportion of the people that they come into contact with would *actually* engage in the behavior. As a data source, self-reports of perceived discrimination experiences are limited by being poten-tially influenced by symptoms or other factors that could lead one to overestimate others' negative intentions. Conversely, studies focusing on community members usually tell us what proportion might be *willing* to engage in a given behavior, but they rarely tell us how many have actually engaged in these behaviors in encounters with people with mental illness. These studies might also be biased by community members' awareness that it might not be "politically correct" to engage in discriminatory behaviors, and therefore to under-report the actual likelihood that they would engage in them. Given these limitations, it is necessary to look at information from multiple sources to try to get the best sense of how often these behaviors are engaged in. In the following sections, I draw on a range of information sources to elaborate on what we know about each of the types of community member manifestations of stigma in greater depth.

Microaggressions

At the lowest level of severity, but possibly the highest level of frequency, are subtle behaviors called "microaggressions." The concept of microaggressions, though relatively new in the study of prejudicial behavior, has nevertheless developed a considerable evidence-base in the area of behavior toward racial/ethnic groups and persons who identify as Lesbian, Gay, Bisexual, or Transgendered (LGBT). Microaggressions are defined as subtle communications of prejudice toward individuals based upon membership in marginalized social groups,[4] and include "communications that convey rudeness and insensitivity," less overt forms of name calling, and "communications that exclude, negate, or nullify ... psychological thoughts, feelings, or experiential reality."[5] An example of a microaggression toward persons who identify as LGBT is well-captured by the title of a book by my colleague Kevin Nadal: *That's So Gay!*[6] Though this phrase (commonly used by teenagers and young adults in the United States to mean that something is ridiculous or silly) might not be directly intended to hurt someone who identifies as LGBT, it is easy to see how it can be perceived as insensitive, rude, or excluding, given that it associates sexual orientation with negative characteristics.

Intrigued by the concept of microaggressions, my colleague Lauren Gonzales and I set out to find out if they are also experienced by people with severe mental illnesses. To explore the topic, we started with a research approach called a "focus group," where a group of people from a given target population gets together to discuss a specific topic. In this case, we convened four focus groups with people who self-identified as having a mental illness from two settings: college students (recruited through a college office that serves students with disabilities) and people receiving services from a public-sector mental health treatment program. After explaining the concept of microaggressions, we asked people if they had had any of these types of experiences and to give specific examples of them. Based on the focus groups, we concluded that people with mental illnesses commonly experience three types of microaggressions: *assumptions of inferiority* (statements indicating that it was assumed that the person is not capable of doing what most people can do), *patronization* (dismissive statements including those suggesting that it is assumed that people with mental illnesses are child-like), and subtle behaviors indicating *fear of mental illness*.[7] An example of assumption of inferiority was voiced by a (at the time four-year) college student, who was told that she should not aspire to go to a four-year college by a high school guidance counselor because she would not be capable of that level of study as a result of her mental illness:

> Because I have a mental illness, that still impacts my ability to do well in school, so when [the college counselor] told me that I should consider a trade or go to community college, I felt as though she was kind of stigmatizing against me and she didn't want to deal with my problems. She's like, "Well, I'm just saying what's true." She didn't apologize.

Another college participant provided an example of patronization when she stated that people often used terms describing mental disorders to characterize behaviors that they find annoying, while at the same time dismissing that someone who is doing well can legitimately have a mental illness:

> I have this thing where I tell people, like I have bipolar and they say "You don't actually because I know people." Or they say to somebody who is behaving a certain way "Oh you're acting so bipolar." And I'm like "Um, really? So there is a way you act?" They don't actually know what it is.

A participant in another study on the experiences of people with mental illness in the criminal justice system indicated how the term "MO" (meaning that someone has been housed in specialized "mental observation" units within the jail) is used as a slur in those settings to indicate that someone should not be taken seriously:

> Basically, a lot of people, they'd see me walking the halls, and "Yeah, he's in MO housing." . . . I experienced it a lot. If I get mad or something, dude be like, "Chill, he MO. Ignore him." Instead of like, let me see what's up.

After conducting focus groups, we decided to explore whether community members would endorse using microaggressions, so we created an assessment scale, based on the types of things that our focus group participants had told us they experienced, to assess whether community members would endorse the intention to engage in these types of behaviors. The resulting scale, called the Mental Illness Microaggression Scale-Perpetrator version (MIMS-P), has been administered to more than 2,000 community participants in three studies (two online and one in-person), and has been found to be significantly related to the endorsement of negative stereotypes about mental illness, indicating that these types of behaviors are part of the stigma constellation.[8] We found that community members most commonly endorse a willingness to use "patronizing" microaggressions. Specifically, in one of our studies, 62% of participants endorsed that, if someone they were "close to" had a mental illness they would "talk to them more slowly," while 81% endorsed that they would "frequently remind them to take their medications." It should be noted that these behaviors, though likely offensive to many people with mental illness, could be well-intentioned and might be the result of a lack of information as well as negative stereotypes.

Another type of "patronizing" interaction that was discussed in our focus groups includes instances in which a person with a mental illness speaks with a community member who is not aware of the first person's psychiatric history and then goes on to make dismissive statements about people with mental illnesses. For example, one individual related having a discussion with a community member in his neighborhood who began to complain about "those people" who live in the community residence for people with mental illness across the street, not realizing that the individual was also one of "those people." A related situation is described by University of Southern California law professor Elyn Saks (who has been diagnosed with schizophrenia) in her book *The Center Cannot Hold*. Saks describes teaching a class on mental health law and discussing the concept of competency, and whether it is appropriate to bar people from mental illness from practicing medicine and law. Saks recounts that a student in the class who was not aware of her psychiatric history stated: "Would you go see a lawyer who was on psychotropic medication? Because I certainly wouldn't."[9]

An interesting window into the extent to which community members regularly engage in insensitive and patronizing statements comes from a recent study of the use of the terms "schizophrenia" and "schizophrenic" on the social media platform Twitter (which, at the time of writing, is regularly used by more than 200 million persons world-wide).[10] This study examined the content of all "Tweets" (or Twitter postings) linked to these terms during a 40-day period and compared them with postings for "diabetes" and "diabetic." It was found that almost 50% of the postings

Figure 6   Mug sold in San Francisco airport in 2017.
Photo by Gerald Lee.

for "schizophrenic" (which were just as common as postings for "schizo-phrenia") were either negative or sarcastic, while this was the case for roughly 22% of those for "schizophrenia." In both cases, negative and sarcastic references were significantly more common for schizophrenia postings than diabetes postings, suggesting that a negative and sarcastic tone is not just a function of the way that people communicate on Twitter. While these findings only tell us about the communication tendencies of people who are active on social media, they do provide a "real-world" window into the degree to which people are prone to make insensitive comments in the context of talking (albeit online) about severe mental illness. An example from another context is demonstrated in a candy bar wrapper (and related products – see Figure 6) I recently saw at San Francisco airport (ironically, after attending an anti-stigma conference). The candy bar wrapper offers an "ALCATRAZ PSYCHO WARD BAR (WITH NUTS!)"

Another type of microaggression discussed by participants in our focus groups was that community members would actively avoid them after discerning that they might have a mental illness. One focus group partici-pant, who dressed in worn clothes (though not malodorous or demon-strating any overt evidence of symptoms) and therefore possibly fit the stereotypical appearance of a homeless person with mental illness, described poignantly how people avoid her when she is in public:

> when I get around people outside in public, I feel like I'm being outnum-bered like hell, they look at me . . . and then they look a second look and start moving away from me, and sit somewhere else, and they see me sitting down, they want to move somewhere else, and move across from me or if I'm sitting on a train you know, they'll move – move somewhere else, and everybody will move far away and sit in a different seat and sit in another seat and then I'm just sitting by myself.

Based on this type of information, we included an item in the MIMS-P stating "if I saw a person who I thought had a mental illness in public, I would keep my distance from them." In a web-based sample of more than 950 US community members, we found that 36% agreed with this item, while 39% of more than 600 people in the New York area (recruited through a street-outreach approach) agreed. This indicates that these types of behavior, while less likely to be endorsed than the "patronization" behaviors just described, are still common.

How often do people with mental illness experience this type of "distancing" from general community members? To address this question, we created a scale of "perceived" microaggressions with community members and included it a study of roughly 350 people with mental illness living in three communities in the New York City area. We found that roughly 20% of the sample agreed with the statement "when I am in public, other member of the community avoid being physically close to me because of my mental illness," while 26% endorsed the statement "members of my community are less friendly toward me after learning of my mental illness." A similar finding emerged in a Swedish study that asked people with mental illness if they had "been avoided by people because they knew you were hospitalized in a mental hospital," which 35% endorsed as happening at least "sometimes."[11] These data support that these experiences are less common than the "patronization" microaggressions described previously, but do commonly occur.

While the above examples relate to interactions with strangers, in other cases community members may demonstrate "distancing" behavior with a person that they see more often as a neighbor, classmate, or coworker. For example, a participant in a study conducted by researcher Nancy Herman discussed how work acquaintances no longer socialized with him after a psychiatric hospitalization: "We all used to go to lunch together, but after my release, they said they no longer eat lunch; neither do they play golf or go out for drinks after work- the things we used to do together."[12] Although we did not collect data on these types of experiences in our study with people with mental illnesses, research with community members supports that many are willing to engage in this type of "distancing." Specifically, findings from recent national surveys (also discussed in Chapter 2) indicate that many Americans try to avoid social contact with people with mental illnesses, with roughly 50% of Americans indicating that they would be unwilling to "socialize with" a hypothetical person with schizophrenia or to have that person "as a neighbor."[13] Similarly, in my research I found that roughly 40% of a national sample of Americans expressed a desire to "stay away" from a hypothetical person with schizophrenia.[14]

Social Rejection

Moving beyond microaggressions on the scale of severity are more overt expressions of social rejection. These are more active efforts to avoid interacting with a prior friend or acquaintance who has a mental illness. In trying to parse out how these behaviors differ from microaggressions, it might be helpful to think of the difference between situations in which others avoid *initiating* relationships with someone and situations in which others actively *end* a relationship. Although the first might be somewhat hurtful, the second requires more effort and is likely to be experienced as a more direct rejection by the target person. A focus group participant explained how he was rejected by the circle of friends that he had grown up around after his first psychiatric episode:

> when I was growing up after my first hospitalization in 1976 my older brother's friends didn't want to include me in their groups any more like when he went to play basketball or just to hang out in general because they thought that I was not in my right frame of mind to be included any more after that first hospitalization.

A number of studies have examined the extent to which people with mental illnesses self-report having been socially rejected. The most comprehensive, conducted by Graham Thornicroft and colleagues for the World Psychiatric Association Global Programme Against Stigma, interviewed more than 700 people diagnosed with schizophrenia in 27 countries. They found that 47% endorsed being "discriminated" against because of mental illness in efforts to make friendships.[15] A substudy with 70 participants from this larger project examined the specific types of rejections people had experienced, and found that the most dominant theme was of being "shunned" by friends and neighbors. For example, one participant from Lithuania, like the participant in our focus group, stated: "All my friends turned away from me ... They just stopped to communicate with me, broke the relations."[16]

Although this research presents a relatively bleak picture, it appears that the reality is more mixed for many people with mental illnesses. For example, in a large survey conducted by researcher Otto Wahl on the stigma experiences of people with mental illnesses in the United States, although 60% of the sample endorsed that they had been shunned or avoided because of their mental illness at least "sometimes," more than 80% *also* endorsed that friends had at least "sometimes" been supportive.[17] In my clinical work with people with severe mental illnesses, I find that many people have some friends who "stand by" them, but may at the same time have had very painful rejection experiences from other friends. For example, one individual has a small circle of "old friends" that he grew up with who he still socializes with, but he is still greatly affected by the experience of a serious girlfriend's rejection of him after his first major psychiatric episode. It is likely that most people with mental illnesses encounter a combination of supportive and rejecting responses from friends.

What do we find if we ask community members about their intention to engage in rejection behaviors? Since it is difficult to find groups of community members that have definitely had contact with people with severe mental illnesses, studies have tended to focus on "intended behavior." For example, a scale called the "Reported and Intended Behavior Scale" (RIBS) asks people if, in the future, they would be willing to continue a relationship with a friend who developed a mental health problem. Obviously, questions about such intentions are more likely to be impacted by "social desirability" or the awareness that it might be seen as inappropriate to socially reject someone on the basis of having a mental illness, as well as the possibility that persons who have engaged in this type of behavior would refuse to participate in research on this topic. Nevertheless, studies in the United States conducted by my research group consistently find that roughly 25% of community members indicate that that they would not be willing to continue a friendship with someone with a mental illness. However, research conducted in other settings suggests that this intention can vary dramatically depending on location. For example, a study that compared responses to the RIBS between community residents in England and the Czech Republic found that while only 18% of respondents in England indicated that they would be unwilling to continue a friendship with someone with a mental illness, nearly 73% of community members in the Czech Republic endorsed this unwillingness.[18] Similarly, a study of university students in Nigeria found that almost 60% endorsed that they would "probably" or "definitely" not continue a friendship with someone with a mental illness.[19] Certainly, it is possible that community members in the Czech Republic and Nigeria were just being more honest than the UK respondents, but it is also possible that willingness to actively reject someone who has developed a mental illness varies by sociocultural context (we will discuss this further in Chapter 4).

Although, on the one hand, findings with community members in the United States and UK are encouraging, since they indicate that a majority of community members would be willing to continue friendships with people with mental illnesses, it should be emphasized that the RIBS does not specify a diagnosis but just asks globally about "mental illness." It is likely that rates of intended rejection would increase with a measure that specified a diagnosis that is more clearly associated with negative stereotypes, such as schizophrenia. Furthermore, as we will see in Chapter 4, there may be particular subgroups of people that are particularly prone to engage in these types of rejecting behaviors, making persons with mental illnesses who live among those groups more likely to experience rejection.

Discrimination

Moving further along on the scale of severity, the term *discrimination* is usually reserved for situations in which others use mental illness as a justification to deny or limit access to essential aspects of community life, such as housing, employment, or educational opportunity. Discrimination is often illegal (although this depends on local laws) so we would certainly expect this to impact the frequency with which this type of behavior would be engaged in, yet even infrequent experiences of discrimination could be expected to have a substantial impact on someone's life. At the most extreme end are instances where someone is denied work or fired simply because it has become known that they have a mental illness. A participant in one of our focus groups described how he lost his job as a building porter after his first psychiatric hospitalization:

> Well, I had discrimination when I was hospitalized and I went back to work and the super didn't want me to work no more because I was in a psych ward. So he didn't like it or he couldn't understand it why I was in a psych ward because of my depression and I lost my job behind that.

Similarly, a participant in a UK study reported being clearly discriminated against because she revealed having a psychiatric history:

> I was dismissed from a job as a psychiatric nursing assistant in a nursing home, as soon as I declared my history, although they said my work was perfectly satisfactory. I was then refused an interview for a psychiatric nursing course, although I had previously worked in three hospitals and the nursing home, and had a degree. At first the Director of Nursing Studies would not tell me why, but when I pursued the matter and met her face-to-face she said it was because I was 'honest enough' to reveal my previous psychosis.[20]

How often do people with mental illnesses report being discriminated against in work, housing, or educational situations? In the Global Programme Against Stigma study, 29% of the sample reported discrimination experiences in both finding and keeping a job, while 19% reported discrimination in education, and 14% in housing. Similarly, in a large study on discrimination experiences of people with mental illness in the United States, roughly 20% reported experiencing employment discrimination related to mental illness, while 12% reported housing discrimination.[21] These proportions might be underestimates, however, as not all participants in these surveys may have sought work or housing. A study that focused specifically on people with mental illnesses who *were* employed, however, found that nearly half reported experiencing workplace discrimination.[22] In a subsequent in-depth study of the types of experiences of those who reported discrimination, experiences included "discrediting the person's professional competence," "prejudicial treatment" in evaluations, lack of advancement, and being "forced out." These findings are concerning, as they suggest that even if more blatant acts of discrimination are not acted upon, there may be many ways in which people with mental illnesses may perceive that they are in a "hostile" work environment.

Of course, readers may wonder how much we can trust these perceptions given that they might be biased by symptoms, such as "persecutory" ideas, which might lead someone to think that a work supervisor is against them when it is not actually the case. On the other hand, we might suspect that surveys with employers or landlords about whether they engage in discriminatory practices might be unlikely to get a forthright response. For this reason, some researchers have used experimental methods that employ deception to find out if employers will discriminate when they are not aware that their willingness to hire people with psychiatric histories is being evaluated. In a group of studies conducted in the 1970s employing this approach, social psychologist Amerigo Farina exposed potential employers to the same individual posing as a prospective employment candidate and varied a "cover story" of whether they were an "ex-mental patient" or had been out of the workforce for some other reason (e.g., that they were "travelling" or that they were a "surgical patient").[23] These studies found strong support that the individual was more likely to be seen as a poor work candidate when they presented as having a psychiatric history than when they did not, even when their interview behavior was deliberately "calm" (but especially when they presented as "tense"). This research provides compelling evidence that employment-related discrimination toward people with mental illnesses is not merely in the "eye of the beholder."

A shortcoming of these findings, however, is that they are dated, as employment discrimination toward persons with disabilities was not illegal in either the United States or the UK in the 1970s. That changed with the passage of the "Americans with Disabilities" (ADA) act in the United States in 1990 and the Disabilities Discrimination Act (DDA) in the UK in 1995, which both made discrimination toward people with a range of disabilities, including "psychiatric" ones, illegal and punishable by civil penalties.[24] However, although a replication of Farina's studies has not been attempted in the post-ADA world, a series of studies conducted by researcher Teresa Scheid indicated that it is unlikely that employment discrimination toward people with mental illnesses has completely disappeared. In the first study, Scheid surveyed 73 prospective employers about their "comfort" with hiring people with a number of background characteristics, and found that 52% expressed "discomfort" with hiring a person who had been to a mental hospital, while 67% expressed "discomfort" with hiring someone taking antipsychotic medication.[25] Another study with 190 prospective employers replicated these findings, and also found evidence that the endorsement of some negative stereotypes about mental illness, such as the belief that "stress at work is a major cause of mental illness," was related to degree of willingness to comply with the ADA.[26]

There is also evidence that the ADA and the DDA are largely ineffective in challenging employment discrimination, when it does occur. For example, an analysis of claims of employment discrimination related to the ADA found that they almost never result in an outcome favorable to the employee[27, a]; similarly, British disability advocate Liz Sayce documented many cases charging employment discrimination under the DDA that were not resolved in favor of the employee, such as the case of a woman whose offer of a job as a fingerprint technician with a police department was withdrawn as soon as her psychiatric history became known.[28] These findings suggest that there are few reasons to expect that biased employers have dramatically altered their practices toward people with mental illnesses, the ADA and DDA notwithstanding.

Although there has been far less research on the willingness of landlords to engage in discrimination toward people with mental illnesses, one experimental study was conducted in Canada that paralleled Farina's work. In this study, prospective landlords advertising vacant apartments were called, and callers randomly engaged in a script where they provided identical background information, varying whether they did or did not mention mental illness. The study found that callers mentioning mental illness were met with a negative response about the availability of the apartment roughly 60–70% of the time, in contrast with those who did

---

[a] Of course, it is not possible to know whether any of these claims lacked legal merit.

not mention mental illness, who were met with a negative response only 17% of the time.[29]

Another way in which discrimination can potentially manifest itself in the area of housing is when there is organized community opposition to the siting of specialized group residences for people with mental illnesses. The process of organized opposition, also known as the "not in my backyard" (or NIMBY) phenomenon, has been documented in many locations in the United States, Canada, and Great Britain. Although proponents of NIMBY often cite neutral concerns such as "traffic" and property values, case studies indicate that community member concerns are often driven by negative stereotypes such as fears that residents will be dangerous. This was supported by a large study conducted in the 1970s by researcher Michael Dear, who found that community members in Toronto, Canada, who were most opposed to the siting of community-based facilities for people with mental illnesses also endorsed the most stigmatizing views. Furthermore, community members who considered the siting of a facility to be "undesirable" were most willing to engage in actions such as "sign petition," "attend meeting," and "join protest group."[30] More recent examples also support that stigma underlies much of the NIMBY phenomenon. For example, in one instance in Great Britain in 2004, families protesting the opening of a community residence held signs stating "Paranoid Schizophrenic Out!" and "Keep Our Children Safe!," indicating that concerns about dangerousness drove opposition.[31] At the time of this writing, a story appeared on a New York City news website and reported an episode of NIMBY opposition to proposed supported housing for people with mental illness in Brooklyn, NY. The article reported a community meeting discussion, in which one concerned resident stated: "You mentioned that these are chronically mentally ill people . . . Do we need to be concerned these people will be out for the day and just grab and stab someone?"[32] Although little recent research has systematically studied what factors predict the likelihood that communities will organize opposition (or that these responses will be successful), it is important to consider NIMBY as a possible manifestation of housing discrimination, as it may lead housing to be located in more economically disadvantaged areas that are less likely to mount organized opposition.

Verbal Harassment/Hate Speech

Verbal harassment and hate speech refer to instances where insulting or threatening language is used in a targeted and aggressive way to undermine members of a specific group. While the two terms are closely aligned, verbal harassment is more likely to be targeted toward an individual, while instances of hate speech are more likely to be characterized by statements targeting an entire group (in some cases threatening violence toward them). In this manner, these actions reflect a more severe manifestation of stigma than social rejection.

The research base on verbal harassment is less comprehensive than it is for other forms of stigma. For example, there are no studies with community members examining self-reported intention to engage in the verbal harassment of people with mental illnesses. Nevertheless, there is ample evidence that instances of verbal harassment occur with some frequency. Examples of verbal harassment include the repeated use of epithets such as "nutter" or "mad" in Great Britain and "psycho" or "schizo" in the United States. In other cases, epithets might not be used, but the reason for the harassment might still be clear. For example, an individual in Great Britain described his experience with a neighbor:

> this place where I used to live a woman came round looking for my brother and said: "Oh you're the one who's been in the psychiatric clinic." Then she went on to give me an earful about how I was likely to be abusing children.[33]

Most research that has been conducted on the verbal harassment of people with mental illnesses has been drawn through advocacy networks and has tended to find very high rates of experiences of this type. For example, a UK-based survey of more than 700 people with mental illnesses found that 47% reported experiencing verbal harassment,[34] while a US survey of more than 400 people with mental illnesses found that more than 80% reported experiencing verbal abuse.[35] Given that they were recruited though advocacy networks, findings from these surveys are not likely to be representative of experiences of people with severe mental illnesses in general, as they plausibly might have been biased toward recruiting people who have had harassment experiences. However, a more well-designed study of verbal harassment, which recruited people with mental illnesses through community mental health teams, was conducted in the UK. This study also had the methodological strength of comparing the verbal harassment experiences of people with mental illnesses to other community members without mental illness. The study found that 34% of people with mental illnesses reported experiencing verbal harassment, in contrast with roughly 14% of the community sample. The most common sources of the harassment were "teenagers" and "neighbors," and the majority of the sample indicated that the harassment targeted their mental health problems.[36] Similarly, another community-based study, conducted with people diagnosed with schizophrenia in India, found that "ridiculing by others" was reported by 22% of the sample.[37] These studies suggest that verbal harassment related to mental illness, though perhaps not as universal as previous surveys suggested, is a real phenomenon for a significant minority of persons.

Hate speech is more difficult to document, as more severe instances of it, which might include violent threats toward an entire group, are more likely to arouse interest from law enforcement. In *Disability Hate Crimes: Does Anybody Really Hate Disabled People?*, Criminologist Mark Sherry documented the existence of hate speech toward a variety of disabled groups, including people with mental illnesses, on targeted "hate" websites and social media platforms. For example, a commenter on one website wrote:

> Schizophrenics really outta [sic] be killed . . . they're horrid and need to be eliminated considering how much of a danger they are to society and how much rights we give them when they really don't deserve any with what they do with them.[38]

Although Sherry concluded that hate speech toward disabled groups is "widespread," it is difficult to draw this conclusion given that there are no studies that firmly establish the prevalence of this type of speech. Nevertheless, his analysis makes it clear that hate speech toward people with mental illnesses is a real phenomenon.

It should also be noted that although speech advocating that people with mental illness be hurt or killed is more likely to occupy the fringes of the internet, there is no shortage of the use of epithets such as "psychos," "schizos," and "crazies" in the mainstream discourse in the media and the internet (see also the headline in Figure 2). It can be argued that the use of these terms in a negative context constitutes a form of hate speech. Some sense of the possible scope of the use of these terms comes from my own research, as the statement "I might sometimes make jokes about people who are 'psychos' or 'schizos' when I'm with friends" was included in the original version of the MIMS-P (the community member micro-aggression scale). This item, which was eventually dropped from the scale because it did not correlate well with the other items (and might be more closely aligned with indirect hate speech than microaggressions), was nevertheless agreed with by 31% of a sample of more than 500 community members. A further example of this type of speech comes from a commentator who has sold more than 3 million books and recently wrote on her internet blog:

> In every one of these mass shootings, there was someone in a position to say before the attack, "Trust me, this person is a psycho." . . . If someone was brought back from the 1950s to today, he'd tell us: "I couldn't help but notice that all the people who committed mass shootings were batsh-t crazy. Why were they not locked up or forced to take medication?"[39]

As noted in Chapter 1, although epithets toward other groups (such as the "n-word") are not tolerated in the mainstream discourse, a similar sense of what is appropriate does not exist with regard to discussions of people with mental illnesses. I will discuss this phenomenon further later in this chapter in the context of media bias, and in Chapter 4.

Hate Crimes

At the highest level of severity in the behavioral expressions of stigma are "hate crimes." Hate crimes are defined as criminal offenses against a person or property that are motivated in whole or in part by an offender's bias against the victim's membership in a specific group.[40] These types of actions are expected to be the least frequently expressed forms of stigma, given their severity and illegality. Placing this into context, however, is the fact that there is clear evidence that people with mental illnesses are at considerably increased risk of being victims of crime compared to the general population.[b, 41] Although this increased risk is arguably related to the secondary consequences of stigma (such as poverty, homelessness, and criminal justice involvement), the question here is how much of this criminal victimization is directly motivated by the victim's mental illness, rather than other "risk factors" for victimization that might be associated with mental illness.

At the time of this writing, the most severe hate crime perpetrated by an individual toward people with mental illnesses occurred in Japan on July 26, 2016, when Satoshi Uematsu broke into a residential treatment program for people with mental illness, stabbing 19 residents to death and injuring 26 others. That Uematsu, a former employee at the program, was motivated by hate was made clear by statements he had made prior to the incident advocating that people with disabilities be "euthanized," and his statement to the police afterward that "it is better that disabled people disappear."[42]

---

[b] For example, one comprehensive survey of crime victimization in the United States found that people with mental illness were 6 to 23 times more likely to be victims of crime than others, depending on the type of crime.

Although Uematsu's actions were horrifying and demonstrate how notions that "people with mental illness do not deserve to live" can potentially lead to violent acts, hate crimes of this caliber are fortunately quite rare.

Information on the extent to which more typical hate crimes are experienced by people with severe mental illnesses comes from two sources: surveys conducted with people about their experience of such incidents, and official reports from law enforcement agencies. Each of these sources has potential problems. Specifically, surveys have the problem that they require the victim of a crime to infer the motivation of the perpetrator, which can be unclear unless the perpetrator made a clear statement of their motives. Official reports, on the other hand, have the problem of relying only on crime that is reported, and there is evidence that much crime goes unreported. Another problem is that most official hate crime reports do not distinguish mental illness from other "mental" disabilities such as intellectual disability (previously called mental retardation), so it is unclear what proportion of crimes were committed against people with mental illnesses.

Surveys with people with mental illnesses have reported varying rates of experience of hate crime. For examples a UK-wide study found that 21% endorsed being "threatened" and 14% "physically attacked" because of mental illness,[43] while a US-based survey found that 45% reported experiencing "physical abuse" related to mental illness.[44] In addition, both studies indicated that a large proportion of individuals (30% and 60%, respectively) did not report the physical "abuse" or attack. Neither of these studies, however, has samples that one can feel confident are "representative," as they were drawn from advocacy organizations.

Official figures on hate crime are hampered by the under-report problem noted in this section, but they provide some sense of the scope and nature of the crimes that are typically committed. The US Federal Bureau of Investigation (FBI) indicated that there were 75 reported crimes against people with "mental" disabilities in 2013 and 69 in 2014.[45] Most of them, in both years, were classified as "simple assault" and "intimidation," and there were no murders reported in either year. In addition, it is likely that some proportion of these reported hate crimes were perpetrated toward persons with intellectual disability rather than mental illness. This suggests that the scope of *reported* hate crime toward people with mental illness is quite small given that there are millions of people with mental illnesses in the United States. Official figures from the "Crown Prosecution Service" of the UK, however, indicate that there is considerably more willingness to report and prosecute this type of crime in the UK, and suggest that the US numbers are likely to represent a significant under-count. Specifically, although the UK has only one fifth the population of the United States, roughly three times as many hate crimes toward disabled persons were reported in 2013 and 2014: In the two years, 574 were charged, with 470 convicted.[c] Types of offenses were primarily "offences against persons," including one homicide. An example of the type of crime prosecuted was offered in the UK report, which described an incident in which a person with combined mental illness and intellectual disability was intimidated by young men who threw stones at him. The crime was prosecuted because it was captured on surveillance video.[46]

What are we to make of the existing data on hate crimes toward people with mental illnesses? Given the limitations of the data sources, it remains unclear what the true scope of the problem is, but the UK numbers suggest that in the United States, anti-mental illness hate crimes might be ten times more common than the official FBI reports suggest. Clearly, more thorough research needs to be done, and the most we can infer from these reports is that *some* proportion of the extensive violent victimization that is experienced by people with mental illnesses is motivated by hatred.

Structural Stigma

The previous section concerned behavioral experessions that are enacted by individuals, but there are also expressions of negative stereotypes that are reflected on a larger level, including laws, social policies, and the practices of public and private institutions. These forms of discrimination, which have been termed "structural stigma" by Patrick Corrigan and others,[47] can affect many aspects of the lives of people with severe mental illnesses. Below, I review two major areas of structural stigma: legal discrimination and media bias. Research in these areas relies on reviews of official documents, which are usually in the public domain, so our analysis in this regard is more straightforward.

Legal Discrminiation

Although laws like the ADA make discrimination in areas such as employment and housing illegal, there are many forms of discrmination toward people with mental illnesses that are completely legal according to state

---

[c] The Crown Prosecution Service report did not provide figures by type of disability, but evidence from the FBI reports suggests that roughly 75% of disability-related hate crimes are likely to be related to "mental" disability. It is therefore likely that roughly 350 of the 470 convictions were for anti "mental" disability hate crime offenses.

and local laws throughout the United States. Five major categories of legal rights that are restricted on the basis of mental illness have been examined in this regard: voting, jury duty, holding office, marriage, and parenting. An analysis of state laws in these areas in 1999 found that 37 of the 50 US states had laws restricting voting rights, 44 restricting jury duty, 24 restricting the ability to hold political office, 27 restricting marriage (i.e., allowing mental illness as grounds for divorce), and 27 restricting parenting rights.[48] In some cases, laws specified that the person had to be found incompetent for rights to be restricted, but in most cases laws did not specify this and allowed rights to be restricted on the basis of mental illness diagnosis without reference to incompetence.

Although we might expect that the legal rights of people with mental illnesses would have expanded since 1999, a later analysis by Patrick Corrigan and colleagues suggests that this has largely not been the case. The analysis found that of 928 mental health bills introduced in US states in 2002, 75% aimed to contract liberties.[49] Examples of laws contracting liberties included a law in Arkansas that "enables the Medical Licensure Commission to revoke or place on probation any physician or osteopath who has been evaluated or received inpatient or outpatient treatment for any psychiatric illness."

Although a comparable examination of laws has not appeared since these two analyses, further examinations in specific areas suggest that there has been no significant change in the number of laws that legally discriminate against people with mental illnesses. In the area of parenting rights, a 2005 analysis of state laws found that 35 states had laws restricting parenting rights on the basis of mental illness (an apparent increase from 1999).[50] Similarly, a 2008 analysis found that 39 states had some restrictions on the voting rights of people with mental illness.[51]

What about the rest of the world? In a recent report, the Mental Disability Advocacy Center, an international legal advocacy organization, documented that 16 European nations (including Russia) employ "legal guardianship" statutes that systematically disenfranchise people with mental illnesses.[52] The statutes, which allow people with mental illness who have been judged incompetent to be deprived of *all* citizenship rights, including the right to marry, vote, and sign a contract, are implemented at rates that vary greatly by country (notably, Eastern European nations Hungary, Croatia, and the Czech Republic placed persons under guardianship at the highest rates).[d] Although

---

[d] The extent to which guardianship can potentially lead to a complete "discrediting" of a person who has been placed under this designation will be familiar to readers of the best-selling *The Girl with the Dragon Tattoo* series.

systematic examinations of laws in other parts of the world are lacking, there are reports of significant legal discrimination in some countries, such as forced sterilization in Kenya.[53] While falling short of forced sterilization, Chinese law includes a provision requiring physicians to advise couples to "cancel their marriage" and not to have children when one member of the couple has a "certain genetic disease of a serious nature which is considered to be inappropriate for child-bearing from a medical point of view," noting that this can include "schizophrenia" and "manic-depressive psychosis."[54]

Of all the restrictions just discussed, in my experience none hits home for people with mental illnesses more than the restriction of parenting rights. As the example that led-off this chapter indicates, in many US states, laws allow parental rights to be lost by a person with a mental illness even when there is no evidence of inappropriate parenting, based on the principle of "presumptive neglect," an idea that is clearly rooted in the negative stereotype that people with mental illnesses are incapable of being responsible. I came into contact with this perspective directly in my work with a client who had asked a family member to care for her children during a psychiatric hospitalization. After returning from the hospital, the client found that she had lost custody of her children on the basis of New York State law,[e] despite no available evidence that she had been an inadequate parent when the children were under her care. After an unsuccessful effort to regain custody, she was even blocked from *supervised visits* with the children. The client, who had financial resources and no history of violence or substance abuse, was devastated by this outcome. I recall speaking with a "forensic psychologist" who evaluated the client's suitability for visitations, and being dumbfounded by the extent to which negative assumptions about people with mental illnesses seemed to permeate his opinions on whether it would be appropriate for the client to even visit her biological children with supervision.

Media Bias

Although not enshrined in law, the actions of major media institutions can arguably also be considered a form of "structural stigma," as they are reflective of the policies and established practices of institutions, rather than individuals.[55] A fairly comprehensive body of literature has examined

---

[e] The law, Social Services Law, Sec.384-b, states that parental rights can be terminated on the basis of: (1) abandonment, (2) permanent neglect, (3) severe and repeated abuse, and (4) "mental illness or mental retardation."

the extent to which media institutions are systematically biased toward the confirmation of negative stereotypes in their reports about people with mental illnesses.

A number of studies were conducted in the 1970s and 1980s that examined the content of US and Canadian television, film, and newsprint. These studies, most of which were summarized by Otto Wahl in his book *Media Madness*,[56] revealed that 70% of TV characters with mental illnesses were shown to be violent, and that the majority of newspaper stories related to mental illness in the United States and Canada emphasized violence as well. These studies led to calls from advocacy organizations for the media to give a more balanced portrayal of people with mental illnesses.

Have these calls led to change in practices in recent years? Analyses of media reporting in the past 15 years suggest that there may have been some change, but that the media is still biased toward negative reports, and gives these reports more prominence. One analysis looked at all stories related to mental illness in major US newspapers (defined as having a circulation greater than 250,000) during six-week-long periods in 2002. The articles were content-coded regarding the primary focus of the article. The authors found that the largest category of stories (39%) concerned dangerousness, and that these stories were more frequently highlighted in the front section of the newspaper (37% of all "front" section mental health stories concerned violent crime). The second most common category (20%) concerned advocacy, and most typically included stories discussing shortages of mental health services, while the least common category (4%) concerned stories of recovery or other positive outcome. A more recent analysis of newspaper reports in Canada between 2005 and 2010 found a similar pattern, with 40% of newspaper articles focusing on crime, violence, or danger, and less than 20% discussing treatment.[57]

An interesting study examining the change in reports about mental illness in major UK newspapers between 1996 and 2005 provided both good and bad news about how media bias changed over that span of time. Although the report found evidence that articles were less likely to use terms equating people with their disorders like "schizophrenic" in 2005 than 1996, they were no less likely to use clearly stigmatizing terms such as "madman," "maniac," "monster," "nutter," "psycho," and "schizo" (14% of articles in both years used these terms). Notably, in almost half of the instances where stigmatizing terms were used, the word appeared in the *headline*.[58] An example of this type of headline from a major UK tabloid is shown in Figure 7.

Figure 7   2003 headline from British tabloid *The Sun* about a professional boxer
who had been hospitalized for psychiatric reasons (photo removed for copyright reasons).
The headline was later replaced by a headline reading "Sad Bruno in Mental Home."
Source: The Sun/News Syndication.

Although no comparable analysis has looked specifically at the use of
stigmatizing language in US newspapers, an analysis that I conducted of
the content of one major US tabloid suggests that the use of such terms is
common. A search of the use of the terms "psycho," "schizo," and
"madman" during 2015 by New York City area newspaper *The New York
Post* (which has an average daily circulation of more than 500,000) revealed
that the newspaper used the term "psycho" in 57 articles, "schizo" in 78
articles, and "madman" in 101 articles during the course of the year.[f] In
many cases, stories suggested that the terms were synonymous with

---

[f] I conducted this search using the newspaper's online database, accessible at www.nypost.com.

violence, implying that mental illness and violence are one and the same. For example, a story about a school stabbing in Sweden described the attacker as a "madman" and a "lunatic," suggesting that they had a mental illness, but provided no specific information of whether the individual had a psychiatric history.

A smattering of recent studies of how news media report on mental illness in other countries suggests that a sensational emphasis on violence is not the norm only in the United States and UK. For example, a study of newspaper reports in Slovakia, Croatia, and the Czech Republic during 2010 found that 35–60% of mental health-related articles were sensational in nature, while the content was judged to be stigmatizing in 30–40% of the articles.[59] Another analysis of articles in the Belgian-Dutch media between 2008 and 2012 found that 42% of articles concerning schizophrenia had a negative emphasis.[60]

Why are media outlets so inclined to sensationalize reports linking mental illness to violence and other negative characteristics? Examinations of this issue have revealed that there is a strong financial incentive to highlight stories that instill fear, as it is believed that this increases sales and viewership (the phrase "if it bleeds it leads" has been used to describe this tendency in the news business). Stories about the intersection of violence and mental illness are most likely to appeal in this regard, as they may relate to violence that is perceived to be "random" and are therefore most likely to generate fear.[61] There may also be an element of "institutional practice" as well. This was expressed by a former UK news editor who, explaining how newpapers could run headlines with terms like "nutter" in them, stated that "such pejorative headlines are not necessarily malicious ... They are grabbed by hard-pressed, lazy or inexperienced sub-editors."[62] This suggests that many news outlets may focus on negative stories whether or not this helps generate sales and viewership because that is simply "what is done."

Summary of Community Stigma

This chapter has provided a broad overview of what we know about the behavioral expressions of community stigma toward people with mental illnesses. As we've seen, stigma is expressed in community member behavior in a number of ways, ranging from small expressions of disregard to acts of violence. Furthermore, it is evident that legally codified discrimination continues to exist in social instutions and laws, even in pluralistic democracies such as the United States and the UK. Nevertheless, it is also evident that rates at which stigmatizing behaviors are expressed vary, raising the question of whether there are particular characteristics of individuals or settings that are most likely to be associated with stigma. In Chapter 4 we will delve further into this issue by examining what is known about the individual and social characteristics that predict the likelihood that one will hold stigmatizing views.

References

1 Wessler, S. F. (2014). Should a mental illness mean you lose your kid? *Propublica*. Accessed online August 23, 2017: www.propublica.org/article/should-a-mental-illness-mean-you-lose-your-kid.

2 Read, J., & Baker, S. (1996). *Not just sticks and stones: A survey of the stigma, taboos and discrimination experienced by people with mental health problems.* MIND. Accessed online August 23, 2017: http://disability-studies.leeds.ac.uk/files/library/MIND-MIND.pdf.

3 Allport, G. W. (1979). *The nature of prejudice* (25th anniversary edition). Reading, MA: Addison-Wesley.

4 Sue, D. W. (2010). Microaggressions, marginality, and oppression: An introduction. In Sue, D. (Ed.), *Microaggressions and marginality: Manifestation, dynamics, and impact* (pp. 3–22). Hoboken, NJ: Wiley.

5 Sue, D. W., Capodilupo, C. M., Torino, G. C., Bucceri, J. M., Holder, A. M., Nadal, K. L., Esquilin, M. (2007). Racial microaggressions in everyday life: Implications for clinical practice. *American Psychologist, 62,* 271–286.

6 Nadal, K. L. (2013). *That's so gay!: Microaggressions and the lesbian, gay, bisexual and transgender community.* Washington, DC: American Psychological Association.

7 Gonzales, L., Davidoff, K., Nadal, K., & Yanos, P. T. (2015). Microaggressions experienced by persons with mental illness: An exploratory study. *Psychiatric Rehabilitation Journal, 38,* 234–241.

8 Gonzales, L., Davidoff, K., DeLuca, J., & Yanos, P. T. (2015). The Mental Illness Microaggressions Scale – Perpetrator Version (MIMS-P): Reliability and validity. *Psychiatry Research, 229,* 120–125.

9 Saks, E. R. (2007). *The center cannot hold: My journey through madness.* New York: Hachette.

10 Joseph, A. J., Tandon, N., Yang, L. H., Duckworth, K., Torous, J., Seidman, L., J., & Keshavan, M. S. (2015). #Schizophrenia: Use and misuse on Twitter. *Schizophrenia Research, 165,* 111–115.

11 Lundberg, B., Hansson, L., Wentz, E., & Bjorkman, T. (2007). Sociodemographic and clinical factors related to devaluation/discrimination and rejection experiences among users of mental health services. *Social Psychiatry & Psychiatric Epidemiology, 42,* 295–300.

12 Herman, N. J. (1993). Return to sender: Reintegrative stigma-management strategies of ex-psychiatric patients. *Journal of Contemporary Ethnography, 22,* 295–330.

13 Pescosolido, B. A., Martin, J. K., Long, J. S., Medina, T. R., Phelan, J. C., & Link, B. G. (2010). A "disease like any other"? A decade of change in public reactions to schizophrenia, depression, and alcohol dependence. *American Journal Psychiatry, 167*, 1321–1330.

14 DeLuca, J., Vaccaro, J., Seda, J., & Yanos, P. T. (Under Review). Political attitudes as predictors of the multiple dimensions of mental health stigma.

15 Thornicroft, G., Brohan, E., Rose, D., Sartorius, N., & Leese, M. (2009). Global pattern of experienced and anticipated discrimination against people with schizophrenia: A cross-sectional survey. *Lancet, 373*, 408–415.

16 Rose, D., Willis, R., Brohan, E., Sartorius, N., Villares, C., Wahlbeck, K., & Thornicroft G. (2011). Reported stigma and discrimination by people with a diagnosis of schizophrenia. *Epidemiology and Psychiatric Sciences, 20*, 193–204.

17 Wahl, O. F. (1999). Mental health consumers' experiences of stigma. *Schizophrenia Bulletin, 25*, 467–478.

18 Winkler, P., Csemy, L., Janouskova, M., Mlada, K., Bankovska-Motlova, L., & Evans-Lacko, S. (2015). Reported and intended behaviour towards those with mental health problems in the Czech Republic and England. *European Psychiatry, 30*, 801–806.

19 Adewuda, A. O., & Makanjuola, R. O. A. (2005). Social distance towards people with mental illness amongst Nigerian university students. *Social Psychiatry and Psychiatric Epidemiology, 40*, 865–868.

20 Read, J., & Baker, S. (1996). *Not just sticks and stones: A survey of the stigma, taboos and discrimination experienced by people with mental health problems.* MIND. Accessed online August 23, 2017: http://disability-studies.leeds.ac.uk/files/library/MIND-MIND.pdf.

21 Corrigan, P., Thompson, V., Lambert, D., Sangster, Y., Noel, J. G., & Campbell, J. (2003). Perceptions of discrimination among persons with serious mental illness. *Psychiatric Services, 54*, 1105–1110.

22 Russinova, Z., Griffin, S., Bloch, P., Wewiorski, N. J., & Rosoklija, I. (2011). Workplace prejudice and discrimination toward individuals with mental illnesses. *Journal of Vocational Rehabilitation, 35*, 227–241.

23 Farina, A., & Felner, R. A. (1973). Employment interviewer reactions to former mental patients. *Journal of Abnormal Psychology, 82*, 268–272; Farina, A., Felner, R. A., & Boudreau, L. A. (1973). Reactions of workers to male and female mental patient job applicants. *Journal of Consulting and Clinical Psychology, 41*, 363–372.

24 Accessed online August 23, 2017 from: www.ada.gov/civil_penalties_2014.htm.

25 Scheid, T. L. (1999). Employment of individuals with mental disabilities: Business response to the ADA's challenge. *Behavioral Sciences and the Law, 17*, 73–91.

26 Scheid, T. L. (2005). Stigma as a barrier to employment: Mental disability and the Americans with Disabilities Act. *International Journal of Law and Psychiatry, 28*, 670–690.

27 Paetzold, R. L. (2005). Mental illness and reasonable accommodations at work: Definition of a mental disability under the ADA. *Psychiatric Services, 56*, 1188–1190.

28 Sayce, K. (2016). *From psychiatric patient to citizen revisited*. London, UK: Palgrave.

29 Page, S. (1977). Effects of the mental illness label in attempts to obtain accommodation. *Canadian Journal of Behavioral Science, 9*, 85–90.

30 Dear, M. J., & Taylor, S. M. (1982). *Not on our street: Community attitudes toward mental health care*. London: Pion.

31 Thornicroft, G. (2006). *Shunned: Discrimination against people with mental illness*. Oxford University Press.

32 Bautista, C. (2016). Planned supportive housing on Gates Avenue draws ire of Bed-Stuy residents. *DnaInfo.com*. Accessed online August 23, 2017: www .dnainfo.com/new-york/20160204/bed-stuy/planned-supportive-housing-on-gates-avenue-draws-ire-of-bed-stuy-residents.

33 Sin, C.H., Hedges, A., Cook, C., Mguni, N., & Comber, N. (2009). *Disabled people's experiences of targeted violence and hostility. Research Report 21*. Manchester: Equality and Human Right's Commission.

34 Read, J., & Baker, S. (1996). *Not just sticks and stones: A Survey of the stigma, taboos and discrimination experienced by people with mental health problems*. MIND. Accessed online August 23, 2017: http://disability-studies.leeds.ac .uk/files/library/MIND-MIND.pdf.

35 Baladerian, N. J., Colemand, T. F., & Stream, J. (2013). *Findings from the 2012 survey on abuse of people with disabilities*. Los Angeles, CA: Spectrum Institute, Disability and Abuse Project. Accessed online August 23, 2017: www.disabilityandabuse.org/survey/findings.pdf.

36 Berzins, K. M., Petch, A., & Atkinson, J. M. (2003). Prevalence and experience of harassment of people with mental health problems living in the community. *British Journal of Psychiatry, 183*, 526–533.

37 Loganathan, S., & Murthy, S. R. (2008). Experiences of stigma and discrimination endured by people suffering from schizophrenia. *Indian Journal of Psychiatry, 50*, 39–46.

38 Sherry, M. (2010). *Disability hate crime: Does anybody really hate disabled people?* Burlington, VT: Ashgate.

39 Coulter, A. (2013). Mental health laws are trouble for democrats. Accessed online August 23, 2017: www.anncoulter.com/columns/2013-12-18.html.

40 Federal Bureau of Investigation (No Date). *Hate crime-overview*. Accessed online August 23, 2017: www.fbi.gov/about-us/investigate/civilrights/hate_ crimes/overview.

41 Teplin, L. A., McClelland, G. M., Abram, K. M., & Weiner, D. A. (2005). Crime victimization in adults with severe mental illness: Comparison with the National Crime Victimization Survey. *Archives of General Psychiatry, 62*, 911–921.

42 McCurry, J. (2016). Japan home care attack: Picture emerges of modest man with horrifying vision. *The Guardian*. Accessed online August 23, 2017: www .theguardian.com/world/2016/jul/26/japan-care-home-attack-satoshi-uematsu-horrifying-vision-disabled-people.

43 Read, J., & Baker, S. (1996). *Not just sticks and stones: A Survey of the stigma, taboos and discrimination experienced by people with mental health problems*.

MIND. Accessed online August 23, 2017: http://disability-studies.leeds.ac
.uk/files/library/MIND-MIND.pdf.

44 Baladerian, N. J., Colemand, T. F., & Stream, J. (2013). *Findings from the
2012 survey on abuse of people with disabilities.* Los Angeles, CA: Spectrum
Institute, Disability and Abuse Project. Accessed online August 23, 2017:
www.disabilityandabuse.org/survey/findings.pdf.

45 Federal Bureau of Investigation (2013). *Hate Crime Statistics, 2013,*
Washington, DC: U.S. Department of Justice. Accessed online August 23,
2017: www.fbi.gov/about-us/cjis/ucr/hate-crime/2013; Federal Bureau of
Investigation (2014). *Hate Crime Statistics, 2014,* Washington, DC: U.S.
Department of Justice. Accessed online August 23, 2017: www.fbi.gov/
about-us/cjis/ucr/hate-crime/2014.

46 Crown Prosecution Service (2014). *Hate crime and crimes against older people
report, 2013–2014.* Accessed online August 23, 2017: www.cps.gov.uk/
publications/docs/cps_hate_crime_report_2014.pdf.

47 Corrigan, P. W., Markowitz, F. E., & Watson, A. C. (2004). Structural levels of
mental illness stigma and discrimination. *Schizophrenia Bulletin, 30,* 481–491.

48 Hemmens, C., Miller, M., Burton, V. S., & Milner, S. (2002). The
consequences of official labels: An examination of the rights lost by the
mentally ill and mentally incompetent ten years later. *Community Mental
Health Journal, 38,* 129–140.

49 Corrigan, P. W., Watson, A. C., Heyrman, M. L., Warpinski, A., Gracia, G.,
Slopen, N., & Hall, L. L. (2005). Structural stigma in state legislation.
Psychiatric Services, 56, 557–563.

50 Lightfoot, E., & LaLiberte, T. (2006). The inclusion of disability as grounds
for termination of parental rights in state codes. *Policy Research Brief, 17,*
1–11.

51 Bazelon Center for Mental Health Law and National Disability Rights
Network (2008). *VOTE. It's your right: A guide to the voting rights of people
with mental disabilities.* Washington DC: Bazelon Center.

52 Mental Disability Advocacy Center (2013). *Legal capacity in Europe: A call to
action to governments and to the EU.* Budapest, Hungary: Mental Disability
Advocacy Center.

53 Mental Disability Advocacy Center (2014). *The right to legal capacity in
Kenya.* Budapest, Hungary: Mental Disability Advocacy Center.

54 Law of the People's Republic of China on maternal and infant health care
(1994), 10th edn. Accessed online August 23, 2017: www.npc.gov.cn/
englishnpc/Law/2007-12/12/content_1383796.htm.

55 Corrigan, P. W., Watson, A. C., Gracia, G., Slopen, N., Rasinski, K., & Hall,
L. L. (2005). Newspaper stories as measures of structural stigma. *Psychiatric
Services, 56,* 551–556.

56 Wahl, O. (1997). *Media madness: Public images of mental illness.* New
Brunswick, NJ: Rutgers University Press.

57 Whitley R, & Berry, S. (2013). Trends in newspaper coverage of mental
illness in Canada: 2005–2010. *Canadian Journal of Psychiatry, 58,* 107–112.

58 Clement, S., & Foster, N. (2008). Newspaper reporting on schizophrenia: A content analysis of five national newspapers at two time points. *Schizophrenia Research*, *98*, 178–183.

59 Vukusic, T., Nawka, A., Brborović, O., Jovanović, N., Kuzman, M. R., Nawková, L., et al. (2012). Development of the PICMIN (picture of mental illness in newspapers): Instrument to assess mental illness stigma in print media. *Social Psychiatry and Psychiatric Epidemiology*, *47*, 1131–1144.

60 Thys, E., Stuyven, C. I., Danckaerts, M., & DeHert, M. (2013). Stigmatization of schizophrenia in Flemish newspapers. *Schizophrenia Research*, *150*, 598–599.

61 Wahl, O. (1997). *Media madness: Public images of mental illness*. New Brunswick, NJ: Rutgers University Press.

62 Wallace, M. (2003). I forgive you, my Sun. *The Independent*. Accessed online August 23, 2017: www.independent.co.uk/news/media/i-forgive-you-my-sun-89169.html.

CHAPTER 4

Who Stigmatizes?

On December 14, 2012, people around the United States were shocked to hear of a horrific mass shooting that occurred in Newtown, Connecticut. Although other shootings have occurred, this one was particularly disturbing because the victims were predominantly small children. In total, 20 children and 6 adults were killed. The shooter, a young man named Adam Lanza who also killed himself before capture, had committed the shooting using his mother's Bushmaster M4-type rifle, a semi-automatic weapon. Later efforts to understand Mr. Lanza's motivation for the killings were inconclusive, but many noted that records indicated that he had been diagnosed with Asperger's Syndrome, a psychiatric disorder that is related to Autism.[a, 1] However, it was difficult for anyone to connect this diagnosis to the shooting, since there had previously been no evidence that Asperger's Syndrome or Autism were related to acts of violence. The official report summarizing the investigation of the shooting found no specific motive or connection to Asperger's Syndrome.[2]

Following the shooting, there were increasing calls from many circles for various forms of gun control, including increased scrutiny in conducting background checks of prospective buyers, as well as bans on certain types of guns, such as assault weapons similar to the type used in the shooting. However, on December 21, 2012, Wayne LePierre, the director of the National Rifle Association (NRA), the United States' leading gun-rights advocacy organization, made a speech where he issued a defiant proposal to instead install armed guards in all schools. In addition, he placed much of the blame for the Newtown incident squarely on the shoulders of people with mental illnesses, stating:

---

[a] With the publication of the *DSM-5* in 2013, Asperger's Syndrome is no longer a diagnostic category as it has been subsumed under the broader category of Autism-Spectrum Disorders. The two main features of Autism-Spectrum Disorders are "Persistent deficits in social communication and social interaction" and "Restricted, repetitive patterns of behavior, interests, or activities." Psychotic symptoms, such as delusions and hallucinations, do not occur in Autism-Spectrum Disorders.

The truth is that our society is populated by an unknown number of genuine monsters – people so deranged, so evil, so possessed by voices and driven by demons that no sane person can possibly ever comprehend them. They walk among us every day . . .

How can we possibly even guess how many [monsters], given our nation's refusal to create an active national database of the mentally ill?[3]

In later statements, Mr. LaPierre used even harsher language about "the mentally ill." Speaking to television reporters he said:

We have no national database of these lunatics . . . We have a completely cracked mentally ill system that's got these monsters walking the streets

And later, to supporters at a rally:

They shouldn't be on the streets, they've stopped taking their medicine and yet they're out there walking around.[4]

As director of a large gun-rights advocacy organization, Mr. LaPierre's insistence that curtailing gun ownership would not prevent future tragedies was certainly to be expected. And it was also not a surprise that he would suggest that more gun ownership would increase public safety, as this is consistent with many of the NRA's past positions. But how do we make sense of his inflammatory rhetoric (reflective of negative stereotypes previously discussed) suggesting that people with mental illnesses are "monsters" who should not be allowed to "walk the streets" (especially when there was no evidence that Adam Lanza, who was not diagnosed with a psychotic disorder and lived in his mother's suburban home, was either "possessed by voices" or "walked the streets")? Where did this come from?

While we may not be able to definitely determine what Mr. LaPierre's thought process was for making these types of statements, one way to make sense of them is to consider the extent to which endorsement of mental health stigma corresponds with certain characteristics of an individual and their worldview. This is also suggested by evidence, mentioned in the previous two chapters, that the endorsement of negative stereotypes about mental illnesses varies by location and is by no means universal in modern societies. In this chapter, we will explore this issue further by examining research on whether and to what extent there are particular characteristics (either of individuals or social contexts) that increase the likelihood that a given individual will endorse or engage in stigma. Thus, we will move beyond the question, raised at the end of Chapter 2, of "*where does stigma come from?*" and instead consider "*why do some people stigmatize, and not others?*"

Table 4.1 *Summary of characteristics predicting mental health stigma*

Domain	Specific characteristic	Nature of relationship
Information about Mental Illness	Education	More education associated with less stigma
	Personal Contact	People with friends, family members and personal experience with mental illness less likely to endorse stigma
Values-Orientation	Cultural Group	Asian-Americans more likely to endorse stigma that other Americans; Eastern and Southern-Europeans more likely to endorse stigma than other Europeans
	Political Ideology	People with socially conservative and authoritarian views more likely to endorse stigma

As we shall see, research suggests that there are a few characteristics that consistently predict the likelihood of endorsing and engaging in stigma. In trying to make sense of what we know, I have organized the characteristics into two broader areas: *information about mental illness*, and *values-orientation*. Table 4.1 summarizes these characteristics and how the research indicates that they are related to stigma. In the following sections, I will summarize the extent to which evidence supports that each of these characteristics is related to stigma, and try to offer theoretical explanations for *why*, which may add further clarification to Mr. LaPierre's motivation for making the statements previously quoted.

It should also be noted that there are some characteristics, such as female gender and younger age, which have been found to be related to a lower likelihood of endorsing stigma in some studies, but less consistently than other characteristics.[5, b] For this reason, I have chosen not to discuss these characteristics in the current chapter.

Information about Mental Illness

Education Level

One of the most consistent findings in research about the predictors of stigma is that it is inversely associated with education level. In other words,

[b] For example, although there is a long history of examining gender as a predictor of stigma, a recent comprehensive review concluded that "with a few exceptions, women do not seem to display more favourable attitudes than men towards people with mental disorder."

the *more* educated a person is, the *less* likely they are to endorse negative stereotypes and the intention to socially avoid people with mental illnesses. For example, in a review of 38 studies examining the predictors of mental health stigma around the world, Matthias Angermeyer and colleagues found that the majority supported the idea that more education was associated with less stigma, and no studies found the opposite relationship.[6] A similar conclusion was reached in a review of the predictors of stigma in the United States.[7]

Why might education, broadly speaking, be associated with less stigma? This finding is certainly consistent with the notion that the more that a person gains access to research-based information, the less likely their beliefs are to be influenced by "common lore," such as sensationalized media accounts. I have certainly encountered this as a college professor teaching 18–20 year olds enrolled in *Abnormal Psychology*, which is, for many students, a first introduction to research-based information about mental illness. Students often tell me that the class led to a major change in their thinking about psychiatric disorders, and a realization that people with mental illness are "people," and not the caricatures that they see presented in popular media.

Findings about the inverse relationship between education and stigma are encouraging, as they suggest that providing a society with more education about mental illness can reduce stigma. However, the potential importance of education should be contextualized by considering that education's impact, though "statistically significant" (meaning that statistical tests indicate that the relationship is highly unlikely to be the result of chance) is actually small. How small? It is difficult to explain this without delving into statistical minutiae, but review studies suggest that only about 1–2% of the variation in measures of stigma is accounted for by education.[8] Furthermore, some studies indicate that education may only be related to some, but not all, aspects of stigma. For example, a national study conducted by Patrick Corrigan and Amy Watson found that while people with a college education or greater were significantly less likely than less educated persons to view a hypothetical person with schizophrenia as "dangerous," they were no less likely to want to avoid the person.[9] Similarly, in my own research, with a street-outreach study of the attitudes of people living in New York City, we found that education was significantly associated with more favorable attitudes toward recovery for people with mental illness and less willingness to engage in microaggressions, but not with intended social avoidance.[10] These findings suggest that education may be helpful, but simply providing greater education is not likely to eliminate the behavioral manifestations of stigma.

The view that education only goes so far is also supported by longitudinal research (also discussed in Chapter 2) indicating that increased population-level education about mental illness has not led to a substantial decrease in stigma over time. For example, in Angermeyer and colleagues' review of research on the "evolution" of stigma over time in Europe and the United States, it was concluded that despite compelling evidence that "the public's literacy about mental disorders clearly has increased," it was also evident that "attitudes towards persons with mental illness have not changed for the better."[11]

Contact

Despite the limited impact of education in general, research indicates that there may be a more powerful source of knowledge about mental illness that may have a greater effect on stigma: direct experience. Direct experience with mental illness is usually determined in surveys by asking whether respondents have had a mental illness themselves, or had a "close friend" or family member with a mental illness. Using this approach, studies have consistently found that persons with any of these types of experiences tend to endorse fewer negative stereotypes and less intended social distance.

The impact of contact has been discussed in several review studies. The first major review indicated that all studies examining the impact of contact found that it was significantly associated with less stigma, and that it was related to both attitudes and behavior.[12] In addition, this review found that the majority of studies that looked at *change over time* in stigma among people who have been exposed to greater contact found that it led to a *decrease* in stigma. Two more recent reviews have also supported the idea that contact is likely to be an important predictor of stigma, but added some qualifications. A review of US studies on stigma supported the concept that contact was significantly associated with less stigma, but noted that evidence suggested that this was only the case for "white" Americans and not persons of other racial backgrounds.[13] Furthermore, in their 2006 international review, Angermeyer and colleagues found that contact was associated with less stigma in 30 of 61 studies, but that there was no relationship found in an equal number of studies (one study also found that contact was associated with more stigma). Although it was unclear from Angermeyer's review if the impact of contact depended on the national context of the study, my own review of more recent studies indicates that contact seems to predict less stigma independent of location. For example, recent studies conducted in Taiwan,[14] Nigeria,[15] the United

States,[16] and the UK[17] have all reported a significant relationship between prior contact with people with mental illness and less stigma.

Why should contact be so important? Certainly, the foundation of the explanation is that it provides compelling "personal experience" that contradicts negative stereotypes and increases one's level of comfort in a way that would decrease intended social distance. For example, by knowing someone with a mental illness as a friend or family member, one may be able to recognize that people with mental illnesses are human beings with talents and strengths independent of their psychiatric problems. Although it may be observed that some negative stereotypes are supported under some circumstances (e.g., the person may have some difficulty caring for themselves when acutely symptomatic), the contact may also provide the opportunity to recognize that the deeper truth is much more complicated. Thus, contact should allow the person to develop a more "nuanced" view of people with mental illnesses that should contradict the monolithic assertions of stigma. In *The Nature of Prejudice*, Gordon Allport supported this perspective in his consideration of whether contact between members of different races and ethnicities could reduce prejudice. He concluded that "prejudice ... may be reduced by equal status contact between majority and minority groups in the pursuit of common goals." However, he noted that prejudice might not be reduced by contact if the prejudice is "deeply rooted in the character structure of the individual" and noted that contact is most likely to be effective if "it is the sort that leads to the perception of common interests and common humanity between members of the two groups."[18]

Allport's last observation raises the point that not all contact will necessarily reduce stigma, and some types of contact may actually increase it. For example, a hypothetically prejudiced police officer who works in a disadvantaged neighborhood might have plenty of interaction with African Americans, but the interactions might not be the kinds that would reduce prejudice, because they would predominantly revolve around intervening when a crime has occurred. Thus, stereotypes that African Americans are criminals might not be contradicted, because the officer would not be involved in observations of people working, going to school, caring for their children, etc. How this might operate in the case of mental health stigma was considered by Jo Phelan and Bruce Link, who, using data from a national survey of people in the United States, tested whether exposure to threat or violence by people with mental illnesses was associated with stigma. Unsurprisingly, they found that people who reported experiencing "harm or threat" from a person with mental illness were, in general, more likely to endorse the negative stereotype that people with mental illness are dangerous. Interestingly, however, Phelan and Link also observed that these types of experiences were only associated with negative stereotypes insofar as they had occurred outside of the context of a more enduring relationship, and that there was only a minimal association between threat experiences and stigma for persons with deeper contact with people with mental illnesses (i.e., friends or family members).[19] This suggests that when there are more enduring connections with people with mental illnesses, negative experiences might not make that much of a difference.

Values-Orientation

Cultural Group

As has already been alluded to in previous chapters, there appear to be large differences between countries in the endorsement of negative stereotypes and willingness to maintain social distance from people with mental illnesses (e.g., the reader may recall that roughly 75% of a sample of people from the Czech Republic expressed a willingness to reject a person with mental illness as a friend, in contrast with fewer than 20% of a sample from the UK). This raises the question of whether "culture," and the complicated mix of values that are attached to it, have a role to play in determining the likelihood that one will endorse and engage in stigma. Furthermore, if there is a role for culture in determining stigma, are there specific types of values that operate across cultural groups with a high endorsement of stigma that explain this relationship?

Before discussing specific findings, it is helpful to consider what is meant by "culture." In psychological research, culture is used to refer to "shared attributes, belief systems, and value orientations that a group of people have in common and that influence their customs, norms, practices, social institutions, psychological processes, and organizations."[20] Although smaller social groups, such as people who like to play fantasy role-playing games, may be said to share a "culture," for the sake of our discussion here we will be thinking of broader groups that are linked to national origin and ethnic/racial heritage. These broader groups are, in turn, presumed to share some belief systems and value orientations. So, for example, as an American I am presumed to share some values and beliefs with other Americans (e.g., a belief that hard work is associated with success), and as a person of Greek ethnic heritage I am also presumed to share some values with other members of my ethnic group (e.g., a belief that one needs to remain loyal to one's family of origin to the greatest extent possible). It should be noted that in most cases, researchers are only able to assess the racial/ethnic group that persons are members of, rather than more specific information about the degree to which they endorse certain cultural values, so there are frequently broad assumptions that are made about the extent to which individuals belong to certain "cultures."

What cultural "belief systems" and "value orientations" might be of relevance to mental health stigma? Some have hypothesized that broad value-orientations such as "individualism" (the value that people should be autonomous and responsible for themselves) versus "collectivism" (the value that people should be interdependent and subordinate their individual needs to those of the group)[21] might have a role to play.[22] Others, however, have hypothesized that more specific aspects of "cultural history, socialization, and culturally-informed attitudes regarding mental illnesses" need to be examined to understand how culture might impact stigma.[23] We will consider both of these possibilities as explanations for cultural differences in degree of stigma next.

Eastern and Southern Europeans. Having defined culture, let us now consider the main patterns that appear in the research about the association between stigma and race/ethnicity/national origin. The first major pattern occurs within a group that is considered to be the same "race" by most (although this was not historically the case[c, 24]) but that differs in important historical and economic ways. Specifically, research has consistently supported that Eastern and Southern Europeans, including residents of historically "Eastern Bloc" countries such as the Baltic States (Lithuania, Latvia, and Estonia) and the Czech Republic, and Eastern Mediterranean countries such as Greece, Cyprus, and Italy, are more likely to endorse stigmatizing attitudes than residents of Northern and Western European countries. This has also been found to hold, when studied, among Eastern and Southern European immigrant groups living in Northern and Western European settings.

Findings in this regard come from a number of sources. The most important source is the 27 country/29,000 participant "Eurobarometer Mental Well-Being" survey conducted by the European Commission in 2005–2006.[25] This study included four questions relating to negative

---

[c] In *The History of White People*, Nell Irwin Painter points out that in the 1800s and early 1900s, Europeans were commonly thought to belong to three different "races": Teutonic, Alpine, and Mediterranean. Present-day Eastern and Southern Europeans would have previously been thought to be members of the Alpine and Mediterranean races.

stereotypes about mental illnesses, including that people with mental illness are dangerous, unpredictable, and never recover. The study found that participating countries with the highest endorsement of the belief that people with mental illnesses were unpredictable were Greece, the Czech Republic, Estonia, Cyprus, Latvia, Lithuania, and Italy (all in the East and South) and that roughly 75% of persons in these countries endorsed the view that people with mental illness were unpredictable, in contrast with the European average of 63%. Similarly, the countries with the highest endorsement of the view that people with mental illnesses are dangerous were Lithuania, Latvia, and Estonia, while the countries with the highest endorsement of the view that people with mental illnesses cannot recover were Italy, Germany, Latvia, the Czech Republic, Lithuania, and Greece (Germany was the sole non-Eastern or Southern European exception in this group, although it should be noted that a large part of Germany had been part of the "Eastern Bloc"). Further evidence supporting regional European differences also comes from the Stigma in Global Context–Mental Health Study, discussed in Chapter 2. Of the seven European countries included in this study, the three countries with the highest degree of stigma across all indicators were Cyprus, Bulgaria, and Hungary, all in Eastern and Southern Europe.[26] Also of note is an earlier study conducted in 1968, which compared the endorsement of negative stereotypes among residents of the UK, West Germany, and Czechoslovakia (as it was known at the time), and found that residents of Czechoslovakia endorsed significantly higher negative stereotypes than residents of the other two countries.[27]

Other evidence for the impact of Eastern/Southern European ethnicity comes from research examining ethnic enclaves within other European countries. Specifically, research with Greek and Greek Cypriot[d] immigrants living in London has found that individuals from these ethnic groups endorse significantly more stigma than "English" Londoners, even when controlling for other factors known to predict stigma such as education and prior contact.[28] Similarly, a study of the predictors of stigmatizing behavior in multi-ethnic Switzerland found that "living in the Italian-speaking part of Switzerland" was a significant predictor of social distance toward people with mental illnesses, even when accounting for a variety of other factors such as prior contact.[29]

---

[d] There are two predominant ethnic groups in Cyprus – Greek and Turkish Cypriots; however, this study focused on Cypriots of Greek heritage.

How might we explain these patterns by cultural background within "White" Europeans? Chris Papadopoulos, who has studied mental health stigma among Greek and Greek Cypriot immigrants in England, hypothesized that stigma might be associated with greater "collectivism" among these groups than the dominant cultures in Britain. Specifically, he hypothesized that "tight-knit" immigrant communities with strong collectivist values, such as Greeks, might be less tolerant of persons who "deviate" from expected norms, as might be the case among persons with mental illness. To test this, Papadopoulos examined the degree of individualism-collectivism among Greeks/Cypriots, "white English," Chinese, and American individuals living in England, and whether scores on this measure were associated with stigma. Contrary to his hypothesis, however, although Greeks and Greek Cypriots were higher both in collectivism and stigma scores than members of the other groups (with the exception of Chinese immigrants, who we'll discuss shortly), collectivism scores were not associated with stigma scores at the individual level. This suggests that some other mechanism is needed to explain high degrees of stigma among Greeks and Cypriots. We will consider other possible explanations shortly.

East and South Asians. The other major ethnic category that has been found to be associated with increased stigma is East and South Asian race/ethnicity. This pattern has been observed both when comparing the scores on stigma measures in East and South Asian countries to those of other countries (when comparative studies have been done), and when comparing people of East Asian heritage living in the United States, the UK, and Australia to people from the dominant (white) ethnic groups in those countries.

With regard to national differences, although there have been a number of studies that have examined stigma in East and South Asia,[30] it is generally difficult to make sense of how these findings compare to findings from other countries, since a variety of different measures and sampling approaches have been used. For this reason, the best source of information is the previously discussed Stigma in Global Context–Mental Health Study, which examined the degree of endorsement of a variety of negative stereotypes and behavioral intentions using the same methods in representative samples from 16 countries. When examining national stigma scores from this study, we find that the three East and South Asian countries included in the study (Bangladesh, the Philippines, and South Korea) had comparatively high levels of stigma, and, along with the three Eastern European countries previously discussed, comprised the "top 6" countries, of those studied, in degree of stigma.[31] People from Bangladesh showed particularly high levels of some aspects of stigma; for example, more than 75% of persons in Bangladesh indicated that they would be unwilling to have a hypothetical person with schizophrenia as a neighbor, the highest level of endorsement of this item globally. Another comparative study that included only health professionals, including medical and nursing staff, compared the attitudes toward mental illness of health professionals working in the United States, Brazil, Nigeria, Ghana, and China.[32] This study found that health professionals working in China endorsed the most stigma in comparison to professionals from all four other countries.

Other studies have examined the extent to which people of East and South Asian heritage living as immigrants in other countries demonstrate a greater degree of stigma than persons of other backgrounds. Here, studies have tended to either focus specifically on Chinese immigrants or have lumped people of South and East Asian heritage into one category (as is typical in the US census), so information on the extent to which people of South Asian heritage endorse stigma is unfortunately unclear. However, at least with regard to people of Chinese heritage, findings are consistent: studies conducted in the United States,[33] UK,[34] and Australia[35] all indicate that individuals of Chinese heritage endorse more mental health stigma than nonimmigrant white individuals from those locations. The Australian study also noted that there was a gradient in endorsement of stigma between different ethnically Chinese groups, with immigrants from mainland China demonstrating more stigma than immigrants from Taiwan, who in turn demonstrated more stigma than Australian-born persons of Chinese heritage.

How do we make sense of these findings? At least with regard to people of Chinese heritage, the explanatory mechanisms are clearer, thanks to the theoretically informed work of Lawrence Yang, a researcher from Columbia University (now at New York University). Yang theorized that Chinese culture places a great emphasis on the primacy of individual and family reputation (or "face"), and that mental illnesses such as schizophrenia pose a powerful potential threat to reputation. In addition, a strong emphasis on the role of genetics, or "lineage," leads to the potential for unaffected family members to be "contaminated" by the presence of a person with mental illness in their family. Pointing toward historical and legal sources, Yang illustrated that public knowledge that one has a relative with schizophrenia can damage the respectability of the family, and even the ability of undiagnosed family members to marry.[36] Yang then tested his theory that culture-specific threat would account for greater stigma among

Chinese-Americans in a series of studies. In the first, he and colleagues examined the extent to which Chinese- and European-Americans endorse "eugenic" attitudes about mental illness, such as the belief that people with a family history of mental illness should not have children, and found that Chinese-Americans showed greater endorsement of these attitudes.[37] In the second, he and colleagues found that the extent to which it was perceived that mental illness is likely to be inherited predicted differences in stigma between Chinese- and European-Americans, suggesting that the belief that mental illnesses are genetic is a major factor in explaining stigma among Chinese-Americans. In the third, he used an experimental design to assign Chinese and European-American college students to vignettes that either did or did not discuss concerns with the effect of mental illness on the reputation of one's family "lineage." He found that Chinese-Americans were significantly more likely to spontaneously recall content related to "lineage" concerns than European-Americans, indicating that they were more attuned to these types of issues.[38] In total, these findings support his theory that a culture-specific concern with the genetic reputation of one's family may partly explain increased mental health stigma among people of Chinese heritage.

Yang's findings suggest that if we are trying to understand the drivers of differences in stigma between cultural groups, it might be more fruitful to examine culture-specific values that can influence stigma, rather than broader value-systems such as individualism or collectivism. There is clearly much more work that needs to be done in this area to understand why other cultural groups, especially South Asians and Eastern/Southern Europeans, are so much more likely to endorse mental health stigma than others. With regard to Greeks specifically, as someone of Greek heritage, I will venture to speculate that some of the mechanisms at play in the Greek community might be similar to those that Yang theorized to be operating among persons of Chinese heritage. Specifically, traditional Greek culture has been found to place great value on family honor and loyalty to one's family above all other social groups.[39] Mental illness can be seen as a blow to a family's reputation, leading to a strong sense of shame when mental illness occurs in one's family.[e] When mental illness occurs, it tends to be hidden, leading to little familiarity with the human face of mental illness. As a result, mental illness is seen as something that is distant

---

[e] In a recent conversation that I had with my mother, she expressed the view that Greek parents might feel "guilty" about having a child with a disability, suggesting that they would feel responsible for damaging the family's reputation.

and unknown, possibly leading to more endorsement of negative stereotypes. When mental illness is encountered among known people, there is a tendency to minimize its seriousness so as not to associate the person with the tainting effects of the label.[f] Although I have yet to conduct research examining this hypothesis, I hope to look further at this issue in the future.

Political Ideology

The final potential factor related to values-orientation that might explain why some people are more likely to endorse stigma, while others are not, is political ideology. Political ideology refers to a collection of attitudes toward a variety of social, economic, and cultural issues. It is believed that people develop their individual political attitudes at an early age in a process that is influenced by family members, peers, and other environmental influences (e.g., media and popular culture). Although attitudes toward specific issues (e.g., gay rights, abortion, government spending) may be unrelated, attitudes typically cluster together in a way that follows ideological patterns. In this regard, researchers have usually focused on two predominant patterns of political ideology, with which readers will undoubtedly be familiar: conservativism, which emphasizes "tradition and stability," and liberalism, which emphasizes "innovation and reform" ("moderates" tend to fall somewhere in between.)[40] So, for example, conservatives would plausibly be expected to oppose same-sex marriage, which deviates with longstanding marital traditions, while liberals would be expected to support it as an example of "reform."

The conservative–liberal distinction is fairly broad, so researchers have also attempted to develop more fine-grained distinctions. Specifically, researchers have identified a sub-type of conservativism known as "right-wing authoritarianism."[41] Right-wing authoritarianism is distinguished by three main components: (1) a high value on "strong" authority figures, (2) an emphasis on upholding traditional values and social norms, and (3) a hostility toward outgroups (such as LGBT persons or immigrants). As

---

[f] I can vividly recall a conversation between my father and his aunt, an immigrant from Greece, which illustrates this. My great-aunt asked for my father's opinion about the son of a Greek friend whose behavior had caused the family concern. My father gave his frank opinion as a psychiatrist that the young man was psychotic. This caused my great-aunt to become enraged, yelling at my father that this was not possible since he was a "good boy" (*kalo paedi*) who just had some emotional problems and was "not a criminal." My father tried to explain that this was not what psychotic meant, but my great-aunt could not get past the negative connotations of the label and refused to talk to him about it further.

such, we might see right-wing authoritarianism as reflecting a particular
strain of "social" conservativism that might well be distinct from "fiscal"
and "libertarian" types of conservativism. As an illustration, at the time of
writing, Donald J. Trump is the US president, and seems to reflect many
of the characteristics that right-wing authoritarians value: the appearance
of "toughness" (exemplified by his frequent use of terminology about
"strength" and "weakness"), a hostility toward outgroups (such as illegal
immigrants and Muslims), and an emphasis on tradition rather than
change (exemplified by his campaign slogan "Make America Great Again,"
suggesting a need to return to the values of the past). A media analysis
supported that the endorsement of authoritarianism significantly predicted
support for Trump over other Republican candidates during the Republican primary process.[42]

What do political attitudes, and right-wing authoritarianism in particular, have to do with mental health stigma? While the connection may not
be inherently apparent, researchers have long felt that authoritarianism
might predict prejudice toward a number of groups. In 1950, a group of
researchers including Theodor Adorno (a philosopher who had fled Nazi
Germany) published a landmark attempt to characterize the type of person
who was more likely to hold prejudicial views toward ethnic groups such as
Jews and "Negros" (the term used at the time) in *The Authoritarian
Personality*. Gordon Allport also echoed some of their assertions in *The
Nature of Prejudice*, published just a few years later. Although many of
their conclusions are dated, it is interesting to consider one of the most
important ones: that prejudices do not tend to operate in isolation.
Specifically, Adorno and colleagues stated that a person "who is hostile
toward one minority group is very likely to be hostile against a wide variety
of others."[43] Similarly, Allport asserted that "prejudice is frequently woven
firmly into a style of life."[44]

What types of lifestyle factors might be important? Adorno and Allport
found that the view that the world was threatening and dangerous (as
evidenced by the endorsement of statements such as "the world is a
hazardous place in which men are basically evil and dangerous") predicted
prejudicial attitudes toward a number of groups. Is this also the case for
attitudes toward people with mental illnesses? Almost all of the research
that has looked at the association between political ideology and stigma
says yes.

Most research on the relationship between political attitudes and stigma
has been fairly atheoretical, simply examining self-reported political identification (e.g., conservative, moderate, or liberal). Nevertheless, research

indicates that self-identified conservativism *is* a consistent predictor of negative stereotypes toward people with mental illnesses. For example, in two US national studies of the predictors of stigma, political conservativism was found to be a significant predictor even when controlling for other important variables such as education and prior contact.[45] In a study that I and two colleagues conducted with a representative sample of New York state residents, we also found that self-reported political conservativism was the strongest overall predictor of the endorsement of negative stereotypes toward people with mental illness, even when accounting for other factors such as education, race/ethnicity, and gender.[46] Furthermore, although most studies of the relationship between political affiliation and stigma have been specific to the United States, a recent study conducted in India found that political conservativism is also a significant predictor of stigma in that context.[47]

A limitation of all of the above studies is that they looked at self-reported conservativism broadly, rather than authoritarianism more specifically. My colleague Joseph DeLuca and I believed that this was problematic, as many people who identify as conservative might do so for fiscal reasons that are unlikely to be related to authoritarianism. We also felt that many people who self-identify as "moderate" or even "liberal" for other reasons might endorse authoritarian views. Furthermore, we wanted to examine whether right-wing authoritarianism would predict not just attitudes but also intended *behavior* toward people with mental illnesses. We therefore conducted two surveys (one with roughly 500 New York State residents, and one with roughly 950 US residents) where we examined peoples' agreement with authoritarian views using the "Right-Wing Authoritarianism" (RWA) scale,[48, g] and the extent to which these views predicted the endorsement of both negative stereotypes and intended social distance (as well as microaggressions, using the scale discussed in Chapter 3). In both studies, we found that the RWA scale was the strongest predictor of the endorsement of negative stereotypes, intended social distance, and microaggression behaviors, and that it was a more powerful predictor than other traditional predictors of stigma such as personal contact, education, and female gender.[49] How powerful? Our analyses suggested that RWA uniquely explained about 7–9% of the

---

g The RWA scale includes a number of items reflecting the need for a "strong" authority, as well as attitudes toward homosexuality and women's rights. For example: "The facts on crime, sexual immorality and the recent public disorders all show we have to crack down harder on deviant groups and troublemakers, if we are going to save our moral standards and preserve law and order."

variation in measures of negative stereotypes and intended social distance, which is a substantial amount in social science research.

What is the theoretical explanation for why RWA predicts mental health stigma? Joseph and I reasoned that something called "Terror Management Theory" might partially explain the relationship. Terror Management Theory proposes that some individuals cling strongly to certain worldviews because of fear of death or other threats to safety.[50] We reasoned that it is probably not always a literal threat to physical integrity that affects people who are high in authoritarianism, but possibly a threat to one's sense of *psychological* integrity and sense of order in the world. Put another way, by seeing people with mental illnesses as essentially less human or "other," people with authoritarian views may feel protected from the sense of uncertainty that an acceptance of the normality of mental illness would pose. These threats might include fears that one's friends, family members, or *self* might not be immune from mental illness, which would lead to a greater feeling of uncertainty about oneself and the world. So, as a means of self-protection, people with mental illnesses might tend to be categorized as dangerous "others," rather than "people like you and me." This interpretation was also supported by a study conducted by Australian researchers, who found that people with authoritarian views were more likely to socially reject people diagnosed with schizophrenia when presented with "biogenetic" explanations of mental illness that reinforce their "otherness."[51]

Although we need to do more work to test our view that Terror Management Theory explains the relationship between RWA and stigma, Joseph and I have already conducted some analyses that support this perspective. First, in our second survey, we included a measure of willingness to seek help for potential psychological problems (the Self-Stigma of Help-Seeking Scale)[52] and found that people who were high in RWA were significantly less likely than others to be willing to seek psychological help if they developed psychological problems themselves. This suggests that RWA is also related to a desire to protect oneself from concerns that "mental illness could happen to me." We also included a scale called the "Dangerous World Scale" that assesses perceptions that the world is unpredictable and dangerous, and found that people who were high in RWA scored high on this scale as well, although it did not statistically explain the relationship between RWA and stigma. This suggests that concerns that the world is unpredictable and dangerous might lead people who are high in RWA to perceive people with mental illnesses as more dangerous (as this might reduce feelings of general threat and danger, since it means that one just needs to avoid those who are "different" and "other" in order to stay safe). In addition to our research, other researchers have also studied how the degree to which one ascribes "humanity" to people with mental illness predicts stigma, and have found that the process of seeing people with mental illnesses as less human is associated with greater endorsement of negative stereotypes and intended social distance.[53]

This brings us back to Wayne LePierre's statements that we discussed at the beginning of this chapter, and possibly provides a way of making sense of them. Advocates for gun rights (who tend to be politically conservative) often argue that the world is dangerous and that gun owners need guns to protect themselves and their families. Mental health advocates point out that mental illness can happen to anyone, perhaps leading some gun owners who start out with good intentions to use their guns in ways other than for self-defense (usually to commit self-harm, but sometimes harming others). However, this perspective poses a threat to the argument that society is neatly divided into groups of "law-abiding citizens" (who should be free to own guns) and "sickos" or "monsters" (who need to be locked away). By calling people with mental illnesses "monsters," LaPierre (and other prominent figures on the right, such as Ann Coulter, who routinely uses dehumanizing terms like "psychos"[54] in reference to people with mental illnesses) is reassuring his followers that violence is a not a problem for them, but rather a problem of not exercising enough control over "those people." This can also be seen as fitting in with the "system justification" argument for what causes stigma, discussed at the end of Chapter 2. Among right-wing authoritarians in the present-day United States, mental health stigma and the view that some people are inherently "different" and should be "kept away" provides justification for a system that proposes to privilege the rights of one group (such as gun owners, who want to maintain their freedom of firearm access) over the rights of another (people diagnosed with mental illnesses, who, it is thought, should lose their freedom to "walk the streets" in the general community).

It should be pointed out that while some of the loudest voices for authoritarianism are conservative white men and women such as LaPierre and Coulter, the reality of who supports authoritarian attitudes is by no means limited to "white America." Specifically, in our research, we found that both African American and Asian-American participants scored sig-nificantly *higher* on average on the RWA scale than white participants, and that higher RWA scores in turn partly explained elevated stigma scores among these groups. At least in the African American community, the endorsement of authoritarian attitudes may be linked to religious

Figure 8   Sign for the Altah Church in New York City.
Photo by Rudy Kagie.

conservativism, which has led to hostility to LGBT rights in some circles. These types of views are exemplified by the "Atlah" church, located in the heart of New York City's Harlem African American community, which posts messages such as the one seen in Figure 8 on a large billboard on a weekly basis.

It should also be emphasized that the use of stigmatizing terms is by no means universal among prominent conservatives, and there is evidence that contact with mental illness (either in oneself or one's family) can override the relationship between right-wing authoritarianism and stigma. For example, despite the loud condemnations of LaPierre and Coulter, other prominent right-wing figures such as Glenn Beck (who has spoken about his personal mental health problems), Sarah Palin (who has spoken publicly about mental health problems among her children), and John Kasich (who has spoken about his brother's experience of mental health problems) have not, to my knowledge, made any such statements. In our own research, we also found evidence that the relationship between right-wing authoritarianism and stigma was diminished and even *reversed* (meaning that participants had lower stigma scores) when they had contact experience with mental illness.[55] Thus, it may be possible to undo the damaging effects of right-wing authoritarianism by providing people with more contact experiences.

Conclusion: Who Stigmatizes?

To summarize, the answer to the question "*why do some people stigmatize, and not others?*" posed at the beginning of this chapter is not a clear-cut one. However, research provides some evidence that a combination of knowledge- and ideology-based factors influences who is more likely to stigmatize. On the one hand, people who lack information about mental illness, either from formal education or personal experience, are more likely to believe negative stereotypes and to act accordingly. On the other hand, people from ethnic backgrounds that see mental illness as a threat to family reputation, and political backgrounds that see mental illness as something that can only happen to "others," are also more likely to endorse stigma. We can also imagine that there may be a cumulative effect for these factors, such that less educated, politically authoritarian members of some ethnic groups who have no contact experiences may be the most likely to endorse stigma. In fact, when we included multiple predictors of stigma into our analyses, we were able to explain roughly 15–20% of the variation in measures of stigma.[56]

One of the implications of the above is that people with mental illnesses are not all equally at risk of encountering stigma. Based on what we've discussed in this chapter, we can presume that people with mental illnesses who live in communities where stigma is more prevalent, such as the Chinese and Greek immigrant communities, or in communities where right-wing authoritarianism and lower education are also common are at greater risk of encountering stigma in their lives. In Chapters 5 and 6, we will begin to consider how encountering stigma impacts the lives of people with mental illnesses.

References

1 American Psychiatric Association (2013). *Diagnostic and Statistical Manual of Mental Disorders*, 5th Edition. Washington, DC: American Psychiatric Association.

2 Wikipedia (no date). Sandy Hook elementary school shooting. Accessed online August 23, 2017: https://en.wikipedia.org/wiki/Sandy_Hook_Elementary_School_shooting.

3 The New York Times (2012). Text of the NRA speech. Accessed online August 23, 2017: www.nytimes.com/interactive/2012/12/21/us/nra-news-conference-transcript.html.

4 Quoted in Lexington (2013). Why the NRA keeps talking about mental illness, rather than guns. *The Economist*. Accessed online August 23, 2017: www.economist.com/blogs/lexington/2013/03/guns-and-mentally-ill.

5 Holzinger, A., Floris, F., Schomerus, G., Carta, M. C., & Angermeyer, M. C. (2012). Gender differences in public beliefs and attitudes about mental disorder in western countries: A systematic review of population studies. *Epidemiology and Psychiatric Sciences, 21*, 73–85.

6 Angermeyer, M. C., & Dietrich, S. (2006). Public beliefs and attitudes toward people with mental illness: a review of population studies. *Acta Psychiatrica Scandinavica*, *113*, 163–179.

7 Parcesepe, A. M., & Cabassa, L. J. (2013). Public stigma of mental illness in the United States: A systematic literature review. *Administration and Policy in Mental Health*, *40*, 384–399

8 Angermeyer, M. C., & Dietrich, S. (2006). Public beliefs and attitudes toward people with mental illness: a review of population studies. *Acta Psychiatrica Scandinavica*, *113*, 163–179.

9 Corrigan, P. W., & Watson, A. C. (2007). The stigma of psychiatric disorders and the gender, ethnicity, and education of the perceiver. *Community Mental Health Journal*, *43*, 439–458.

10 Gonzales, L., Yanos, P. T., Stefancic, A., Alexander, M. J., & Harney-Delehanty, B. (In Press). Predictors of community participation among persons with psychiatric disabilities, Part 2: Neighborhood factors and community stigma. *Psychiatric Services.*

11 Schomerus, G., Schwahn, C., Holzinger, A., Corrigan, P. W., Grabe, H. J., Carta, M. G., & Angermeyer, M. C. (2012). Evolution of public attitudes about mental illness: A systematic review and meta-analysis. *Acta Psychiatric Scandinavica*, *125*, 440–452.

12 Coutoure, S. M., & Penn, D. L. (2003). Interpersonal contact and the stigma of mental illness: A review of the literature. *Journal of Mental Health*, *12*, 291–305.

13 Parcesepe, A. M., & Cabassa, L. J. (2013). Public stigma of mental illness in the United States: A systematic literature review. *Administration and Policy in Mental Health*, *40*, 384–399.

14 Song, L.-Y., Chang, L.-Y., Shih, C.-W., Lin, C.-H., & Yang, M.-J. (2005). Community attitudes towards the mentally ill: The Results of a national survey of the Taiwanese population. *International Journal of Social Psychiatry*, *51*, 162–176.

15 Adewuda, A. O., & Makanjuola, R. O. A. (2005). Social distance towards people with mental illness amongst Nigerian university students. *Social Psychiatry and Psychiatric Epidemiology*, *40*, 865–868.

16 Kobau, R., DiIorio, C., Chapman, D., & Delvecchio, P. (2010). Attitudes about mental illness and its treatment: Validation of a generic scale for public health surveillance of mental illness associated stigma. *Community Mental Health Journal*, *46*, 164–176.

17 Papadopoulos, C., Foster, J., & Caldwell, K. (2013). "Individualism-Collectivism" as an explanatory device for mental illness stigma. *Community Mental Health Journal*, *49*, 270–280.

18 Allport, G. W. (1979). *The nature of prejudice* (25th anniversary edition). Reading, MA: Addison-Wesley.

19 Phelan, J. C., & Link, B. G. (2004). Fear of people with mental illnesses: The role of personal and impersonal contact and exposure to threat or harm. *Journal of Health and Social Behavior*, *45*, 68–80.

20 Abdullah, T., & Brown, T. L. (2011). Mental illness stigma and ethnocultural beliefs, values, and norms: An integrative review. *Clinical Psychology Review, 31,* 934–948.
21 Triandis, H. C. (2001). Individualism-collectivism and personality. *Journal of Personality, 69,* 907–924.
22 Papadopoulos, C. Foster, J., & Caldwell, K. (2013). "Individualism-Collectivism" as an explanatory device for mental illness stigma. *Community Mental Health Journal, 49,* 270–280.
23 Abdullah, T., & Brown, T. L. (2011). Mental illness stigma and ethnocultural beliefs, values, and norms: An integrative review. *Clinical Psychology Review, 31,* 934–948.
24 Painter, N. I. (2010). *The history of white people.* New York: Norton.
25 European Union (2006) Mental well-being: Special Eurobarometer 248/ Wave 64.4. Accessed online August 23, 2017: http://ec.europa.eu/health/ ph_information/documents/ebs_248_en.pdf.
26 Pescosolido, B. A., Medina, T. R., Martin, J. K., & Long, J. S. (2013). The "backbone" of stigma: Identifying the global core of public prejudice associated with mental illness. *American Journal of Public Health, 103,* 853–860.
27 Levine, D. (1972). A cross-national study of attitudes toward mental illness. *Journal of Abnormal Psychology, 80,* 111–114.
28 Papadopoulos, C., Leavey, G., & Vincent, C. (2002). Factors influencing stigma: A comparison of Greek-Cypriot and English attitudes towards mental illness in north London. *Social Psychiatry and Psychiatric Epidemiology, 37,* 430–434; Papadopoulos, C., Foster, J., & Caldwell, K. (2013). "Individualism-Collectivism" as an explanatory device for mental illness stigma. *Community Mental Health Journal,* 49, 270–280.
29 Lauber, C., Nordt, C., Falcato, L., & Rossler, W. (2004). Factors influencing social distance toward people with mental illness. *Community Mental Health Journal, 40,* 265–274.
30 Lauber, C., & Rossler, W. (2007). Stigma towards people with mental illness in developing countries in Asia. *International Review of Psychiatry, 19,* 157–178.
31 Pescosolido, B. A., Medina, T. R., Martin, J. K., & Long, J. S. (2013). The "backbone" of stigma: Identifying the global core of public prejudice associated with mental illness. *American Journal of Public Health, 103,* 853–860.
32 Stefanovics, E., He, H., Ofori-Atta, A., Cavalcanti, M., T., Neto, H. R., Makanjuola, V., Ighodaro, A., Leddy, M., & Rosenheck, R., (2016). Cross-national analysis of beliefs and attitude toward mental illness among medical professionals from five countries. *Psychiatric Quarterly, 87,* 63–73.
33 Yang, L. H., Purdie-Vaughans, V., Kotabe, H., Link, B. G., Saw, A., Wong, G., & Phelan, J. (2013). Culture, threat and mental illness stigma: Identifying culture-specific threat among Chinese American groups. *Social Science & Medicine, 88,* 56–67.

34 Papadopoulos, C., Foster, J., & Caldwell, K. (2013). "Individualism-Collectivism" as an explanatory device for mental illness stigma. *Community Mental Health Journal, 49,* 270–280.

35 Mellor, D., Carne, L., Shen, Y-C, McCabe, M., & Wang, L. (2012). Stigma toward mental illness: A cross-cultural comparison of Taiwanese, Chinese immigrants to Australia and Anglo-Australians. *Journal of Cross-Cultural Psychology, 44,* 352–364.

36 Yang, L. H., & Kleinman, A. C. (2008). "Face" and the embodiment of stigma in China: The cases of schizophrenia and AIDS. *Social Science & Medicine, 67,* 398–408.

37 WonPat-Borja, A., Yang, L. H., Link, B. G., & Phelan, J. C. (2012). Eugenics, genetics, and mental illness stigma in Chinese Americans. *Social Psychiatry and Psychiatric Epidemiology, 47,* 145–156.

38 Yang, L. H., Purdie-Vaughans, V., Kotabe, H., Link, B. G., Saw, A., Wong, G., & Phelan, J. (2013). Culture, threat and mental illness stigma: Identifying culture-specific threat among Chinese American groups. *Social Science & Medicine, 88,* 56–67.

39 Scourby, A. (1984). *The Greek-Americans.* Boston: Twayne Publishers.

40 Hibbing, J. R., Smith, K. B., & Alford, J. R. (2014). Differences in negativity bias underlie variations in political ideology. *Behavioral & Brain Sciences, 37,* 297–350.

41 Altemeyer, R. A. (1996). *The authoritarian specter.* Cambridge, MA: Harvard University Press.

42 McWilliams, M. (2016). The best predictor of Trump support isn't income, education, or age. It's authoritarianism. *Vox.* Accessed online August 23, 2017: www.vox.com/2016/2/23/11099644/trump-support-authoritarianism.

43 Adorno, T. W., Frenkel-Brunswick, E., Levinson, D. J., & Sanford, R. N. (1982). *The authoritarian personality* (Abridged Edition). New York: Norton. 9

44 Allport, G. W. (1979). *The nature of prejudice* (25th anniversary edition). Reading, MA: Addison-Wesley. 396.

45 Phelan, J. C., & Link, B. G. (2004); Anglin, D., M., Link, B. G., & Phelan, J. C. (2006). Racial differences in stigmatizing attitudes toward people with mental illness. *Psychiatric Services, 57,* 857–862.

46 Gonzales, L., Chan, G., & Yanos, P. T. (2017). Individual and neighborhood predictors of mental illness stigma in New York state. *Stigma and Health, 2,* 175–181.

47 Hunter, K. N., Rice, S., MacDonald, J., & Madrid, J. (2014). What are the best predictors of opinions of mental illness in the Indian population? *International Journal of Mental Health, 43,* 35–51.

48 Altemeyer, R. A. (1996). *The authoritarian specter.* Cambridge, MA: Harvard University Press.

49 DeLuca, J. S., & Yanos, P. T. (2016). Managing the terror of a dangerous world: Political attitudes as predictors of mental health stigma. *International Journal of Social Psychiatry, 62,* 21–30.; DeLuca, J. S., Vaccaro, J., Seda, J., &

Yanos, P. T. (Under Review). Political attitudes as predictors of the multiple dimensions of mental health stigma.

50 Greenberg, J., Simon, L., Pyszcynski, T., Solomon, S., & Chatel, D. (1990). Evidence for terror management theory II: The effects of mortality salience on reactions to those who threaten or bolster the cultural worldview. *Journal of Personality and Social Psychology, 58*, 308–318.

51 Kvaale, E. P., & Haslam, N. (2016). Motivational orientations and psychiatric stigma: Social motives influence how causal explanations relate to stigmatizing attitudes. *Personality and Individual Differences, 89*, 111–116.

52 Vogel, D. L., Wade, N. G., & Ascheman, P. L. (2009). Measuring perceptions of stigmatization by others for seeking psychological help: Reliability and validity of a new stigma scale with college students. *Journal of Counseling Psychology, 56*, 301–308.

53 Martinez, A. G., Piff, P. K., Mendoza-Denton, R., & Hinshaw, S. P. (2011). The power of a label: Mental illness diagnoses, ascribed humanity, and social rejection. *Journal of Social and Clinical Psychology, 30*, 1–23.

54 Accessed online August 23, 2017: www.anncoulter.com/columns/2015-10-07.html.

55 DeLuca, J. S., Vaccaro, J., Seda, J., & Yanos, P. T. (2016). Can intergroup contact with mental illness trump the relationship between politics and mental health stigma? Presentation at the American Public Health Association Annual Convention, Denver, CO, October 31, 2016.

56 DeLuca, J. S., Vaccaro, J., Seda, J., & Yanos, P. T. (Under Review). Political attitudes as predictors of the multiple dimensions of mental health stigma.

CHAPTER 5

Responses to Stigma among People Diagnosed with Mental Illnesses

In the early 1970s, Patricia Deegan was a 17-year-old high school senior living in rural New England. She was a promising athlete and looked forward to a future working as a women's athletic coach. However, during the winter of her senior year she began to have unusual perceptual experiences that led to a fundamental change in how she acted in and experienced the world. She explains that:

> during basketball practice it became harder and harder to catch a ball. My depth perception and coordination seemed strangely impaired and I found myself being hit in the head with passes rather than catching the ball. Objects around me also began to look very different ... A similar shift in my perception and understanding occurred when people spoke to me. Language became hard to understand. Gradually I could not understand what people were saying at all. It became difficult to believe that people were really who they said they were. What I remember most was the extraordinary fear that kept me awake for days and the terrible conviction I was being killed and needed to defend myself.[1]

Soon after, Deegan was taken to a psychiatric hospital, where she was given an explanation for the disturbing experiences that she had been having: She had a mental illness called schizophrenia. Although this provided a medical explanation for the experiences, Deegan did not feel relieved. Rather, she recalls feeling a different kind of terror in response to hearing the diagnosis:

> All I knew were the stereotypes I had seen on television or in the movies. To me, mental illness meant Dr. Jekyll and Mr. Hyde, psychopathic serial killers, loony bins, morons, schizos, fruitcakes, nuts, straight jackets, and raving lunatics. They were all I knew about mental illness, and what terrified me was that professionals were saying I'm one of them.[2]

As a result of this reaction, Deegan remembers that she "could feel the weight of [the words describing the diagnosis] crushing my already fragile hopes and dreams and aspirations for my life."[3]

A similar process is described by Elyn Saks in her memoir *The Center Cannot Hold*. Saks, who was a student at Yale law school at the time and had been valedictorian of her graduating class at Vanderbilt University, recalls her reaction to finding out that her diagnosis was "chronic paranoid schizophrenia" with a "grave" prognosis: "now I was being told that whatever had gone wrong inside my head was permanent and, from all indication, unfixable." She also indicates that she realized that negative stereotypes about mental illnesses that she had encountered throughout her youth now applied to her:

> And then there was the whole mythology of schizophrenia, aided and abetted by years of books and movies that presented people like me as hopelessly evil and helplessly doomed. I would become violent ... Maybe I'd end my life in an institution; maybe I'd *live* my life in an institution.[4]

So far, we have been concerned with the extent to which community members hold negative stereotypes about people with mental illnesses and how these stereotypes impact their behavior toward labeled individuals. However, both of these examples illustrate that awareness of these negative stereotypes can have a profound impact on the people who are *diagnosed* with these disorders. This, in turn, can greatly impact their expectations for how others will view them and treat them, and their views about themselves and their value as human beings.

Figure 9 presents a conceptual model for two distinct, but related, processes involving stigma that are hypothesized to occur among people diagnosed with mental illness. In step 1 (which essentially represents the *modified labeling theory* developed by Bruce Link and colleagues[5]), when people become diagnosed with a severe mental illness, this occurrence interacts with an awareness of negative stereotypes about mental illness that were acquired during the socialization process; this interaction, in turn, leads to a concern about the implications of being labeled with a mental illness, including the assumption that others would reject one as a friend, neighbor, etc. In step 2 (which is similar to what has been put forth by Patrick Corrigan and Amy Watson[6]), a belief in the legitimacy of negative stereotypes interacts with a self-identification that one has a mental illness, leading to a belief that negative stereotypes are true about oneself (as reflected in Saks' statements "I would become violent ... I'd end my life in an institution"). This part of the process is now commonly referred to as internalized or self- stigma.[7]

In this chapter, we will review evidence supporting the idea that each part of the process represented in Figure 9 commonly occurs. One of the

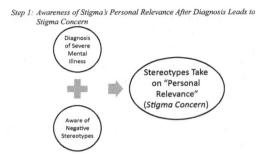

Step 1: Awareness of Stigma's Personal Relevance After Diagnosis Leads to Stigma Concern

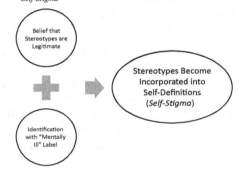

Step 2: Belief in Legitimacy of Stereotypes and Identification with the Label Lead to Self-Stigma

Figure 9   Model for how awareness of stigma impacts people with mental illness

important implications of this discussion will be that stigma does not *only* impact the lives of people with mental illnesses through the direct denial of opportunity for social relationships, work, and other aspects of community participation, as we learned in Chapter 3. Rather, we will learn that stigma *also* exerts an impact more insidiously, both by leading people with mental illnesses to fear social rejection, and therefore avoid many potentially fruitful opportunities for social support, and by leading them to feel that they are less valuable than others. In this way, people with mental illnesses can come to be "written off" by themselves as part of the stigma process.

The Development of Stigma Concern

The first important part of the process discussed in the previous section is the development of significant "stigma concern." Our understanding of this area is deeply indebted to the work of Bruce Link and colleagues, who developed "modified labeling theory" in the late 1980s and have continued to refine it in recent years.[8] As originally summarized by Link, modified labeling theory proposes that people who go on to develop a mental illness are likely already aware of negative stereotypes prior to becoming diagnosed, and that these stereotypes take on "personalized relevance" after diagnosis. This awareness then impacts social behavior and self-perceptions. In the next section, I will review evidence for each aspect of the "stigma concern" process.

Children's Awareness of Negative Stereotypes

A key assumption of modified labeling theory is that exposure to negative stereotypes about mental illness starts in childhood, so that people are already aware of them if they develop mental illness in adolescence or later. Is there evidence to support the idea that children become aware of negative stereotypes during the socialization process? Research summarized in two reviews of this topic indicates that, at least in the United States, children are indeed aware of negative stereotypes about mental illness.[9] Although the youngest children who have been studied frequently do not know the meaning of technical terms such as mental illness, they are almost always aware of terms such as "crazy" and their negative implications. For example, in one study, school-aged children were asked how they thought "crazy" people should be treated by society, and one seventh-grade child responded: "crazy people have to stay away from people. The real crazy people like killers should be kept in special homes for the mentally disturbed or in jail."[10] Although there have been few studies with very young children, the research that has been conducted suggests that an awareness of negative stereotypes about "crazy people" appears as early as age five.[11] Furthermore, although the majority of the research on stigma among children has been conducted in the United States, there is also evidence for widespread stigma among children in other locations, including Kenya[12] and Jamaica.[13]

While longitudinal research is generally lacking, there appears to be a decline in the endorsement of negative stereotypes among children between ages 5 and 13, presumably as children become more educated and their thinking matures. However, the degree to which children actually endorse negative stereotypes about mental illnesses is not really the point here. The main point, insofar as modified labeling theory is concerned, is that children are socialized to be *aware* that mental illness is something that one does not want to have, as it is associated with significantly diminished social status and negative assumptions from others.

How do children learn about these stereotypes? Research has not been able to clearly answer this question, but it is hypothesized that children become aware of stereotypes about mental illness in the same way that they learn about gender and race-related stereotypes (evidence consistently demonstrates that children are aware of gender and race-related stereotypes at a young age).[14] These stereotypes are rarely formally "taught," either by parents or schools, but they are absorbed through interactions with peers, media influence, and observations of how people who are labeled are treated (e.g., if a parent or care-giver moves a child away from someone who appears disturbed in public and says "that person is crazy"). Certainly, cultural factors described in Chapter 4 may also play an important role as they transmit important messages about how mental disorders are regarded. For example, consider the experience related in Chapter 4 about my great-aunt's reaction that it was not possible that her friend's son could be psychotic. By observation, I learned that psychosis is something that is considered to be shameful and unacceptable in my cultural group.

Media geared toward children (books, cartoons, movies, and digital games) may also have a particular impact in this regard, given that children spend a substantial amount of time watching TV or movies and playing digital games (according to a recent estimate, children in the United States spend an average of six hours per day watching TV or playing digital games).[15] Although research has not explored the extent to which digital games communicate negative stereotypes, there is clear evidence that negative stereotypes are frequently reinforced in cartoons and movies geared toward children. Specifically, one review found that roughly one in every four children's films depicted a character with mental illness in some way, and that two-thirds of these characters were depicted as being violent,[16] while another study found that 85% of Disney films contained negative verbal references to mental illness.[17] Exposure to these media is likely to also influence children's impressions of what "crazy" and related terms mean, and how someone who is "crazy" is regarded by others. As my children have grown up and I have become immersed in the media that they are exposed to, I have noted that many child-focused films now use the word "psychotic" in a negative manner, which likely provides children with their first introduction to the term. For example, in the popular 2005 film *Madagascar* (a story of animals who escape from the zoo) the word "psychotic" is used at least three times, and always in a way that equates it with "violent" or "out-of-control." The most memorable usage occurs during a culminating scene in the film, where main character Alex the lion goes on a rampage; during his rampage, another character exclaims "he's psychotic!"

"Personalized Relevance"

Given that children are socialized to have an awareness that mental illness is something that carries the "baggage" of negative stereotypes, what happens when someone enters adolescence or young adulthood and starts to become aware (or be told by others) that they might have a psychological problem themselves? Modified labeling theory proposes that, at this point, the negative stereotypes that one has previously been aware of start to take on "personalized relevance," meaning that the person starts to become aware that these stereotypes are relevant to how others might view *them*. This awareness then leads to some sensitivity about the issue of mental illness, which can have a range of effects that we will discuss shortly.

Why should people be sensitive to an awareness of what others might think of them? Although it is probably intuitively obvious to most readers that people often care to some extent about others' opinions about them, sociologists and social psychologists have formalized this idea by asserting that people tend to internalize a sense of how they are perceived by a "generalized other" (a sort of average person who does not know them).[18] So, for example, when I travel in a foreign country I might be dimly aware that I might be perceived as a "foreigner" or "clueless tourist" by people who see me walking around looking confused. No one has to directly tell me that I am a "foreigner" for me to have this sensitivity.[a] Of course, the views of the "generalized other" are only one consideration in how people behave (so, for example, I'm not going to avoid travelling just so that I'm not perceived as a clueless tourist). But the point is that there is some impact of this concern on people's assumptions about how they are perceived, and that this is particularly likely to be the case for something as strongly associated with negative stereotypes as severe mental illness. This process was described by one of the participants in sociologist Nancy Herman's ethnographic study of how people diagnosed with mental illnesses become aware of stigma:

> I knew about mental illness and the stigma or negative effects that goes with it, before anyone had to hospitalize me ... You see, I've lived in the world for many years before going to the hospital. During that time I learned from the kids on my block, my friends, and on TV, and even from my folks what is healthy normal behavior and what ain't ... And no one had to shun me to make me realize the results of being mentally ill. I knew that my friends would treat me badly if they knew. You just know![19]

---

[a] Although sometimes they do. A few years ago, while walking around in my parents' home town of Kastoria, Greece, some adolescents shouted "*Xenos!*" (Greek for foreigner) at me and my family.

A similar sentiment was expressed by a participant in a focus group study of the stigma experiences of people who identify as both LGBT and having a mental illness, conducted by my colleague Lauren O'Connor. Highlighting how both types of statuses were ones that he knew were "bad," while growing up, the participant made it clear that he was aware that mental illness was definitely "worse."

> You know, growing up, the thing that – next to being gay, which is the second worst thing growing up to be, was being crazy.[20]

Stigma Concern before Diagnosis. Modified labeling theory initially proposed that stigma concern begins to take shape after people are formally diagnosed with a mental illness. However, more recent research suggests that concern may develop before people are formally labeled, but when they start to experience symptoms that indicate that they might be labeled in the near future. A window into how stigma concern develops at this early stage is offered by some informative recent studies on people who are judged to be at "high risk" of developing a psychotic disorder. These are usually young individuals who do not meet the full technical criteria for a psychotic disorder such as schizophrenia, but are demonstrating early warning signs, such as the experience of unusual ideas, suspiciousness, grandiosity, and perceptual disturbances, but at a lower level of frequency or intensity than what is necessary to make a diagnosis.[21] There has recently been an emphasis on the importance of identifying, monitoring, and treating such individuals with the hope of minimizing some of the negative potential impacts of developing a "full-blown" psychotic disorder. However, a potential risk of this identification is that it might increase stigma concern as young people become aware that they have been identified as being "at risk" of developing a major mental illness.

German researcher Nicolas Rüsch and colleagues conducted a series of studies on this issue with a group of people found to meet "high risk" criteria at a clinic in Zurich, Switzerland. Rüsch found that these individuals were highly aware of negative stereotypes about mental illness, and that the degree to which they were aware of them was significantly associated with more "stigma stress," defined by Rüsch as the extent to which people thought that the negative impact of stigma would outweigh their abilities to deal with it.[22] Although there was some evidence that "self-labeling" oneself as someone with a mental health problem had the positive impact of increasing willingness to take medication, stigma stress was actually associated with *negative* attitudes toward treatment, including taking medication and receiving psychotherapy (I will discuss the association between stigma concern and treatment-seeking further in a bit).[23] An additional, and worrying, finding was that increased "stigma stress" at the beginning of the study was associated with a higher likelihood that an individual would actually "transition" from "high risk" to diagnosable schizophrenia one year later, even when accounting for the severity of their initial symptoms and whether they received medication.[24] A similar finding emerged from another study of "high risk" individuals in the United States, which found that concern about stigma related to the "high risk" label was associated with significantly increased anxiety symptoms.[25] These studies suggest that stigma concern is common during the early stages of developing a mental disorder, and that it can both deter one from receiving services and possibly make symptoms worse.

The Impact of Stigma Experiences on the Development of Stigma Concern. Although modified labeling theory presumes that people are aware that being diagnosed with a mental illness leads one to be socially devalued, some research suggests that this is not always the case, but that an awareness of the devaluation of mental illness may sometimes develop in response to experiences one has after one is diagnosed. In her ethnographic study, Nancy Herman found that a significant minority (about 20%) of her participants expressed that they expected that everything would "be the same" once they were discharged from an initial hospitalization, but that they were instead met with what could be described as a "rude awakening." For example, one participant stated:

> The first time I got out, I was so naïve, I thought things would be like they once were. How wrong I was. I now know the truth . . . each time I got out friends or people that I thought were friends treated me like I had the plague or made cruel jokes. I finally got it into my head that I had something that was disgraceful![26]

An interesting window into how this unfolds over time comes from research conducted by social work professor Tally Moses with adolescents discharged from their first psychiatric hospitalization for a nonpsychotic disorder (the most typical diagnosis was depression).[27] When interviewed seven days after their discharge, these adolescents were only moderately concerned about what others would think of them after finding out about their mental health problems, with 33% reporting concern that their peers would tease or harass them (an experience that is consistent with the concept of "microaggressions" discussed in Chapter 3). However, six months after hospitalization discharge, roughly 70% reported that they *had* been teased or harassed, and the extent to which they had experienced social rejection was related to the likelihood that they perceived more stigma in the community in general.[28] This suggests that many people might not be concerned about stigma after initial treatment experiences, but that concern might grow over time as others' behavior indicates that they *are* regarded differently.

Other studies have also suggested that the extent to which people experience stigma concern is influenced by their experience of social rejection or more subtle expressions of stigma. In one of the first studies that I conducted related to stigma, I found that experiencing that others "treated you like there is something wrong with you" (again, consistent with the concept of microaggressions discussed in Chapter 3) significantly predicted the extent to which people diagnosed with mental illnesses perceived stigma in the community at large, even after accounting for symptoms and other factors.[29] Similarly, Swedish researchers found that social rejection experiences related to having a mental illness were strong predictors of perceived stigma.[30] These findings are consistent with the notion that concern about others' stigma is not only impacted by assumptions based on early socialization experiences, but that it is also impacted by actual experiences of subtle or overt social rejection.

The Ubiquity of "Stigma Concern" after Diagnosis

The studies discussed in the previous section largely relate to people who are in the very early stages of experience with symptoms and treatment, but most people who receive mental health services have been experiencing symptoms and treatment for much longer. What do we know about the extent to which the "average" person with a severe mental illness is concerned about stigma? Here, we have a large body of research to draw on using the "devaluation-discrimination" scale developed by Bruce Link when he originally conceptualized modified labeling theory.[31] This scale measures the extent to which one agrees that "most people" (meant to represent the "generalized other") would reject someone with a mental illness as a close friend, dating partner, job applicant, etc. As such, when administered to people with mental illnesses, it captures the extent to which they presume that most people hold stigmatizing views (though not necessarily the extent to which they have actually encountered this type of stigma).

What does research with the devaluation-discrimination scale indicate? Studies conducted in the United States, Europe, and elsewhere convincingly show that the majority of people with severe mental illnesses presume that most people would reject them. For example, a study of the views of more than 2,400 people with schizophrenia, bipolar disorder, and depression in 14 European countries found that approximately 70% of participants scored in the moderate to high range on the devaluation-discrimination scale (meaning that they usually agreed that "most people" would not accept a person with a mental illness in the social roles indicated on the scale).[32] Similarly, another study of more than 700 people with a variety of diagnoses in six other countries (five in Europe, one in Asia) found that 67% of participants scored in the moderate-high range.[33] Although no comparably large study has been conducted in the United States, studies conducted by Link and others also indicate that roughly 60–70% of people diagnosed with mental illnesses in the United States agree with most statements regarding the devaluation of people with mental illness.[34] Furthermore, large studies conducted in China and Korea also confirm that comparable proportions of individuals outside of the European and North American contexts also show moderate-high stigma concern.[35]

In addition to research using the devaluation-discrimination scale, a related body of research has studied "anticipated discrimination" (this was examined in the Global Programme Against Stigma study previously discussed in Chapter 3). Although "anticipated discrimination" does not necessarily assess the extent to which people expect that "most people" would reject them, it does assess whether they expect that *someone* will discriminate against them in the future because of mental illness. Research on anticipated stigma indicates that globally, roughly 70% of persons with schizophrenia anticipate discrimination in some area of life, while this was the case for 87% of a sample of people with various severe mental health diagnoses in the UK.[36] When taken in combination with research using the devaluation-discrimination scale, these findings suggest that whether they develop it through assumptions based on the socialization process or direct experience, the majority of people with severe mental illnesses develop a high degree of "stigma concern."

The Impact of Stigma Concern on Social Behavior

Even given that stigma concern is extremely common, many may not be convinced that it is important. However, modified labeling theory proposes that stigma concern has a major impact on social behavior. This is because modified labeling theory expects that being concerned about others' potential rejection will lead to "secrecy" and "social withdrawal." Essentially, it is expected that people will try to hide their mental illness diagnosis from others based on the expectation that this would lead them to be "discredited," or seen in a different light. In Link's original studies on modified labeling theory, he found that roughly 70% of participants endorsed that they would try to hide the fact that they have a mental illness when meeting new people, and roughly 68% endorsed that they would avoid interacting with someone that they thought "might" think less of them because of their mental illness.[37]

Going a step further, however, is the possibility that this means that people who are concerned about stigma might avoid social contact *in general,* based on the assumption that "most people" hold stigmatizing views. This was the situation confronted by Jose (the individual discussed in Chapter 1), who very much wanted to attend religious services, but did not dare to go because he feared that he would be asked questions about his personal history that would lead others to deduce that he had a mental illness. This was also expressed by a participant in a qualitative study of stigma, who stated flatly: "if I did get into relationships then I could be rejected, that's why I keep myself to myself."[38] Link's research investigated the possibility that stigma concern leads to general social withdrawal by looking at the association between the endorsement of the devaluation-discrimination scale and people's number of social contacts. His research supported that higher scores on the devaluation-discrimination scale were significantly associated with smaller social networks[39] and with a greater tendency to avoid social contact in general.[40]

Despite the above findings, a criticism of Link's early studies is that they did not adequately address alternate explanations for the relationship between perceived stigma and social withdrawal. For example, it might be that people with increased stigma concern also have more symptoms, such as "persecutory" beliefs, which lead them to think that others have the intention of harming them, and withdraw from social contact. However, research that has attempted to address this as a possible "alternate" explanation has confirmed that stigma concern effects social withdrawal even when considering the impact of symptoms. Specifically, in a study that statistically controlled for a range of objectively rated symptoms, including psychotic ones, German researcher Brigit Kleim found that perceived stigma was the strongest predictor of social withdrawal.[41] This study indicates that concern about others' stigma is a significant contributor to the social withdrawal that is pervasive among so many people with severe mental illnesses.

Stigma Concern and Treatment Avoidance. Another possible effect of "stigma concern" that was not considered initially by Link, but that has been considered by many others, is the avoidance of *treatment.* Essentially, the thinking here is that individuals who are concerned about stigma might avoid treatment to prevent having others see them as someone who is mentally ill. In some cases, such as rural communities, this might be *literally* the case, if there is only one mental health service center in the area and it is difficult to not be recognized by others when driving or walking to it. This is the aspect of stigma that many policymakers have been concerned with, such as the various US federal task forces discussed in Chapter 1, which all emphasized the need to combat stigma because of its presumed negative impact on help-seeking.

Does the research support the idea that concern about stigma deters people from seeking psychiatric help? A recent systematic review of all studies (more than 100) that were published on the topic between 1980 and 2011 provides a qualified "yes."[42] Overall, the review revealed a "small negative relationship" between concern about mental health stigma and the decision to seek help, but there was no observed relationship for some types of stigma and some subgroups of people. However, the study noted that stigma concern had a clearer impact on help-seeking among particular groups, including people of Asian, African American or Arabic ethnicity, men, and people serving in the military, suggesting that members of these groups might be particularly reluctant to seek help for a mental health problem because of concern about stigma. These findings suggest that there is evidence that diminished willingness to seek help is a consequence of stigma for at least some subgroups of people, although it is by no means the only consequence.

The Gap between What Is Experienced and Expected

A final note about "stigma concern" regards a common finding in research on "anticipated" stigma, which is that people with mental illnesses often anticipate stigma even when they do not report having experienced it. This was a major finding of the Global Programme against Stigma study, which revealed that roughly 35% of the people who anticipated discrimination had not reported actually experiencing it.[43] Similarly, a qualitative study of people diagnosed with mental illnesses living in community-based housing in Washington DC found that stigma was discussed as being an ever-present concern, but was rarely experienced.[44] Why might this be? One reason might be that most studies that have noted the gap between anticipated and experienced stigma have not studied more subtle manifestations of stigma, such as the "microaggressions" discussed in Chapter 3, which are not blatantly discriminatory but are likely to provide strong cues to people with mental illnesses that rejection or discrimination is forthcoming. This can also include "overheard" communications, such as jokes and other derogatory statements that might be made about "psychos," though not necessarily directed at anyone in particular. It is also possible that aspects of the broader social environment, such as the media (which is clearly biased toward negative reports, as discussed in Chapter 3), might influence perceptions that most people would reject someone with a mental illness. As discussed in Chapter 1, one can easily imagine how encountering a headline like "Get the Violent Crazies Off Our Streets!" could impact the perception that a person with mental illness has about the extent to which they are welcome in the broader community. The possible impact of the media was well-expressed by a participant in a qualitative study on stigma, who stated: "you don't see much about a schizophrenic who's been working hard for charity and done some really nice things, but you will see one sword-wielding maniac."[45] Although sensationalist media accounts are not likely a true reflection of the public's views, they might still be experienced by many individuals as a representation of "what people really think."

There is also evidence that stigma concern may condition people diagnosed with mental illnesses to perceive more negative evaluation from others when they think that they are aware of their diagnosis, even if they have not directly experienced discrimination or rejection. A classic study conducted by social psychologist Amerigo Farina shed light on this. In the study, people with mental illnesses were instructed to play a cooperative board game with college students; half of the participants with mental illnesses were randomly assigned to be told that the college student knew that they were a "mental patient," while the other half were told that the college student was told that they were a "surgical patient" (the college students were actually not told either). The study found that when participants with mental illnesses were assigned to believe that their psychiatric status was known, they spoke less and experienced more anxiety (and performed more poorly in the game).[46] This indicates that for people with mental illnesses who assume that community members know about their psychiatric status, anxiety about social rejection may be heightened. This may be especially the case if they live in community-based housing facilities, where all residents have a mental illness, making their labeled status more "visible." In fact, some residences loudly proclaim that they are community-based housing facilities for people with "problems" (see Figure 10). Supporting that this can have an impact on perceptions of stigma are findings from my research study with people with mental illness living in New York City, which found that participants living in group-based housing perceived significantly more social exclusion from community members than people living in "scatter-site" apartments in the same neighborhoods.[47] This indicates that

Figure 10 A community residence in Manhattan's East Harlem announces itself.
Photo by author.

expectations of social exclusion may permeate the lives of people with mental illnesses when they live in types of housing that make their diagnosis clear to community members.

Finally, there is the reality that many people diagnosed with mental illnesses often do not directly encounter rejection or discrimination related to mental illness because they do such a good job of hiding it. As a result, although stigma is not encountered, it remains part of the subtext of every social interaction, because an undercurrent of fear of being "found out" pervades them. This reality goes back to the "discreditable" nature of social interactions experienced by those with invisible stigmas that Erving Goffman discussed (mentioned in Chapter 1). The irony of this, however, is that secrecy and social avoidance, though to some extent adaptive strategies for reducing the likelihood of directly encountering stigma, work to maintain stigma on a societal level, because people in society do not realize that they know someone with a severe mental illness and consequently do not acquire the "contact" experiences that so effectively counter-act negative stereotypes (as we learned in Chapter 4). We will discuss possible ways to remedy this problem to reduce stigma on a societal level in a Chapter 10.

The Development of Self-Stigma

As mentioned earlier in this chapter and represented in Figure 11, the development of "stigma concern" is only one part of the way in which awareness of others' stigma impacts people with mental illnesses. An even

Response 1: Indifference

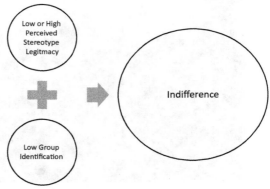

Response 2: Righteous Anger

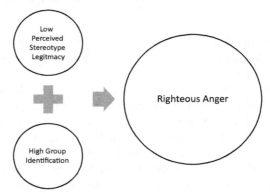

Response 3: Self-Stigma

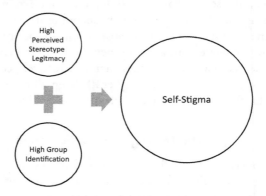

Figure 11   Possible identity responses to stigma

more insidious process can occur when a belief in the validity of negative stereotypes interacts with a self-identification that one has a mental illness, which in turn can lead to the internalization of stigma, or "self-stigma." Essentially, this means that people with mental illnesses can come to believe that the negative stereotypes that others hold about them are *true*, to at least some extent. In addition, there is a strong component of "alienation" in the experience of self-stigma, in which people come to feel that they are fundamentally different from, and worth less than, others. In her personal account titled *Self-Stigmatization* (arguably the first time that the term "self-stigma" was discussed in an academic journal), Kathleen Gallo, a woman who had been diagnosed with schizophrenia, poignantly described how her self-perception had reflected an internalization of others' negative stereotypes:

> I perceived myself, quite accurately, unfortunately, as having a serious mental illness and therefore as having been relegated to what I called "the social garbage heap." ... Thinking of myself as garbage, I would even leave the sidewalk in what I thought of as exhibiting the proper deference to those above me in social class. The latter group, of course, included all other human beings.[48]

The Internalization Process

As we shall learn in what follows, research suggests that Gallo's experience of feeling like she counted for less than others as a result of having a mental illness is by no means unique. How do people with mental illnesses come to internalize negative stereotypes that they are incompetent, unpredictable, and incapable of recovering? For a long time, social psychological theory assumed that it was human nature for the self-image of people who are members of stigmatized categories to be impacted by the views of the "generalized other." For example, in *The Nature of Prejudice*, Allport predicted that exposure to prejudice would "destroy the integrity of the ego" and "create a groveling self-image" among members of prejudiced groups.[49] In fact, the opinion that racially-segregated schools damaged the self-images of African American students formed a major part of the argument for school desegregation in the 1950s.[b, 50]

---

[b] In the *Brown* v. *Board of Education* decision, the Supreme Court stated: "To separate [African American children] from others of similar age and qualifications solely because of their race generates a feeling of inferiority as to their status in the community that may affect their hearts and minds in a way unlikely ever to be undone."

Despite this assumption, it is important to note that the large amount of research that has been conducted with people with stigmatized statuses other than mental illness (such as overweight persons and members of negatively stereotyped ethnic and racial groups such as African Americans) indicates that it is most typically *not* the case that negative stereotypes are internalized.[51] In fact, members of these other stigmatized groups usually have self-esteem that is equal to or better than others, apparently due to an ability to "disengage" self-image from others' approval. However, contrary to this pattern, people diagnosed with mental illnesses consistently have *worse* self-esteem than others without mental illnesses. This suggests that there may be something particularly powerful about mental health stigma that makes it especially difficult to "disengage" from an awareness of others' presumed negative views. This was articulated by participants in the study conducted by my colleague Lauren O'Connor on the stigma internalization experiences of people who identified as both LGBT and mentally ill. Several participants indicated how it was more difficult to accept having a mental illness than being LGBT. This was exemplified by participants' statements that mental illness is more difficult to accept because "you're getting into the mind, you're not getting an aspect of sexuality, you're dealing with the whole person and the potential is to themselves and to others," and "mental, that's your brain, mental illness is something bad, that's how I look at it, it is what it is ... but, your [LGBTQ] lifestyle, there is nothing wrong with that at all."[52]

How does the internalization of negative stereotypes occur among people who've been diagnosed with mental illnesses? In one of the first studies to document the process of self-stigmatization (which he called "engulfment"), psychologist Stephen Lally conducted interviews with 60 residents of a state psychiatric hospital, exploring how their self-images were impacted by having a diagnosis of mental illness and what life events had been pivotal in that process.[53] He found that a majority of the participants had developed what he called an "identity crisis," leading their self-concepts to become increasingly dominated by "the mental patient role." Events that emerged as being particularly important in this process were: (1) the experience of symptoms, such as hallucinations, that could not easily be dismissed as "normal," (2) hospitalization and the experience of being around other "mental patients," (3) being told that one has a diagnosis that is strongly associated with negative stereotypes, such as schizophrenia, and (4) applying for federal benefits programs, such as Supplemental Security Income (SSI), which require that one proclaim that one are disabled.

Experiencing symptoms, such as auditory hallucinations, appears to be an important part of the process of developing a stigmatized identity, especially as people become aware that what they are hearing is "not real." This realization, coupled with an awareness that hearing things that are not real is "not normal," can lead to a heightened sensitivity to the meaning of the experience. This was explicitly stated by one of Lally's participants, who said "I hear these inner voices and I know it's not normal and it affects my conception of myself in terms of being able to function in a normal way." Similarly, another participant stated: "It scared me to death, I thought, well, I'm going completely insane. I'm completely insane. I was more scared than I'd ever been in my whole life."

The impact of hospitalization or other experiences of being grouped together with others with mental illness has rarely been studied, but it appears that there is some degree of "socialization" to the role of how one acts as a person with mental illness that is transmitted through contact with others who have been diagnosed. For example, one of the participants in Nancy Herman's study stated: "by virtue of the fact that you're on the ward every day with 50 other 'mentals' – they're the ones who teach you what it means to be mentally ill."[54] Thus, through observation or more explicit means, people may learn how one is expected to act from others who have longer experience in the mental health system. Being hospitalized or surrounded by others with mental illnesses can also serve as a reminder of one's lower social status. This was described by a participant in an ethnographic study conducted by sociologist Linda Shaw, who stated: "at [the boarding home], everything is a constant reminder that you've failed."[55]

Hearing one's diagnosis, and possibly being told that it means that one needs to diminish one's life expectations, may have a particularly powerful impact on the development of self-stigma. This was also discussed by Patricia Deegan, who described how she was told by her psychiatrist that "if you continue to take your medications for the rest of your life and you avoid stress, then you might be able to cope,"[56] and that this statement, which implied that she should give up on her dreams of having a normal life, made her feel that her life was a "closed book." After hearing her diagnosis, Deegan recalls "losing the will to live" since her "future had been reduced to a prognosis of doom."[57] Similarly, one of Lally's participants stated that after hearing that his diagnosis was schizophrenia, he felt that "it was kind of like I had no hope, there was no purpose in trying anything else ... like it made me feel as if I was going to be sick for the rest of my life."

Applying for federal benefits programs for income support also seems to have a powerful impact on one's expectation that one does not have the ability to work in the future. In the United States, applying for SSI requires one to attest that one is "unable to do any substantial gainful activity,"[58] which seems to lead many to believe that it must be true. This was clearly described by one of Lally's participants, who said:

> The doctors here put me on social security disability. It disappointed me because I wanted to work. I thought, "I'm not able to work, I might as well accept it" . . . it's had a lot of effect on me. It did. I was younger then and I was certainly disappointed because I couldn't work because of it.

Common Reactions to Stigma: Not Everyone Internalizes

Although the internalization of stigma is common, it should be emphasized here that it is by no means the only reaction to finding out that one is diagnosed with a mental illness. In fact, Patrick Corrigan and Amy Watson theorized that there are three primary responses to being diagnosed with a mental illness insofar as identity is concerned: indifference, righteous anger, and self-stigma.[59] In their conceptualization, the two key factors in determining one's reaction are "group identification" (or the extent to which people believe that they are part of the category of "mentally ill") and "perceived legitimacy of stigma" (or the extent to which people believe that negative stereotypes are correct). An elaboration of how these factors interact to lead to these three possible outcomes in provided in Figure 11.

As can be seen in Figure 11, indifference, or a "no big deal" attitude, is expected to result when people have low group identification, meaning that they either do not believe that they have a mental illness, or believe that they are somehow different from others in this category. These individuals may or may not believe in the legitimacy of negative stereotypes, but this is not really important, since they do not feel that the stereotypes apply to them regardless. Some people who develop an "indifferent" response may be individuals who are believed by professionals to "lack insight." This raises the question of whether there may be some adaptive functions to "lacking insight," which we will consider more in Chapter 6.

Righteous anger, on the other hand, occurs when people do identify as members of the group, but reject the legitimacy of negative stereotypes. These individuals may become involved in advocacy or other means of protesting the injustice of stigma. In some cases, a righteous anger response may develop over time. This was described by Patricia Deegan, who explained how she eventually came to reject the "prognosis of doom" that she had initially accepted, thinking: "I am more than that, more than a schizophrenic."[60] We will learn more about how certain intervention approaches attempt to nurture this type of response in Chapter 8.

Finally, as already indicated, self-stigma can result when individuals both identify as members of the group ("yes, I have a mental illness") and believe in the legitimacy of negative stereotypes ("it is true that people with mental illnesses are dangerous and can't recover, so this must be true of me.") Based on what we know about human nature, it might seem counterintuitive that people would sometimes accept the view that having a mental illness means that they are incompetent and cannot recover, rather than find some way to "deflect" the negative stereotypes, as most with other stigmatized statuses do. To make sense of this, it is helpful to consider that there may be some self-protective functions to taking on a stigmatized identity after one has experienced repeated struggles. Mental illness is rarely associated with a quick-and-easy path of recovery, and in many cases there may be a series of setbacks and disappointments. After experiencing many difficulties related to psychiatric symptoms, people may find that agreeing with the (inaccurate) idea that people with mental illness "cannot" do certain things in society gives them a feeling of relief in that they cannot be blamed for no longer trying. This was expressed by one of Lally's participants, who stated:

> Before I used to see myself as very able, able to handle things, very strong person. Now I see myself as just the opposite. Just have to accept it.[61]

How Common Is Elevated Self-Stigma?

In the past ten years or so, researchers have become increasingly concerned with how often people with mental illnesses develop identities that are strongly influenced by "self-stigma," especially given its potentially profound impact on self-esteem. In order to answer this question, researcher Jennifer Boyd developed the *Internalized Stigma of Mental Illness* scale to assess the extent to which people with mental illnesses agree with negative stereotypes (e.g., "People with mental illness shouldn't get married"), and feel alienated from others (e.g., "I feel inferior to others who don't have a mental illness").[62] This scale has now been translated into dozens of languages and administered to thousands of people with mental illnesses around the world, so we now have a good idea of how common the experience of self-stigma is. Using predetermined cutoffs on the measure, studies conducted in countries across Europe, North America, Africa, and East Asia have consistently found that between 20–40% of people with severe mental illnesses demonstrate "clinically significant" self-stigma.[63] Research with the largest samples suggests that people diagnosed with schizophrenia are generally more likely to experience self-stigma than persons with major depression and bipolar disorder (although a study conducted in Taiwan found that people with bipolar disorder had even higher self-stigma scores on average than people with schizophrenia[64]), but that other background factors such as gender, age, and education level do not make much of a difference in influencing whether one will develop it.

Is Self-Stigma More Common When There Is More Community Stigma?

An interesting question that researchers have begun to contend with is whether people with mental illnesses are more likely to experience self-stigma in locations where there is more community stigma. To date, only one study has addressed this question – a study conducted by Sara Evans-Lacko of London's Kings College, which combined data on community stigma from the Eurobarometer survey (discussed in Chapter 4) with data on the extent to which self-stigma was endorsed by people with mental illnesses who were surveyed in 14 of the countries. This study revealed that there was, in fact, a relationship between "country-level" stigma and "individual-level" self-stigma, such that people with mental illnesses living in countries where stigma is more prevalent (i.e., the Eastern and Southern European countries of Greece, the Czech Republic, Lithuania, and Estonia) were also more likely to experience self-stigma.[65] This suggests that self-stigma is particularly likely to be a concern for individuals living in settings and cultural contexts where negative stereotypes are more prevalent.

Conclusion: Stigma Gets under Your Skin

In summary, along with the considerable evidence for the direct impact of stigma through discrimination and social exclusion that we reviewed in Chapter 3, in this chapter we have seen that stigma also impacts people with mental illnesses in more insidious ways, through the development of "stigma concern" (which impacts roughly 60–70% of diagnosed individuals) and "self-stigma" (which impacts roughly 20–40%). Though heightened by experiences of social rejection and discrimination, research indicates that is not necessary for one to have these experiences in order to develop stigma concern or self-stigma. These manifestations of stigma may, in turn, have a profound impact on the ability of people with mental illnesses to participate in community life and reach their full potential as humans. In Chapter 6, we will examine in detail how self-stigma exerts a pervasive impact on the lives of many people with severe mental illnesses that goes above and beyond the direct effects of mental illness itself.

References

1 Deegan, P. E. (2001). Recovery as a self-directed process of healing and transformation. In C. Brown (Ed.) *Recovery and wellness: Models of hope and empowerment for people with mental illness.* Haworth Press: New York.

2 Deegan, P. E. (1993). Recovering our sense of value after being labeled mentally ill. *Journal of Psychosocial Nursing and Mental Health Services, 31,* 7–11.

3 Deegan, P. E. (1996). Recovery as a Journey of the Heart. *Psychiatric Rehabilitation Journal, 19,* 91–97.

4 Saks, E. R. (2007). *The center cannot hold: My journey through madness.* New York: Hachette.

5 Link, B. G., Cullen, F. T., Struening, E., Shrout, P. E., & Dohrenwend, B. P. (1989). A modified labeling theory approach to mental disorders: An empirical assessment. *American Sociological Review, 54,* 400–423.

6 Corrigan, P. W., & Watson, A. C. (2002). The paradox of self-stigma and mental illness. *Clinical Psychology: Science & Practice, 9,* 35–53; Watson, A. C., Corrigan, P. W., Larsen, J. E., & Sells, M. (1997). Self-stigma in people with mental illness. *Schizophrenia Bulletin, 33,* 1312–1318.

7 Gallo, K. M. (1994). First person account: Self-stigmatization. *Schizophrenia Bulletin, 20,* 407–410.

8 Link, B. G., Cullen, F. T., Struening, E., Shrout, P. E., & Dohrenwend, B. P. (1989). A modified labeling theory approach to mental disorders: An empirical assessment. *American Sociological Review, 54,* 400–423; Link, B. G., & Phelan, J. C. (2014). Stigma power. *Social Science and Medicine, 103,* 24–32.

9 Wahl, O. F. (2002).Children's views of mental illness: A review of the literature. *Psychiatric Rehabilitation Skills, 6,* 134–158.; Corrigan, P. W., & Watson, A. C. (2007). How children stigmatize people with mental illness. *International Journal of Social Psychiatry, 53,* 526–546.

10 Spitzer, A., & Cameron, C. (1995). School-age children's perceptions of mental illness. *Western Journal of Nursing Research, 17,* 398–415.

11 Weiss, M. F. (1985). Children's attitudes toward mental illness as assessed by the Opinions About Mental Illness Scale. *Psychological Reports, 57,* 251–258.

12 Ndetei, D. M., Mutiso, V., Maraj, A., Anderson, K. K., Musyimi, C., & McKenzie, K. (2016). Stigmatizing attitudes toward mental illness among primary school children in Kenya. *Social Psychiatry and Psychiatric Epidemiology, 51,* 73–80.

13 Jackson, D., & Heatherington, L. (2006). Young Jamaicans' attitudes toward mental illness: Experimental and demographic factors associated with social distance and stigmatizing opinions. *Journal of Community Psychology, 34,* 563–576.

14 Corrigan, P., W., & Watson, A. C. (2007). How children stigmatize people with mental illness. *International Journal of Social Psychiatry, 53,* 526–546.

15 Rideout, V.J., Foher, U.G., & Roberts, D.F. (2010). *Generation M2: Media in the Lives of 8-18-Year-Olds: A Kaiser Family Foundation Study.* Menlo Park, CA: Henry J. Kaiser Family Foundation.

16 Wahl, O. F. (2003). Depictions of mental illness in children's media. *Journal of Mental Health, 12,* 249–258.

17 Lawson, A., & Fouts, G. (2004). Mental illness in Disney animated films. *Canadian Journal of Psychiatry, 49,* 310–314.

18 Mead, G. H. (1934). *Mind, self, and society.* Chicago: University of Chicago Press; Burkitt, I. (2008). *Social selves: Theories of self and society.* London: Sage.

19 Herman, N. (1993). Return to sender: Reintegrative stigma management strategies of ex-psychiatric patients. *Journal of Contemporary Ethnography, 22,* 295–330.

20 O'Connor, L., Pleskach, P., & Yanos, P. T. (Under Review). Dual self-stigma: Lesbian, Gay, Bisexual, Transgender and Queer persons with severe mental illness.

21 Fusar-Poli, P., Borgwardt, S., Bechdolf, A., Addington, J., Riecher-Rössler, A., Schultze-Lutter, F., et al. (2013). The psychosis high-risk state: A comprehensive state-of-the-art review. *JAMA Psychiatry, 70,* 107–120.

22 Rüsch, N., Corrigan, P.W., Heekeren, K., Theodoridou, A., Dvorsky, D., Metzler, S., Müller, M., Walitza, S., & Rössler, W., (2014b). Well-being among persons at risk of psychosis: The role of self-labeling, shame and stigma stress. *Psychiatric Services, 65,* 483–489.

23 Rüsch N., Heekeren, K., Theodoridou, A., Dvorsky, D., Müller, M., Paust, T., et al. (2013) Attitudes towards help-seeking and stigma among young people at risk for psychosis. *Psychiatry Research, 210,* 1313–1315.

24 Rüsch, N., Heekeren, K., Theodoridou, A., Müller, M., Corrigan, P. W., Mayer, B., et al. (2015). Stigma as a stressor and transition to schizophrenia after one year among young people at risk of psychosis. *Schizophrenia Research, 166,* 43–48.

25 Yang, L. H., Link, B. G., Ben-David, S., Gill, K. E., Girgis, R. R., Brucato, G., Wonpat-Borja, A. J., & Corcoran, C. M. (2015). Stigma related to labels and symptoms in individuals at clinical high-risk for psychosis. *Schizophrenia Research, 168,* 9–15.

26 Herman, N. (1993). Return to sender: Reintegrative stigma management strategies of ex-psychiatric patients. *Journal of Contemporary Ethnography, 22,* 295–330.

27 Moses, T. (2011). Stigma apprehension among adolescents discharged from brief psychiatric hospitalization. *Journal of Nervous and Mental Disease, 199,* 778–789.

28 Moses, T. (2014). Determinants of mental illness stigma for adolescents discharged from psychiatric hospitalization. *Social Science & Medicine, 109*, 26–34.

29 Yanos, P. T., Rosenfield, S., & Horwitz, A. V. (2001). Negative and supportive social interactions and quality of life among persons diagnosed with severe mental illness. *Community Mental Health Journal, 37*, 405–419.

30 Lundberg, B., Hansson, L., Wentz, E., & Bjorkman, T. (2007). Sociodemographic and clinical factors related to devaluation/discrimination and rejection experiences among users of mental health services. *Social Psychiatry & Psychiatric Epidemiology, 42*, 295–300.

31 Link, B. G., Cullen, F. T., Struening, E., Shrout, P. E., & Dohrenwend, B. P. (1989). A modified labeling theory approach to mental disorders: An empirical assessment. *American Sociological Review, 54*, 400–423.

32 Brohan, E., Elgie, R., Sartorius, N., & Thornicroft, G. (2010). Self-stigma, empowerment and perceived discrimination among people with schizophrenia in 14 European countries: The GAMIAN-Europe study. *Schizophrenia Research, 122*(1–3), 232–238; Brohan, E., Gauci, D., Sartorius, N., & Thornicroft, G. (2011). Self-stigma, empowerment and perceived discrimination among people with bipolar disorder or depression in 13 European countries: The GAMIAN–Europe study. *Journal of Affective Disorders, 129*, 56–63.

33 Krajewski, C., Burazeri, G., & Brand, H. (2013). Self-stigma, perceived discrimination and empowerment among people with a mental illness in six countries: Pan European stigma study. *Psychiatry Research, 210*(3), 1136–1146.

34 Rosenfield, S. (1997). Labeling mental illness: The effects of received services and perceived stigma on life satisfaction. *American Sociological Review, 62*, 660–672; Link, B. G., Cullen, F. T., Struening, E., Shrout, P. E., & Dohrenwend, B. P. (1989). A modified labeling theory approach to mental disorders: An empirical assessment. *American Sociological Review, 54*, 400–423.

35 Chien, W-T., Yeung, F. K. K., & Chan, A. H. L. (2014). Perceived stigma of patients with severe mental illness in Hong Kong: relationships with patients' psychosocial conditions and attitudes of family caregivers and health professionals. *Administration and Policy in Mental Health, 41*, 237–251; Jung, S. H., & Kim, H. J. (2012). Perceived stigma and quality of life of individuals diagnosed with schizophrenia and receiving psychiatric rehabilitation services: A comparison between the clubhouse model and a rehabilitation skills training model in South Korea. *Psychiatric Rehabilitation Journal, 35*, 460–465.

36 Thornicroft, G., Brohan, E., Rose, D., Sartorius, N., & Leese, M. (2009). Global pattern of experienced and anticipated discrimination against people with schizophrenia: A cross-sectional survey. *Lancet, 373*, 408–415; Farrelly, S., Clement, S., Gabbidon, J., Jeffrey, D., Dockery, L., Lassman, F., et al. (2014). Anticipated and experienced discrimination amongst people with

schizophrenia, bipolar disorder and major depressive disorder: A cross sectional study. *BMC Psychiatry*, *14*, 157.

37 Link, B. G., Cullen, F. T., Struening, E., Shrout, P. E., & Dohrenwend, B. P. (1989). A modified labeling theory approach to mental disorders: An empirical assessment. *American Sociological Review*, *54*, 400–423.

38 Burke, E., Wood, L., Zabel, E., Clark, A., & Morrison, A. P. (2016). Experiences of stigma in psychosis: A qualitative analysis of service users' perspectives. *Psychosis*, *8*, 130–142.

39 Link, B. G., Cullen, F. T., Struening, E., Shrout, P. E., & Dohrenwend, B. P. (1989). A modified labeling theory approach to mental disorders: An empirical assessment. *American Sociological Review*, *54*, 400–423.

40 Link, B. G., Wells, J., Phelan, J. C., & Yang, L. (2015). Understanding the importance of "symbolic interaction stigma": How expectations about the reactions of others adds to the burden of mental illness stigma. *Psychiatric Rehabilitation Journal*, *38*, 117–124.

41 Kleim, B., Vauth, R., Adam, G., Stieglitz, R.-D., Hayward, P., & Corrigan, P. (2008). Perceived stigma predicts low self-efficacy and poor coping in schizophrenia. *Journal of Mental Health*, *17*, 482–491.

42 Clement, S., Schauman. O., Graham, T., Maggioni, F., Evans-Lacko, S., Bezborodovs, N., Morgan, C., Rüsch, N., Brown, J. S. L., & Thornicroft, G. (2015). What is the impact of mental health-related stigma on help-seeking? A systematic review of quantitative and qualitative studies. *Psychological Medicine*, *45*, 11–27.

43 Thornicroft, G., Brohan, E., Rose, D., Sartorius, N., & Leese, M. (2009). Global pattern of experienced and anticipated discrimination against people with schizophrenia: A cross-sectional survey. *Lancet*, *373*, 408–415.

44 Whitely, R., & Campbell, R. D. (2014). Stigma, agency and recovery amongst people with severe mental illness. *Social Science & Medicine*, *107*, 1–8.

45 Burke, E., Wood, L., Zabel, E., Clark, A., & Morrison, A. P. (2016). Experiences of stigma in psychosis: A qualitative analysis of service users' perspectives. *Psychosis*, *8*, 130–142.

46 Farina, A., Gliha, D., Boudreau, L. A., Allen, J. G., & Sherman, M. (1971). Mental illness and the impact of believing others know about it. *Journal of Abnormal Psychology*, *77*, 1–5.

47 Yanos, P. T., Stefancic, A., Alexander, M. J., Gonzales, L., & Harney, B. (Under Review). Housing and personal capacity predictors of community participation among persons with psychiatric disabilities.

48 Gallo, K. M. (1994). First person account: Self-stigmatization. *Schizophrenia Bulletin*, *20*, 407–410.

49 Allport, G. W. (1979). *The nature of prejudice* (25th anniversary edition). Reading, MA: Addison-Wesley. 152.

50 Accessed online August 23, 2017: www.naacpldf.org/brown-at-60-the-doll-test

51 Crocker, J., & Quinn, D. M. (2000). Social stigma and the self: Meanings, situations, and self-esteem. In T. F. Heatherton et al. (Eds.) *The Social*

Psychology of Stigma. New York: Guilford; Major, B., & O'Brien, L. T. (2005). The social psychology of stigma. *Annual Review of Psychology, 56,* 393–421.

52 O'Connor, L., Pleskach, P., & Yanos, P. T. (Under Review). Dual self-stigma: Lesbian, Gay, Bisexual, Transgender and Queer persons with severe mental illness.

53 Lally, S. J. (1989). Does being in here mean there is something wrong with me? *Schizophrenia Bulletin, 15,* 235–265.

54 Herman, N. (1993). Return to sender: Reintegrative stigma management strategies of ex-psychiatric patients. *Journal of Contemporary Ethnography, 22,* 295–330.

55 Shaw, L. N. (1991). Stigma and the moral careers of ex-mental patients living in board and care. *Journal of Contemporary Ethnography, 20,* 285–305.

56 Deegan, P. E. (1997). Recovery and empowerment for people with psychiatric disabilities. *Social Work in Health Care, 25,* 11–24.

57 Deegan, P. E. (1993). Recovering our sense of value after being labeled mentally ill. *Journal of Psychosocial Nursing and Mental Health Services, 31,* 7–11.

58 Social Security Administration (2016). Understanding Supplemental Security Income SSI Eligibility Requirements – 2016 Edition. Accessed online August 23, 2017: www.ssa.gov/ssi/text-eligibility-ussi.htm.

59 Corrigan, P. W., & Watson, A. C. (2002). The paradox of self-stigma and mental illness. *Clinical Psychology: Science & Practice, 9,* 35–53.

60 Deegan, P. (2001). Recovery as a self-directed process of healing and transformation. In C. Brown (Ed.) *Recovery and wellness: Models of hope and empowerment for people with mental illness.* New York: Haworth Press.

61 Lally, S. J. (1989). "Does being in here mean there is something wrong with me?" *Schizophrenia Bulletin, 15,* 235–265.

62 Boyd Ritsher, J., Otilingam, P. G., & Grajales, M. (2003). Internalized stigma of mental illness: psychometric properties of a new measure. *Psychiatry Research, 121,* 31–49.

63 Brohan, E., Elgie, R., Sartorius, N., & Thornicroft, G. (2010). Self-stigma, empowerment and perceived discrimination among people with schizophrenia in 14 European countries: The GAMIAN-Europe study. *Schizophrenia Research, 122,* 232–238; Brohan, E., Gauci, D., Sartorius, N., & Thornicroft, G. (2011). Self-stigma, empowerment and perceived discrimination among people with bipolar disorder or depression in 13 European countries: The GAMIAN–Europe study. *Journal of Affective Disorders, 129,* 56–63; Krajewski, C., Burazeri, G., & Brand, H. (2013). Self-stigma, perceived discrimination and empowerment among people with a mental illness in six countries: Pan European stigma study. *Psychiatry Research, 210,* 1136–1146; West, M. L., Yanos, P. T., Smith, S. M., Roe, D., & Lysaker, P. H. (2011). Prevalence of internalized stigma among persons with severe mental illness. *Stigma Research and Action, 1,* 54–59; Assefa, D., Shibre, T., Asher, L., & Fekadu, A. (2012). Internalized stigma among

patients with schizophrenia in Ethiopia: a cross-sectional facility-based study. *BMC Psychiatry*, 12, 239; Lu, Y., Wolf, A., & Wang, X. Experienced stigma and self-stigma in Chinese patients with schizophrenia. (2013). *General Hospital Psychiatry*, 35, 83–88.

64 Chang, C.-C., Wu, T.-H., Chen, C.-Y., & Lin, C.-Y. (2016). Comparing self-stigma between people with different mental disorders in Taiwan. *Journal of Nervous and Mental Disease*, 204, 547–553.

65 Evans-Lacko, S., Brohan, E., Mojtabi, R., & Thornicroft, G. (2012). Association between public views of mental illness and self-stigma among individuals with mental illness in 14 European countries. *Psychological Medicine*, 42, 1741–1752.

CHAPTER 6

Discredited
The Impact of Self-Stigma on Identity and Community Participation

In an ethnographic study of people with mental illnesses living in a large community residence in Los Angeles, sociologist Linda Shaw discussed in detail the case of "Robert," an "intelligent, outgoing person in his early 30's" from a "middle-class" background, who had at one time aspired to become an accountant.[1] As described by Shaw, Robert is not actively demonstrating symptoms and is in fact told that he is "high functioning" by residence staff, but he nonetheless appears to be desperately struggling. What is he struggling with, if not the symptoms of mental illness? As described by Shaw, and Robert's own words, he is grappling with the dramatic impact that the internalization of negative stereotypes about mental illness has had on his self-image, leading him to develop a "stigmatized self." Robert states that he sees a "futureless future" for himself as a resident of the housing facility, and denigrates the passivity of residents by calling them "human rocks," but also notes that he is becoming "like one of those rocks." Keenly aware of the gap between what he aspired to become and where he is, he states "I got no hope." Despite being offered the opportunity to leave the residence and live more independently, Robert eventually gives up, saying "I don't even want to try to be on the outside anymore." Shaw sadly noted that Robert committed suicide some months after she completed her research.

In her retrospective discussion of how she initially responded to being told that she was diagnosed with schizophrenia, Patricia Deegan also drew a distinction between the impact of symptoms and the impact of stigma.[2] Deegan recounted how she could see her younger self "sit[ting] in a chair" smoking "cigarette after cigarette," seeing "no way to achieve the valued roles she once dreamed of." However, Deegan was clear that as she observed her younger self "it is not so much mental illness that I am observing," but rather "the flame of a faltering human spirit." What accounted for the faltering of this flame? Deegan attributed it to the impact of the "prognosis of doom" that others had ascribed to her when they told her that she had schizophrenia, and the effect of "putting on those warped glasses" that lead to "viewing yourself as others see you." She concluded that this had resulted in her transforming from "being a person to being an illness."

The above examples illustrate a crucial contention of this book that was alluded to in Chapter 1: that the internalization of stigma exerts a powerful impact above and beyond the impact of the symptoms of mental illness themselves. I never knew Robert and have never met Patricia Deegan, but their stories are very familiar to me from my clinical work. Over and again, I have been struck by how people with what I recognize to be great potential (who are also symptomatically "stable") feel that they have no hope for the future. In the winter of 2006, this became the topic of a discussion that I had with my colleague David Roe (also a clinical psychologist and researcher) when we met at a coffee shop in New Jersey, where we both worked at the time, to talk about the possibility of working on research together. We agreed that we both had worked with many people who had "given up" on themselves when they had so much yet to offer, and that the internalization of stigma was a major reason for this. Energized by the belief that we had identified something important, David and I agreed that what we had observed in our clinical work had to be documented in research and addressed in a systematic way by the mental health system, and a collaborative journey that has continued for the past ten years began.

Another important point of this book that was mentioned in Chapter 1 should be highlighted here. The individuals that we knew who had been profoundly impacted by the internalization of stigma were not people who had failed to receive mental health services. In fact, in many cases they were considered to be "insightful" (or highly aware) of the extent to which mental illness affected their lives. Thus, the problem of stigma was not, for them, a problem of refusing to recognize the seriousness of mental illness or refusing to seek help for it. Rather, the problem was, in some respects, a by-product of taking the admonitions of the mental health system (such as recommendations to "avoid stress") too deeply to heart. Hence this book's emphasis on the need for the field to move beyond the typical focus on encouraging (or even *forcing*, as advocated by some[3]) help-seeking as the solution to stigma, since there is compelling evidence that receiving help can cause other problems *if* it is not sensitive to the issue of self-stigma.

One of the products of my discussion with David was a diagram for a "theoretical model" explaining how the internalization of stigma exerts its effects. Figure 12 shows the "Illness Identity" model that eventually developed out of that discussion and later discussions with our colleague Paul Lysaker.[4] This model proposes that the interaction between awareness that one has a mental illness and agreement with the negative stereotypes that are attached to it sets off a cascade of problematic outcomes. First, hope and self-esteem are diminished, as people come to believe that having a mental illness means that they cannot get better and have less value than others. This increases risk for suicide and leads to the development of a more passive attitude toward coping with psychiatric symptoms (including disengagement from treatment, as people come to believe that "there is no point in trying"). Furthermore, feeling that one has less value than others increases social avoidance. Passive coping and disengagement in treatment, in turn, diminish the likelihood that people will seek or maintain employment, even if they are offered services intended to provide work opportunities. Finally, the model proposes that social avoidance and passive coping also increase the severity of psychotic and other symptoms. This stems from the view that while these factors do not cause symptoms, their frequency and severity can be heightened by social isolation and disengagement in treatment.

The assertion that the far-reaching effects shown in Figure 12 are independent of the symptoms of mental illness themselves does not mean that symptoms are not also important in other ways, but they are largely irrelevant in the model, which is only concerned with responses to the social phenomenon of stigma. Thus, the model insists that a large amount of the social disability that is associated with mental illnesses can be attributed to the internalization of societal stigma. Although this view is now much more likely to be taken seriously in the field, when we first made these contentions we were met with skepticism from many colleagues. Is it really possible, I recall one senior colleague asking me, that stigma makes a difference after one has considered the impact of things like

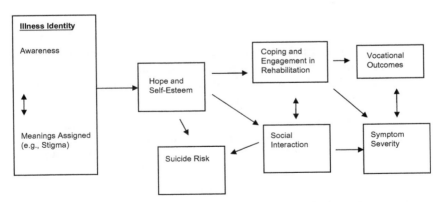

Figure 12   The illness identity model (Used by Permission of Taylor & Francis)

psychotic symptoms and substance abuse? We knew that we thought so, but research had to be conducted to test this view. Others also questioned whether what we were talking about was really something that was not already known and being addressed by the mental health system.

In fact, there is a long history of the discussion of impairments in "sense of self" among people with schizophrenia (going back even to the initial descriptions of the disorder by Emil Kraepelin and Eugen Bleuler in the early 1900s). Essentially, these early discussions observed that people with schizophrenia struggle to understand who they are and how they fit in the world. However, as summarized by Paul and John Lysaker in their book *Schizophrenia and Fate of the Self*, these discussions characterized "fragmentation" of the self as a *symptom* of the disorder, and almost never connected it to stigma.[5] In retrospect, it seems that statements that people with schizophrenia experience a "rent in [their] relations with [the] world"[6] (made by R. D. Laing in the 1960s) are crying out for a consideration of the role of stigma. Nevertheless, stigma was not mentioned in these discussions. Thus, while it may be true to say that disturbances in "sense of self" have long been recognized by psychiatry, the belief that they were symptoms of the disorder rather than the results of the internalization of stigma made a world of difference in how they were responded to.

In this chapter, I will review research supporting each of the assertions of the "Illness-Identity" model, considering the extent to which evidence supports that the internalization of stigma has a substantial effect on extent to which many people diagnosed with severe mental illnesses are able to achieve their full human potential.

Hope and Self-Esteem

The first major contention of the "Illness Identity" model is that the combination of internalized stigma and an awareness that one has a mental illness leads to diminished hope for the future and reduced self-esteem. The way that this manifests itself was well-articulated by a participant in Nancy Herman's ethnographic study, who stated:

> Having been diagnosed as a psychiatric patient with psychotic tendencies is the worst thing that has ever happened to me. It's shitty to be mentally ill; it's not something to be proud of. It makes you realize how different you are from everyone else – they're normal and you're not.[7]

In the first study that we worked on together, Paul Lysaker, David Roe, and I decided to empirically test the prediction that the combination of internalized stigma and awareness of mental illness would lead to diminished hope and self-esteem.[8] We used scores on scales of internalized stigma and insight to divide a sample of people diagnosed with schizophrenia into three groups: people who believed they had a mental illness and attached negative stereotypes to it (high insight/high self-stigma), people who believed they had a mental illness but *did not* attach negative stereotypes to it (high insight/low self-stigma), and people who essentially did not think that they had a mental illness (low insight/low self-stigma). We found that people in the high insight/ high self-stigma group demonstrated markedly less hope and self-esteem in comparison with people with high insight/low self-stigma. In addition, there was almost no difference in hope and self-esteem between the high insight/ low self-stigma group and the low insight/low self-stigma group. This showed that being aware that one has a mental illness can come at a great cost to hope and self-esteem *if* it is paired with an acceptance of self-stigma. This finding also shed some light on a possible reason why some individuals might not want to accept that they have a mental illness, since to do so might suggest that they would have to apply all of the negative implications associated with stigma to their self-definition.[a, 9]

Since our first study, a host of others have confirmed that there is a strong association between self-stigma and diminished hope and self-esteem, although the importance of "insight" has not always been replicated. Summarizing these findings was a 2010 review article, which found that 30 of 34 studies investigating a relationship between self-stigma and self-esteem found a significant negative relationship between the two, while all five studies examining the relationship between self-stigma and hope found a significant negative relationship.[10] Several other studies have been conducted since the review was published, including studies in the United States,[11] Korea,[12] Austria,[13] Ethiopia,[14] and Israel,[15] and results continue to demonstrate a strong negative relationship between self-stigma and both self-esteem and hope.

Suicide Risk

The next major contention of the "Illness Identity" model is that self-stigma increases suicide risk by way of its impact on self-esteem and hope. Essentially, we believed that self-stigma leads individuals to feel that they

---

[a] Other studies have also supported that "denial" can have some paradoxically positive effects. An analysis of data from the nationally representative sample of US residents found that among those determined to have a serious mental illness, people who rejected the view that they had a mental illness scored lower on measures of psychological distress.

are less valuable than others and to have less hope for the future, increasing the likelihood that they will feel that there is no point in living and contemplate or attempt suicide. This was certainly evident in the case of "Robert," described previously. Increased risk for suicide among people with schizophrenia and other severe mental illnesses has long been recognized, and it is estimated that people with schizophrenia are roughly 20 times more likely to commit suicide than members of the general population (roughly 5% of people with schizophrenia commit suicide).[16] Suicide is arguably the worst possible outcome for someone with a severe mental illness, as it ends all possibility that one will be able to achieve their future promise.

Suicide is a difficult phenomenon to study since completed suicides occur infrequently and it is usually not possible to determine what someone's internal state was after a suicide has occurred. Therefore, most studies investigating suicide do not focus on completed suicides but rather suicide attempts or degree of preoccupation with suicide ("suicidal ideation"), both of which are established "risk factors" for suicide completion. Based on this research, there is compelling evidence for a connection between insight into having a mental illness, increased self-stigma, decreased hope/self-esteem, and suicide risk, although most studies have not "connected the dots" between these variables.

To begin with, both hopelessness and insight are clearly major suicide risk factors. Two comprehensive reviews of the risk factors for suicide in schizophrenia indicated that there is consistent evidence that both insight and hopelessness are major risk factors, with one review clarifying that insight is only a risk factor when it is associated with hopelessness (which would correspond with the "high insight/high self-stigma" group identified in the study previously described).[17]

Is there also evidence that self-stigma plays a role in decreases in hope and self-esteem that are associated with suicide attempts? To date, only a handful of studies have directly investigated this, but all have found strong evidence to support that self-stigma plays a potentially major role in predicting suicide risk. A study of people with schizophrenia in Egypt found that internalized stigma was the strongest overall factor in predicting suicide risk, and that it fully accounted for the relationship between insight and suicide risk.[18] Furthermore, a study of people with schizophrenia in Korea found that internalized stigma and low self-esteem were the two strongest predictors of suicide attempts, while a study in Ethiopia found that self-stigma was significantly associated with likelihood of having attempted suicide.[19] Another study, conducted in Switzerland with young people judged to be at "high risk" of developing schizophrenia, did not directly assess self-stigma, but it found that people who had self-labeled themselves as "mentally ill" had lower self-esteem, and that both low self-esteem and self-labeling were significantly associated with the presence of more thoughts about suicide.[20] Taken together, these studies indicate that there is compelling evidence for the "Illness Identity" model's contention that self-stigma is associated with increased suicide risk, by way of its impact on hope and self-esteem.

Coping and Treatment Engagement

Another assertion of the "Illness Identity" model is that decreased hope and self-esteem related to self-stigma lead to a tendency to use "avoidant" or "passive" ways to cope with life's problems, including decreased engagement in mental health treatment. "Coping" is a term that is used to describe intentional efforts to manage stressful experiences that one encounters. The term "avoidant" is typically used to describe coping efforts that involve trying to get away from or escape a problem rather than actively trying to solve it.[21] Examples of avoidant coping efforts include using substances to numb one's feelings, socially isolating when experiencing depression, or staying away from situations that are associated with anxiety. The idea that people who accept the negative implications of having a mental illness would tend to use more avoidant coping strategies was termed the "why try?" effect by Patrick Corrigan and colleagues.[22] This view argues that people will be more inclined to use passive, rather than effortful, strategies to deal with life's problems if they do not believe that they have a promising future.

Not much research has directly assessed whether self-stigma leads to more avoidant coping by way of its impact on self-esteem and hope, but the research that has been conducted to date supports our model. Specifically, in 2008, my colleagues and I tested this prediction with a group of approximately 100 people diagnosed with schizophrenia using a statistical method called "path analysis."[23] This analysis found support that there was a strong relationship between self-stigma and the use of avoidant coping strategies to deal with stress that was largely explained by low self-esteem and hope. In addition to the studies I and my colleagues conducted, an interesting study conducted by social work researcher Tally Moses examined the relationship between self-stigma and coping in a group of adolescents who had recently been hospitalized. This study found that adolescents who endorsed more self-stigma were also significantly more likely to use a form of coping called "disengagement," which included strategies like "avoiding people" and "trying not to feel anything."[24] Examining these processes over a six-month period, she also found evidence that adolescents using more avoidant strategies at the beginning of the study were more likely to experience greater self-stigma later on, suggesting that there may be a "vicious cycle" effect in which self-stigma and avoidant coping mutually influence each other.

Although it has tended to be studied separately, engagement in professional treatment, including taking medication, can also be seen as a form of coping, as people usually have the opportunity to make a choice about whether they will regularly attend therapy or other psychosocial treatment sessions, and if they will regularly take medication that has been prescribed to them. Time and again, the mental health service system finds that people often "vote with their feet" and do not regularly attend scheduled service appointments or regularly take medication as prescribed. Is it possible that self-stigma and the "why try?" effect could be one of the reasons for inconsistent engagement in treatment? The belief that this would be the case might seem counterintuitive, since we usually assume that people do not attend services because they think that they "don't have a problem," and people with elevated self-stigma generally, by definition, agree that they have a mental illness. However, keep in mind that people who have accepted the negative stereotypes linked to self-stigma often do not believe that there is much hope for their improvement, and they therefore might not see the point of investing time and energy into attending services and taking medication.

A number of studies have examined whether self-stigma is related to both decreased engagement in psychosocial services and "compliance" with taking psychiatric medication, and have found strong support for both. The 2010 review article previously discussed found that all seven studies on the relationship between self-stigma and "treatment adherence" observed that increased self-stigma was moderately but significantly associated with less engagement in treatment.[25] Studies conducted since this review was published have continued to find this to be the case, for both attendance of psychosocial services and willingness to take medication as prescribed. For example, studies conducted by Chinese researcher Kelvin Fung and colleagues found that decreased self-esteem related to self-stigma significantly predicted the likelihood that people diagnosed with schizophrenia would be rated as low "attenders" and "participators" in mental health services by program staff.[26] With regard to medication, studies conducted in Turkey,[27] the Czech Republic,[28] and New York City[29] all found that self-stigma significantly predicted lower likelihood of taking psychiatric medication as prescribed. These studies suggest that there are compelling reasons to be concerned that self-stigma can lead to disengagement in the types of services that are intended to alleviate the effects of psychiatric symptoms.

Social Avoidance

Social isolation, or diminished engagement in social relationships with others, is a major concern among people with mental illnesses. It has been well-established that people with severe mental illnesses tend to have smaller social networks, on average, than others in the community.[30] Going back to the 1950s, researchers have been interested in whether this phenomenon is a cause or consequence of the symptoms of schizophrenia (with the consensus in the field now largely that it is a consequence).[31] It should be clear from reading the earlier chapters of this book, though, that although psychiatric symptoms are no doubt important, it is likely that stigma also plays a role in social isolation insofar as it is associated with both an increased likelihood of *social rejection* from community members (as discussed in Chapter 3) and increased *concern* about future rejection that leads to avoidance of others (as discussed in Chapter 5). In addition, the "Illness Identity" model proposes that the internalization of stigma can also increase the likelihood that one will socially withdraw. Essentially, the expectation here is that people who have accepted the negative stereotypes associated with the mental illness label will feel that they are not worthy of having relationships with others. This view was exemplified by Kathleen Gallo's statement that she "would even leave the sidewalk in what I thought of as exhibiting the proper deference to those above me in social class" in her personal account of the self-stigma experience.[32] Similarly, a participant in a qualitative study stated: "when I am around people I am very anti-social because I feel inadequate. I feel like I am not up to their standard in a conversation ... I really lower myself when I am around a crowd of people."[33]

Does research support the idea that self-stigma is associated with an increased likelihood of social avoidance? A number of studies have examined this question and provide support that self-stigma is associated with both decreased social network size and a reduced frequency of social interaction. In the initial study that I conducted with Paul Lysaker and David Roe, we found that people in the "high insight/high self-stigma" group had significantly poorer interpersonal functioning than those with "high insight/low self-stigma," although their functioning was virtually identical to those with "low insight" (which makes it clear that lack of insight also has its costs in the interpersonal arena.)[34] Later, in our "path analysis" study, we found strong support that self-stigma had an impact on social avoidance by way of its impact on hope and self-esteem.[35] Notably, the second study adjusted for the impact of psychiatric symptoms, indicating that the relationship between self-stigma and interpersonal functioning holds even when accounting for the impact of symptoms.

Others have also found support for a relationship between self-stigma and diminished social contacts among people with severe mental illnesses, suggesting that this relationship is not just a function of our research approach. For example, a study of more than 700 people with severe mental illnesses in six countries found that individuals with moderate to high self-stigma were significantly more likely to have very few (zero to two) social contacts than persons with low self-stigma.[36] Similarly, a study conducted in Nigeria found that people endorsing high levels of self-stigma were ten times more likely to be rated as having "poor" social support than persons with low self-stigma.[37] Furthermore, a study conducted in Spain found that self-stigma was strongly related to poorer social functioning (including interpersonal relationships) and that this impact held even when accounting for the impact of self-reported discrimination experiences.[38] In sum, although a comprehensive study weighing the relative impacts of symptoms, experiences of social rejection, stigma concern, and self-stigma on social isolation has yet to be conducted, there is ample evidence to indicate that self-stigma plays at least some role in the increased likelihood of social isolation among people with severe mental illnesses.

Vocational Outcomes

In the United States, it is estimated that between 39 and 68% of people with severe mental illnesses are unemployed.[39] These rates are certainly higher than the general population, but are also quite a bit higher than rates of unemployment among people with physical and other disabilities.[40] Certainly, there are a number of factors that impact the high rates of unemployment among people with severe mental illnesses, including symptoms, disincentives related to the Social Security system, and employment discrimination (previously discussed in Chapter 3). However, the "Illness Identity" model also proposes that the incorporation of negative stereotypes (such as the belief that people with mental illness cannot work) into one's identity, which is further compounded by an avoidant coping stance, can also impact unemployment in this population. Certainly, this has been my experience working with people with mental illnesses with a variety of vocational skills (and sometimes extensive work histories and educational qualifications) who have been symptomatically "stable" for an extended period. Often, efforts to encourage these individuals to consider applying for jobs hits a "brick wall," as clients express that they either "cannot" or "don't want to" work. In many cases, people will express a wish to work, but will state that they are too concerned about how they will handle anticipated stressors, and therefore choose a more avoidant path.

Does self-stigma play a role in unemployment among people with severe mental illnesses? There is evidence from several studies that there is a strong relationship between endorsement of self-stigma and unemployment. This was supported by all four studies examining this association that were noted in the 2010 review previously discussed,[41] as well as two studies conducted since then.[42] However, a problem with interpreting these findings is that the "direction" of the relationship is difficult to interpret, meaning that it is completely plausible that people's endorsement of self-stigma is elevated *because* they are not working, rather than the other way around. To address this problem, my colleagues (Paul Lysaker and David Roe) and I used data from a unique group of people diagnosed with schizophrenia who were all involved in a work rehabilitation program (and were all offered work opportunities as part of the program) and had data collected over the course of five months. We focused on the extent to which self-stigma at the beginning of the study predicted their work functioning five months *later*, to address the problem of the "direction" of the relationship (based on the well-established rationale that something in the present cannot cause something in the past). Consistent with what the "Illness Identity" model would predict, we found that the extent to which people endorsed self-stigma at the beginning of the study was significantly associated with less improvement in vocational functioning over the course of five months, and that the impact of self-stigma was greater than that of psychiatric symptoms.[43] This suggested that self-stigma leads people to be less likely to keep and do well in a job, even when they are offered work opportunities.

Unfortunately, no other study that we are aware of has examined the association between self-stigma and work functioning over time. Given the crucial importance of work to the participation of people with severe mental illnesses in the community, further research is needed to test this important prediction of the "Illness Identity" model.

Symptom Severity

A final prediction of the "Illness Identity" model is that self-stigma impacts the severity of psychotic symptoms. The model specifically predicts that this occurs because people who accept that negative stereotypes apply to them are more likely to be socially withdrawn and use avoidant coping strategies, since both of these factors have been consistently found to predict the severity of psychotic symptoms. For example, research that used "daily diary" methods (where people are queried about their mood, thoughts, and activity once or more times per day for several consecutive days) with people with severe mental illnesses has found that they are more likely to experience psychotic symptoms, such as delusions, when they are alone.[44] Does evidence support that self-stigma can play a role in this process?

Although there is no shortage of studies finding an association between self-stigma and psychotic symptom severity (e.g., all 50 studies included in the 2010 review found evidence for a small but significant relationship between self-stigma and symptom severity[45]), most research in this area suffers from the interpretation problem discussed in the previous section. That is, are we to infer that people have more symptoms because they experience more self-stigma, or that they experience more self-stigma because they have more symptoms? To date, only two studies have moved past some of the methodological problems inherent in studying these issues. The first, conducted by Swiss researcher Mariluisa Cavelti and colleagues, looked at the relationship between self-stigma and psychotic symptoms over the course of a year.[46] This study found that higher levels of self-stigma at the *beginning* of the study were significantly related to having more psychotic symptoms one year later, suggesting that it is unlikely that the relationship between the two variables is only the result of symptoms leading to more self-stigma. The other study, conducted by researcher Dror Ben-Zeev, used an innovative "smart-phone" based assessment method to look at the complex interplay between thoughts about self-stigma and psychotic symptoms in a group of 24 people with schizophrenia over the course of one week.[47] By "checking in" with participants about these variables multiple times per day, the investigators could see how they related to each other over time, within the microcosm of the week. Interestingly, the study found support that the relationship between psychotic symptoms and thoughts about self-stigma went both ways; that is, when one increased, it was likely that the other would as well immediately afterward. This suggests that, as in the case of avoidant coping, there may also be a "vicious cycle" relationship between symptoms and self-stigma that can lead to an exacerbation of both issues. Although the findings from the above study are intriguing, a definite limitation is that it examined the experiences of a small sample of people over a small period of time. More research is definitely needed to better clarify the nature of the relationship between self-stigma and psychotic symptom severity.

Can Self-Stigma Change over Time?

Given the compelling evidence we have just reviewed that self-stigma impacts multiple outcomes among people with severe mental illnesses, an important question for the field is whether self-stigma can be alleviated over time, and if this alleviation is associated with related improvements in some of the areas identified in the "Illness Identity" model. We will specifically address the question of what types of interventions show evidence for reducing self-stigma in Chapters 8 and 9, but here I will restrict my discussion to the question of change, independent of intervention.

The good news is that there is evidence available that identity, and self-stigma, can change over time, and that the process of identity change is associated with a host of other positive changes. One of the first studies to confirm this was a qualitative study conducted by my colleague David Roe in 2001, who examined changes in the "narratives" of people with severe mental illnesses after they had been discharged from a psychiatric hospital (interviews were conducted every two months over the course of a year).[48] Roe found that among those who showed the most functional improvement during that time period, there was a progression from what he called "patienthood" to "personhood" in people's characterizations of themselves. This meant that their definitions of themselves changed from primarily focusing on their role as recipients of mental health treatment to primarily focusing on their roles in wider society. This suggests that reduction in symptoms, improvements in functioning (including work) and changes in identity are intimately linked.

Quantitative studies examining change in self-stigma over time also indicate that self-stigma does often decrease, and decreases in it are associated with improvements in both self-esteem and functioning. The first study, conducted by my colleague Paul Lysaker and others (including me) examined change in self-stigma and its correlates over one year in a group of 70 people diagnosed with schizophrenia (all were involved in rehabilitation services).[49] The study found that 38% of the sample showed a significant decrease in self-stigma over time, and that these decreases were

associated with a related increase in self-esteem. The second study, conducted by me and my colleagues, examined whether change in self-stigma
over the course of seven months was associated with changes in measures
of community functioning, including interpersonal relationship.[50] This
study found that people whose self-stigma decreased over time also tended
to improve their community functioning, and that this change was independent of the effects of psychiatric symptoms that often predict functioning. These studies indicate that there is good reason to expect that
stigmatized identities can be changed, and that reducing self-stigma will
be associated with other positive changes.

Conclusion: It's Not Just about Getting Help

As indicated at the beginning of this chapter, the "Illness Identity" model
theorizes that self-stigma is a major barrier to the community participation
of people with severe mental illnesses. Community participation consists
of multiple components, including social relationships, work, and engagement in leisure activities in the general community. The "Illness Identity"
model argues that self-stigma negatively impacts the community participation of people with severe mental illnesses across multiple domains.

Furthermore, the "Illness Identity" model argues that the impact on
community participation can occur whether or not one seeks help. In fact,
community participation could be made worse by services that transmit
the message that severe mental illnesses are "life-sentences" that one cannot
hope to recover from. This raises the question about how service providers
and others who support people with severe mental illnesses might come to
transmit these types of messages. In Chapter 7 we will consider a possible
mechanism for this by examining how stigma impacts family members and
professionals, and whether the ways that they manage stigma increase the
likelihood that they will transmit demoralizing messages to the people they
support. We will then discuss approaches to reducing and preventing the
development of identities that are impacted by self-stigma in Chapters 8
and 9.

References

1 Shaw, L. N. (1991). Stigma and the moral careers of ex-mental patients living
   in board and care. *Journal of Contemporary Ethnography*, *20*, 285–305.
2 Deegan, P. E. (1993). Recovering our sense of value after being labeled
   mentally ill. *Journal of Psychosocial Nursing and Mental Health Services*, *31*,
   7–11.

3 Treatment Advocacy Center (2014). What is the main cause of stigma against people with serious mental illness? Accessed online August 16, 2017: www.treatmentadvocacycenter.org/storage/documents/backgrounders/what%20is%20the%20main%20cause%20of%20stigma%20against%20individuals%20with%20serious%20mental%20illness%20final.pdf.

4 Yanos, P. T., Roe, D., & Lysaker, P. H. (2010). The impact of illness identity on recovery from severe mental illness. *American Journal of Psychiatric Rehabilitation*, *13*, 73–93.

5 Lysaker, P., & Lysaker, J. (2008). *Schizophrenia and the fate of the self*. New York: Oxford University Press.

6 Laing, R. D. (1969). *The divided self*. New York: Pantheon Books.

7 Herman, N. (1993). Return to sender: Reintegrative stigma management strategies of ex-psychiatric patients. *Journal of Contemporary Ethnography*, *22*, 295–330.

8 Lysaker, P. H., Roe, D., & Yanos, P. T. (2007). Toward understanding the insight paradox: Internalized stigma moderates the association between insight and social functioning, hope and self-esteem among people with schizophrenia spectrum disorders. *Schizophrenia Bulletin*, *33*, 192–199.

9 Thoits, P. A. (2016). "I'm not mentally ill": Identity deflection as a form of stigma resistance. *Journal of Health and Social Behavior*, *57*, 135–151.

10 Livingston, J. D., & Boyd, J. E. (2010). Correlates and consequences of internalized stigma for people living with mental illness: A systematic review and meta-analysis. *Social Science & Medicine*, *71*, 2150–2161.

11 Drapalski, A. L., Lucksted, A., Perrin, P. B., Aarke, J., M., Brown, C. H., DeForge, B. R., & Boyd, J. E. (2013). A model of internalized stigma and its effects on people with mental illness. *Psychiatric Services*, *64*, 264–269.

12 Kim, J. W., Song, Y. J., Ryu, H.-S., Ryu, V., Kim, J. M., Ha, R. Y., et al. (2015). Internalized stigma and its psychosocial correlates in Korean patients with serious mental illness. *Psychiatry Research*, *225*, 433–439.

13 Schrank, B., Amering, M., Grant Hay, A., Weber, M., & Sibitz, I. (2014). Insight, positive and negative symptoms, hope, depression and self-stigma: a comprehensive model of mutual influences in schizophrenia spectrum disorders. *Epidemiology and Psychiatric Sciences*, *23*, 271–279.

14 Girma, E., Tesfaye, M., Froeschl, G., Möller-Leimkühler, A. M., Dehning, S., & Müller, N. (2013). Facility based cross-sectional study of self stigma among people with mental illness: Towards patient empowerment approach. *International Journal of Mental Health Systems*, *7*, 21.

15 Mashiach-Eizenberg, M., Hasson-Ohayon, I., Yanos, P. T., Lysaker, P. H., & Roe, D. (2013). Internalized stigma and quality of life among persons with severe mental illness: The mediating roles of self-esteem and hope. *Psychiatry Research*, *208*, 15–20.

16 Hor, K., & Taylor, M. (2010). Suicide and schizophrenia: A systematic review of rates and risk factors. *Journal of Psychopharmacology*, *24*, 81–90.

17 Hor, K., & Taylor, M. (2010) Suicide and schizophrenia: A systematic review of rates and risk factors. *Journal of Psychopharmacology*, *24*, 81–90.; Popovic, D.,

Benabarre, A., Crespo, J. M., Goikolea, J. M., Gonzalez-Pinto, A., Gutierrez-Rojas, L., Montes, J. M., & Vieta, E. (2014). Risk factors for suicide in schizophrenia: Systematic review and clinical recommendations. *Acta Psychiatrica Scandinavica*, *130*, 418–426.

18 Sharaf, A. Y., Ossman, L. H., & Lachine, O. A. (2012). A cross-sectional study of the relationships between illness insight, internalized stigma, and suicide risk in individuals with schizophrenia. *International Journal of Nursing Studies*, *49*, 1512–1520.

19 Yoo, T., et al. (2015). Relationship between suicidality and low self-esteem in patients with Schizophrenia. *Clinical Psychopharmacology and Neuroscience*, *13*, 296–301.; Assefa, D., Shibre, T., Asher, L., & Fekadu, A. (2012). Internalized stigma among patients with schizophrenia in Ethiopia: A cross-sectional facility-based study. *BMC Psychiatry*, *12*, 239.

20 Xu, Z., Müller, M., Heekeren, K., Theodoridou, A., Metzler, S., Dvorsky, D., et al. (2016). Pathways between stigma and suicidal ideation among people at risk of psychosis. *Schizophrenia Research*, *172*, 184–188.

21 Roe, D., Yanos, P. T., & Lysaker, P. H. (2006). Coping with psychosis: An integrative developmental framework. *Journal of Nervous and Mental Disease*, *194*, 917–924.

22 Corrigan, P. W., Larson, J. E., & Rusch, N. (2009). Self-stigma and the "why try" effect: Impact on life goals and evidence-based practices. *World Psychiatry*, *8*, 75–81.

23 Yanos, P. T., Roe, D., Markus, K., & Lysaker, P. H. (2008). Pathways between internalized stigma and outcomes related to recovery in schizophrenia-spectrum disorders. *Psychiatric Services*, *59*, 1437–1442.

24 Moses, T. (2015). Coping strategies and self-stigma among adolescents discharged from psychiatric hospitalization: A 6-month follow-up study. *International Journal of Social Psychiatry*, *61*, 188–197.

25 Livingston, J. D., & Boyd, J. E. (2010). Correlates and consequences of internalized stigma for people living with mental illness: A systematic review and meta-analysis. *Social Science & Medicine*, *71*, 2150–2161.

26 Fung, K. M., Tsang, H. W. H., & Corrigan, P. W. (2008). Self-stigma of people with schizophrenia as predictor of their adherence to psychosocial treatment. *Psychiatric Rehabilitation Journal*, *32*, 95–104; Tsang, H. W. H., Fung, K. M., & Chung, R. C. (2010). Self-stigma and stages of change as predictors of treatment adherence of individuals with schizophrenia. *Psychiatry Research*, *180*, 10–15.

27 Yilmaz, E., & Okanli, A. (2015). The effect of internalized stigma on the adherence to treatment in patients with schizophrenia. *Archives of Psychiatric Nursing*, *29*, 297–301.

28 Vrbová, K., Prasko, J., Holubova, M., Kamaradova, D., Ociskova, M., Marackova, M., et al. (2015). Self-stigma, adherence and discontinuation of medication in patients with psychotic disorders – Cross-sectional study. *Česká a Slovenská Psychiatrie*, *111*, 119–126.

29 West, M. L., Vayshenker, B., Rotter, M., & Yanos, P. T. (2015). The influence of mental illness and criminality self-stigmas and racial self-concept on

outcomes in a forensic psychiatric sample. *Psychiatric Rehabilitation Journal, 38,* 150–157.

30 Albert, M., Becker, T., McCrone, P., & Thornicroft, G. (1998). Social networks and mental health service utilisation: A literature review. *International Journal of Social Psychiatry, 44,* 248–266.

31 Kohn, M. L., & Clausen, J. A. (1955). Social isolation and schizophrenia. *American Sociological Review, 20,* 265–273.

32 Gallo, K. M. (1994). First person account: Self-stigmatization. *Schizophrenia Bulletin, 20,* 407–410.

33 Roe, D. (2001). Progressing from patienthood to personhood across the multidimensional outcomes in schizophrenia and related disorders. *Journal of Nervous and Mental Disease, 189,* 691–699.

34 Lysaker, P. H., Roe, D., & Yanos, P. T. (2007). Toward understanding the insight paradox: Internalized stigma moderates the association between insight and social functioning, hope and self-esteem among people with schizophrenia spectrum disorders. *Schizophrenia Bulletin, 33,* 192–199.

35 Yanos, P. T., Roe, D., Markus, K., & Lysaker, P. H. (2008). Pathways between internalized stigma and outcomes related to recovery in schizophrenia-spectrum disorders. *Psychiatric Services, 59,* 1437–1442.

36 Krajewski, C., Burazeri, G., & Brand, H. (2013). Self-stigma, perceived discrimination and empowerment among people with a mental illness in six countries: Pan European stigma study. *Psychiatry Research, 210*(3), 1136–1146.

37 Adewuda, A. O., Owoeye, A. O., Erinfolami, A. O., & Bolanle, A. O. (2010). Correlates of self-stigma among outpatients with mental illness in Lagos, Nigeria. *International Journal of Social Psychiatry, 57,* 418–427.

38 Muñoz, M., Sanz, M., Pérez-Santos, E., & de los Ángeles Quiroga, M. (2011). Proposal of a socio–cognitive–behavioral structural equation model of internalized stigma in people with severe and persistent mental illness. *Psychiatry Research, 186,* 402–408.

39 Cook, J. (2006). Employment barriers for persons with psychiatric disabilities: Update of a report for the President's Commission. *Psychiatric Services, 57,* 1391–1405.

40 Bureau of Labor Statistics (2012). *Persons with a Disability: Labor Force Characteristics Summary.* Accessed online August 23, 2017: www.bls.gov/news.release/disabl.nro.htm.

41 Livingston, J. D., & Boyd, J. E. (2010). Correlates and consequences of internalized stigma for people living with mental illness: A systematic review and meta-analysis. *Social Science & Medicine, 71,* 2150–2161.

42 Corrigan, P. W., Powell, K. J., & Rusch, N. (2012). How does stigma affect work in people with serious mental illnesses? *Psychiatric Rehabilitation Journal, 35,* 381–384; Krajewski, C., Burazeri, G., & Brand, H. (2013). Self-stigma, perceived discrimination and empowerment among people with a mental illness in six countries: Pan European stigma study. *Psychiatry Research, 210*(3), 1136–1146.

43 Yanos, P. T., Lysaker, P. H., & Roe, D. (2010). Internalized stigma as a barrier to improvement in vocational functioning among people with schizophrenia-spectrum disorders. *Psychiatry Research, 178,* 211–213.

44 Myin-Germeys, I., Nicolson, N. A., & Delespaul, P. A. E. G. (2001). The context of delusional experiences in the daily life of patients with schizophrenia. *Psychological Medicine, 31,* 489–498.

45 Livingston, J. D., & Boyd, J. E. (2010). Correlates and consequences of internalized stigma for people living with mental illness: A systematic review and meta-analysis. *Social Science & Medicine, 71,* 2150–2161.

46 Cavelti, M., Rusch, N., & Vauth, R. (2014). Is living with psychosis demoralizing? Insight, self-stigma, and clinical outcome among people with schizophrenia across 1 year. *Journal of Nervous and Mental Disease, 202,* 521–529.

47 Ben-Zeev, D., Frounfelker, R., Morris, S. B., & Corrigan, P. W. (2012). Predictors of self-stigma in schizophrenia: New insights using mobile technologies. *Journal of Dual Diagnosis, 8,* 305–314.

48 Roe, D. (2001). Progressing from patienthood to personhood across the multidimensional outcomes in schizophrenia and related disorders. *Journal of Nervous and Mental Disease, 189,* 691–699.

49 Lysaker, P. H., Roe, D., Ringer, J., Gilmore, E. M., & Yanos, P. T. (2012). Change in self-stigma among persons with schizophrenia enrolled in rehabilitation: Associations with self-esteem and positive and emotional discomfort symptoms. *Psychological Services, 9,* 240–247.

50 Yanos, P. T., West, M. L., Gonzales, L., Smith, S. M., Roe, D., & Lysaker, P. H. (2012). Change in internalized stigma and social functioning among persons diagnosed with severe mental illness. *Psychiatry Research, 200,* 1032–1034.

CHAPTER 7

Stigma by Association
The Impact of Stigma on Family Members and Professionals

In a powerful account that was included in the book *Breaking the Silence*, Jeffrey Liew (currently a professor at Texas A & M University) described his experience growing up as an immigrant from China with a mother with bipolar disorder. Although the impact of his mother's symptomatic behavior is an important part of the story, the account's main theme is how stigma related to his mother's mental illness impacted him and his family. Liew specifically recalled how, when he was nine years old, one of his friends taunted him by stating "your mother was talking crazy, and the police took her away."[1] The message he received from this interaction was that mental illness was something to be ashamed of, and that his mother's being "crazy" was something that had negatively affected his family's reputation. Liew discussed how the belief that mental illness was shameful led his family to hide, deny, and delay seeking treatment for his mother's disorder, and led him to delay seeking help himself when he later experienced panic disorder and depression. Liew's account illustrates how the awareness of negative stereotypes about mental illness impacts not only people who have been diagnosed, but their family members as well.

Another potential source of stigma experience for family members can be mental health professionals. My friend and colleague Barbara Felton (former professor at New York University) wrote about the experience of providing a "family history" to a psychiatrist after her younger brother was hospitalized with a psychotic disorder for the first time in the early 1970s.[2] As she provided explanations of their family's religious views and her brother's relationships with their parents, she recalled the psychiatrist spitting back formulaic summaries of the information she provided, such as "religiosity" and "domineering mother, passive father." Felton recalled that the psychiatrist seemed oblivious to the fact that these statements were clearly insulting to her (and would be to anyone). Her conclusion was that the psychiatrist had labeled her as a "patient family member," so she was seen and treated as a clinical entity, rather than as a full person.

Mental health professionals who work with people diagnosed with severe mental illnesses may also experience some degree of "stigma by association" themselves, from friends, family members, or others who work outside the mental health system. In a qualitative study I conducted with my colleague Beth Vayshenker, which focused on the experiences of mental health professionals, one participant shared: "I had family members once tell me that I had the job that others didn't want, like a garbage collector. They all laughed about it."[3] This suggests that professionals can also experience some degree of devaluation related to their association with a stigmatized group.

These accounts illustrate an aspect of the stigma process that was first discussed by Erving Goffman in *Stigma: Notes on the Management of a Spoiled Identity*.[4] In explaining the broad-reaching effects of stigma, Goffman asserted that persons who are "related through the social structure to a stigmatized individual" (such as family members) "share some of the discredit of the stigmatized person to whom they are related." How this works was not made totally clear, but Goffman suggested that there is an almost contaminative effect to the discrediting of stigmatized individuals that taints those with whom they associate. To illustrate this, he described the effects of stigma as "spread[ing] out in waves, but of diminished intensity."

So far, we have been primarily concerned with understanding how the negative stereotypes and related behaviors of community members impact people who have been diagnosed with severe mental illnesses. However, as suggested by Goffman, it may also be important to understand the impact of these negative stereotypes and behaviors on those who are part of the "inner circle" of people who have been diagnosed, including family members and mental health professionals (a phenomenon that is now usually called "associative stigma"). The reader may question whether we should be so concerned about the impact of the "diminished" waves of mental health stigma on family members and professionals to devote an entire chapter to the issue. However, I intend to demonstrate that this area is ultimately of considerable importance, because there is evidence that how family members and professionals *respond* to associative stigma affects not only them, but how they interact with diagnosed individuals as well. These interactions, in turn, can have a significant impact on important processes such as the internalization of stigma. Thus, in this chapter we will review what we know about associative stigma, and will find out whether it can be more than just a form of "collateral damage" inflicted

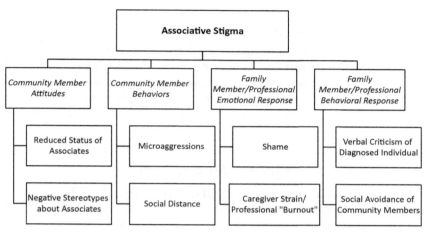

Figure 13   Forms of associative stigma

by stigma, but also a mechanism through which stigma can further affect people with mental illnesses themselves.

Components of Associative Stigma

The literature on associative stigma is sparse in comparison with the literature on mental health stigma more broadly. In addition, there is a general lack of conceptual clarity in many discussions, with distinctions infrequently made between components of the construct, such as the attitudes and behaviors of community members versus the attitudinal and behavioral responses of family members and professionals. As a result, I have organized what we know about associative stigma into a set of categories, which are represented in Figure 13.

As can be seen in Figure 13, the larger concept of associative stigma can be divided into two main categories: community member attitudes and behaviors, and the associates' emotional and behavioral responses to these attitudes and behaviors. Community member attitudes include impressions of reduced status among the associates, and negative stereotypes about the associates (e.g., that mental health professionals are "crazy"). Community member behaviors include subtle "microaggression" behaviors such as jokes and remarks communicating negative stereotypes about the stigmatized group (e.g., that people with mental illnesses are dangerous or hopeless), and social avoidance of the associates. The associates' responses to awareness of stigma include emotional responses such as shame and emotional exhaustion, and behaviors such as verbal criticism of diagnosed individuals, as well as social avoidance of others to minimize instances in which mental illness is discussed. As in Chapter 3, we will draw on evidence from a variety of research approaches, including surveys with community members about their attitudes and behaviors, and surveys with family members and professionals about the experiences that they have had.

Community Member Attitudes

Reduced Status of Associates. Several studies indicate that affiliation with people with mental illnesses is related to a perception of reduced "status" or reputation among both family members and professionals. One of the first studies of the experience of associative stigma among family members, conducted by Marian Yarrow and colleagues in 1955, concerned the experiences of the wives of men who had been admitted to a state psychiatric hospital. This study found that a major concern was diminished "family reputation" or "name."[5] One of the participants poignantly expressed great concern that knowledge of her husband's hospitalization would be used to mock their child: "I live in horror – a perfect horror – that some people will make a crack about it to Jim (child)."

How common is the perception that having a family member with a severe mental illness diminishes a family's "status"? Estimates vary, but findings suggest that close to half of some types of family members may perceive this. A study conducted with more than 400 family members in the New York City area found that approximately 50% endorsed the statement that "most people look down on families that have a member that is mentally ill."[6] However, another study of the relatives of people who had been hospitalized for psychotic disorders found that perceptions of being devalued might partly depend on which member of the family is asked. Specifically, although only 15% of participants overall were concerned that they were regarded "differently" by others in the community, spouses of diagnosed individuals were significantly *more* likely to express this concern than parents.[7] A similar finding emerged from a study conducted in Sweden with relatives of people admitted for a variety of psychiatric disorders, with more than 50% of spouses expressing this concern, in contrast with 20–30% of parents and adult children.[8] While it is unclear why spouses would experience more concern with diminished status, it is possible that this might be related to the view that they have "chosen" to affiliate with someone with a mental illness, in contrast with biological relatives. Thus, having chosen to affiliate with a "discredited" person might be perceived as reflecting poorly on one in a more personal way.

Studies conducted outside of the United States and Western Europe also support that approximately half of family members of people with severe mental illnesses perceive devaluation, and it is possible that concern with devaluation might be even greater in cultural settings where stigma is more pronounced (such as China and Eastern Europe). For example, the majority of caregivers of people with mental illnesses in Hong Kong agreed with the statement "My reputation is damaged because I have a family member with mental illness at home."[9] Similarly, a qualitative study of the relatives of people diagnosed with schizophrenia in the former Soviet country of Belarus found that nearly half spontaneously reported concern that the entire family's reputation was damaged by the presence of a "mentally ill" family member. One participant indicated that she was concerned that knowledge of mental illness within the family would damage the "marriage prospects" of her daughter: "We are afraid of it. It is a stigma of the whole family. I am a mother and I have a younger daughter who has good prospects, who is a respected person."[10]

Since the above studies all relied on the perceptions of family members, the reader might question whether concerns about diminished status or reputation reflect actual community member attitudes, or merely perceptions of them. Unfortunately, no study has specifically assessed the extent to which community members endorse believing that having a family member with a mental illness diminishes status. However, two investigations looked at community member perceptions of the children of people with mental illnesses and suggest that perceptions of them are relatively more negative than perceptions of children whose parents have other types of health issues. Specifically, one study found support that community members (college students, to be specific) were more likely to regard a hypothetical student with a father with a mental illness to be more "hard to get along with" than a hypothetical student whose father had another potentially discredited status (such as an amputated leg).[11] Furthermore, another study found that the extent of associative stigma expressed toward people with a parent with mental illness was predicted by "genetic attributions" (i.e., beliefs that mental illness is genetic and it is likely that having a parent with mental illness increases the risk that the child will develop it).[12]

Although genetic attributions may be one mechanism explaining associative stigma, it is clear that this cannot be the only mechanism, as spouses lack a genetic relationship with their husband or wife and, as previously indicated, they may be most prone to concerns about diminished reputation. Furthermore, there is also strong evidence that mental health professionals, who lack any familial relationship to the people that they assist, also experience significantly diminished "status" relative to other health professionals. For example, a study of more than 1000 medical faculty in 15 countries found that approximately 25% endorsed the view that "psychiatry has low prestige" and that they "would not encourage a bright student to enter psychiatry."[13] Similarly, a study of the perceptions of more than 3,000 psychiatrists and general practitioners in 12 countries found that the psychiatrists perceived significantly more negative stereotypes about their profession than general practitioners, and that nearly 20% thought that the general public had a negative impression of psychiatry.[14]

What might account for perceptions of diminished status in the cases of unrelated individuals, including professionals, who associate with people with mental illnesses? In our previously mentioned study of professionals' experiences with associative stigma, "job devaluation" was a frequently mentioned theme, and it was usually explained as being related to the view that being a mental health professional does not require any skill, since people with mental illness are assumed to be hopeless (as suggested by the "garbage collector" statement quoted previously).[15] For example, a participant stated: "A lot of people think that Psychiatry is a non-essential kind of profession, and continue to believe a psychiatric patient is somebody who spends his whole life in institutions." The belief that mental health professions do not involve any skill was also communicated by another participant, who stated that people frequently state that the "job of a psychologist merely requires you to 'sit there and listen.'" These responses suggest that diminished status may be partly explained by the belief that people who support persons with mental illness, either as spouses or professionals, are "wasting their time" conducting unskilled "babysitting" with people who have no hope of getting better. We also found support for this idea in a follow-up survey we did with more than 450 mental health professionals. We found that 58% of respondents endorsed that they had at least sometimes heard others state that their work "must be sad because people with serious mental illness don't improve in treatment."[16] Thus, the discrediting negative stereotype that people with mental illness cannot recover can come to be extended to those who spend their time trying to help those who are considered to be "hopeless."

Negative Stereotypes about Associates. In addition to diminished status, there is also evidence that community members sometimes hold specific negative stereotypes about the associates of people with mental illnesses. These negative stereotypes might actually be more common with regard to professionals, since they are likely to be viewed as having "chosen" to work with a stigmatized group, and might be assumed to have done so for reasons that reflect negatively upon them.

One potential attitude that has been suggested by the literature that might apply to both family members and professionals is the idea of "contamination," in which being around someone with mental illness can somehow make the person mentally ill.[17] Although the vast majority of community members are aware that mental illness is not contagious in the literal sense, there may be perceptions that spending time with someone who has a mental illness can "drive you crazy." A large survey of community members in the United States found generally low endorsement of the statement "a person's illness could rub off on the family member" (on average people disagreed with the statement), but there was evidence that community members were more likely to endorse this statement when the illness in question was schizophrenia than when it was emphysema.[18]

In a related vein, the most common negative stereotype about professionals expressed by participants in our research was that mental health professionals are themselves "crazy" (half of the participants in our qualitative study spontaneously reported encountering this stereotype, while more than 50% of participants in our survey of more than 450 mental health professionals endorsed encountering this stereotype at least "sometimes").[19] As one participant stated: "Many people assume that if 'you work with the crazy then you must be crazy.'" The existence of this stereotype was also supported by the survey of medical faculty previously discussed, which found that more than 20% of participants endorsed the statement that "students are attracted to psychiatry because of their own personal problems."[20] A more recent study conducted with community members in the UK about their perceptions of mental health professionals also found evidence that the "crazy psychiatrist" stereotype is widely endorsed. In this study, which used both a survey and focus groups with general community members, participants rated mental health professionals who work with people with schizophrenia as significantly more "eccentric" than other health professionals, and expressed awareness of the stereotype that "other branches of medicine will make fun of psychiatrists, saying like 'oh they're all mad'."[21]

There is also evidence that a substantial proportion of the general public endorses cynical attitudes about mental health professionals, such as the view that they "don't know what they are doing," and at the same time are greedy. This view was exemplified by a Fox News commentator, who told a caller diagnosed with bipolar disorder that her problem was not real, but was "something made up by the mental health business just to be able to give people prescriptions and keep them coming in, and keeping you paying them money."[22] Although we might be inclined to attribute this type of attitude to a "fringe" element in the general public, there is evidence that such views are prevalent. Specifically, a research study that I conducted with Master's student Stephanie Freitas of the attitudes of people in predominantly Latino low-income communities in New York City also found that large numbers of individuals in these communities endorsed negative views about mental health professionals. For example, 32% of participants disagreed (many of them strongly) with the statement "psychiatrists and psychologists have the knowledge and skills needed to effectively treat mental illness."

Cynical attitudes about the effectiveness of professional services also dovetail with the belief that mental health professionals are responsible, due to negligence, when people with mental illness commit acts of violence. This perception was exemplified by one of the participants in our study of clinicians' views of associative stigma, who stated: "I feel like there's tremendous responsibility or blame placed on people's mental health professionals when/if these individuals engage in violent crimes or acts. Somehow these professionals are the cause." Polling data conducted by the Gallup organization suggests that this is not just the clinician's perception, but is in fact a view shared by a substantial proportion of the US population. Specifically, following a widely publicized mass shooting incident in 2013, Gallup found that *nearly half* of those polled endorsed the belief that the inadequacy of the mental health system in "identifying individuals who are a danger to others" was the *most important* "factor . . . to be blamed" for the incident.[23] Thus, cynical attitudes regarding the efficacy of mental health services seem to create something of a "double-bind," since, on the one hand, professionals are perceived to be providing unnecessary services for their own enrichment, while on the other they are perceived to be negligent in their responsibility to protect the community from the presumed "dangerousness" of people with mental illness.

Community Member Behaviors

Microaggressions. Many professionals and family members may come into contact with associative stigma in their interactions with community members who make jokes or comments that communicate negative assumptions about people with mental illnesses or their associates. This was illustrated in the experience that Jeffrey Liew had when he was a child (described previously), when another child stated that his mother had been "talking crazy." I have sometimes experienced this myself as a mental health professional when I explain my work to others. For example, I vividly recall talking to a relative about my work area after they had inquired about "what I do" at a family gathering. After explaining that I worked with and studied issues related to people with severe mental illnesses, the family member immediately began talking about a mass shooting that had recently occurred and the presumed strong association between mental illness and violence, and the need to "lock up" people in this population to prevent such incidents. As I tried to explain that this was not what my work concerned, and that, in fact, the belief that there was a strong association between mental illness and violence was not accurate, the family member seemed annoyed and abruptly ended the discussion. I recall feeling greatly upset by this interaction.

It is interesting to consider these types of interactions (where a family member or professional is the receiver of jokes or statements that demean people with mental illnesses) as a form of associative stigma, since these comments are not directly about the family member or professional themselves, but about the people that they support or serve. However, it is important to understand that family members and professionals are usually strongly invested in supporting the people that they "associate" with, and therefore can be expected to experience emotional upset when these types of comments are communicated. How often do family members and professionals report experiencing these types of comments? Unfortunately, there has not been much research conducted in this area, but research suggests that it is commonly, if not necessarily frequently, experienced. In an early study conducted by Harriet Lefly with family members of people with mental illnesses who were also mental health professionals, 90% of the participants reported that they had heard colleagues make "negative or disparaging remarks" about their relative.[24] More recently, in a study of family members of people with schizophrenia conducted in Germany, 65% of relatives reported these types of experiences, often from community members, but also sometimes from professionals (the article noted that particularly mean-spirited comments such as "if Hitler was still alive . . ." were reported to be "rare").[25] In the study with relatives of people with schizophrenia conducted in Belarus that was previously discussed, it was noted that there was a high degree of *concern* about stigmatizing comments from community members, but that they were rarely reported to have been experienced.[26]

There is also evidence that jokes and other negative comments are often encountered among professionals. In a study of the associative stigma experiences of more than 500 mental health professionals in Belgium, 58% reported that they had at least "sometimes" experienced "people making jokes" and approximately 30% endorsed that "people react negatively when they hear you work here."[27] In our own survey of mental health professionals in the United States, we found that approximately a third endorsed hearing jokes to the effect that working with people with mental illness is a job that "no one would want to do if they had the choice," while more than 60% endorsed hearing comments that their job must be "scary." These studies indicate that it is fairly common for professionals to hear disparaging comments about the people that they have devoted themselves to helping.

Social Distance. In addition to experiences of negative comments or demeaning jokes, a number of studies have indicated that family members find that others tend to avoid social interaction with them (this has not been studied in the case of professionals, so here our discussion will focus only on studies with family members). In the 1950s study with the wives of men who had been hospitalized, feeling "ostracized" by others emerged as a major theme. For example, one participant described how a friend had made plans to visit and then repeatedly broken them, leading the participant to conclude that she was being "brushed off."[28]

In more recent research conducted in a variety of locations (including the United States, Sweden, the Netherlands, and Hong Kong), between a quarter and one-half of family members endorsed being avoided by others, including being "treated differently."[29, 30, 31, 32] Relatively few investigations have specifically assessed community member behaviors toward family members of people with mental illnesses from the perspective of the community member, however. In the survey of community members in the United States previously discussed, there was generally low endorsement of the statement "I would not want to socialize with family member" (on average people disagreed with the statement), but there was again evidence that they were more likely to endorse this statement when the illness in question was schizophrenia rather than emphysema.[33] With the exception of this one study, no other research has examined community members' intentions to avoid the family members of people with mental illnesses, so further research is needed to better understand the extent to which this occurs.

Family Member/Professional Emotional Response

Although the previous section documented that family members and professionals often encounter associative stigma from community members, as indicated at the beginning of this chapter, a more important issue is how the family members and professionals *respond* to the stigma. This is the case because one's response to stigma can potentially impact diagnosed individuals who may be particularly sensitive to their supporters' reactions. In the next subsection, I discuss what the research supports are common reactions to associative stigma, and we will then consider their possible effects on people diagnosed with mental illnesses.

Shame. In addition to literature on "associative stigma," a parallel and sometimes overlapping body of research has developed around the idea of "family burden" related to having a relative with a mental illness. Although these studies do not always address the impact of stigma on family burden, a theme in many of them is the experience of "shame" related to having someone with mental illness as a member of one's family. Shame, by definition, implies some awareness of the perceptions of the "generalized other" (discussed in Chapter 5), so discussions of shame are inherently connected to an awareness of others' perceptions of what it means to have a family member with a mental illness. This was articulated by a participant in a British qualitative study on the topic, who indicated that because others knew of his brother's mental illness, he experienced embarrassment related to the awareness that others might have some insight into his deeper self that he'd rather they not have, stating:

> it is embarrassing and I don't like talking about it . . . obviously for your brother to be in that condition means that you can't be as strong as all that. In that you do have a problem deep down.[34]

Responses of shame or embarrassment often also appear to connect directly to perceptions of diminished status or reputation. This was also expressed by Jeffrey Liew, who related his experience of shame to the Chinese value of "face," or family reputation. Specifically, he indicated that one of the hardest things for him to do was to discuss his own or his mother's problems in therapy, since they require one to speak publicly about issues that families prefer to keep "private."

A famous example of the impact of shame related to mental illness concerns the Kennedy family in the United States. As described by E. Fuller Torrey in his book *American Psychosis*, Rosemary Kennedy (younger sister of future president John) began to demonstrate psychotic symptoms during her early twenties. According to Torrey, the perception that having a daughter with mental illness who might potentially behave erratically would damage the family's "respectability" eventually led her father Joe to make the rash decision to have Rosemary "lobotomized" when she was only 25 years old, leading her to become completely incapacitated, and unable to engage in any self-care activities.[35]

There have been few studies that have directly examined the proportion of family members who endorse experiencing shame, and most of these studies have focused on parents' experiences. On the whole, findings are variable and make it difficult to estimate how frequently these reactions occur. The largest study addressing this emotional response was conducted by Yaar Zisman-Ilari with nearly 200 family members in Israel, and used a version of the Internalized Stigma of Mental Illness scale adapted to the family member perspective. This study found that approximately a quarter of the sample agreed with the statement "I am embarrassed or ashamed that I have a son or daughter with a mental illness."[36] It also noted that shame seemed to vary depending on cultural background: Specifically, Jewish Israeli parents were more likely to endorse shame than Arab Israeli parents. This suggests that cultural background may influence whether one experiences shame or not, but it is unclear why parents of Arab background would be less likely to endorse shame.

Other research has found varying rates of endorsement of shame. In a study of parents of adolescents recently hospitalized in a suburban US community, only about 20% endorsed experiencing shame related to their child's mental illness,[37] while a small study of the relatives of people experiencing their first psychotic episode in New York City found that approximately half endorsed "feeling ashamed or embarrassed."[38] In other cultural contexts, higher rates of shame endorsement appear to emerge. Specifically, in the Belarusian study previously discussed, approximately 50% of participants spontaneously discussed themes of "shame or guilt" in relation to their family member,[39] while in the Hong Kong-based study, approximately half of participants endorsed the statement that "having a family member with mental illness makes me think that I am lesser to others."[40] Furthermore, another study conducted in Hong Kong found that endorsement of "face concern," or preoccupation with being embarrassed by loss of status in others' eyes, correlated significantly with self-reported experiences of associative stigma.[41]

Although it did not directly assess "shame" per se, the Swedish study previously discussed illustrated the potential intensity of the emotions that are often experienced by family members, by asking them if they "sometimes" wished that their affected family member had "never been born/never been met" or would be "better off dead."[42] This study found that approximately 20% of family members endorsed these two sentiments. Interestingly, however, these responses varied by family relationship, with spouses the most likely to endorse wishing that their partner had "never been born/never been met" and adult children most likely to think that the relative would be "better off dead."

Caregiver Strain/Professional "Burnout." Related to experiences of shame is the phenomenon of subjective "strain" among caregivers of people with mental illness. In addition, there is the concept of "burnout" among mental health professionals. Both cases concern feelings of being overwhelmed, drained, and defeated. Although strain and burnout can undoubtedly result from fatigue related to symptomatic behavior from people with mental illnesses, there is also evidence that they can be significantly affected by experiences of associative stigma.

Three studies conducted with family members have suggested that perceptions of associative stigma increase perceptions of "burden" or "strain." The previously discussed study conducted in Hong Kong also examined the relationship between experiences of associative stigma and perceived "burden" among family members of people with mental illness[43] and found that there was a moderate relationship between the amount of associative stigma the family member perceived and the amount of stress or "burden" they reported experiencing related to caring for their relative. Similarly, research conducted in Israel found that the degree of family members' internalization of stigma (including feelings of shame) was a strong predictor of perceived burden.[44] A third investigation conducted with more than 500 family members in the Netherlands shed light on the mechanisms by which associative stigma can increase family burden. This study examined not just experiences of associative stigma and perceived family burden, but also ways of coping with these issues. It found that degree of associative stigma was indeed strongly significantly associated with both increased perceptions of burden and increased psychological distress, but that associative stigma was more likely to lead to strain and distress when it was coped with in a "maladaptive" way (e.g., through self-blame, denial, or behavioral disengagement).[45] This suggests that family burden is a product of not just associative stigma, but how one copes with it.

Among professionals, the main outcome of interest has been something called "emotional exhaustion," which is an important component of the larger construct of "burnout." Burnout may also be linked to a reduction in one's empathy, as one becomes fatigued with the task of helping others. It is plausible that associative stigma could increase emotional exhaustion as one tries to distance oneself from the negative implications of working with people with "discredited" conditions. Only two studies have been conducted, to date, which examined whether associative stigma is related to emotional response, and both have found support for a connection. The first study, conducted with professionals in Belgium found that experiences of associative stigma had a moderate but significant relationship with self-reported burnout.[46] The other study, recently conducted by me and colleagues, also supported that there is a moderate but significant relationship between experiences of associative stigma and self-reported burnout (and its emotional exhaustion component in particular).[47] These studies suggest that experiences of associative stigma may indeed be a factor in leading to the deterioration in the degree to which professionals are able to continue to express empathy toward the people that they are tasked with serving.

A related area of interest concerns the degree to which professionals endorse stigmatizing attitudes and behavior toward people with mental illnesses. A growing body of research suggests that while professionals usually endorse less stigma than general community members, many clinicians do still endorse negatives stereotypes and intended social distance.[48] While a number of possible factors might explain this persistence (including the endurance of outdated views that schizophrenia is "incurable" in many professional training programs), one that should be considered in future research is the possibility that emotional exhaustion precipitated by associative stigma leads professionals to endorse more negative attitudes toward mental illnesses. Although this link has yet to be explicitly studied, it was suggested by an anthropological study of psychiatrists described in T. M. Luhrmann's book *Of Two Minds*.[49] In the book, Luhrmann describes how psychiatric training encourages emerging physicians to use the biomedical model as a kind of shield against having to identify too much with persons with mental illnesses. For example, one psychiatric resident stated that an advantage of prescribing medication is "the ability to maintain a comfortable distance from the patient. When I'm prescribing medicine, I don't have to establish this real close relationship with the patient." A focus on biology and medical categories may also lead to types of "cold" interactions with family members like the one related in Barbara Felton's account described at the beginning of this chapter.

Family Member/Professional Behavioral Response

Ultimately, it is expected that increased strain related to associative stigma will impact not only one's emotional state, but also one's behavior. This can include behavior toward one's affected family member or client, as well as behavior toward other community members (such as a tendency to generally avoid others who "won't understand").

Verbal Criticism of Diagnosed Individual. It has been well-documented that family members of people with mental illnesses sometimes express anger toward or verbally criticize their diagnosed relatives. This is, to some extent, to be expected, given that family members usually lack training in interacting with people with emotional difficulties, and working with individuals who experience mental illness can understandably provoke frustration. In the 1970s, a large amount of research was conducted on what was called "expressed emotion" among family members of people with schizophrenia, which consisted of the expressions of criticism, emotional over-involvement, and hostility.[a, 50] These studies found that one-third to one-half of family members demonstrated "high" expressed emotion, and that greater expressed emotion was associated with a higher likelihood that the diagnosed family members would experience an increase in symptoms and return to the hospital. This research did not usually consider whether critical comments and expressed hostility could potentially be impacted by associative stigma; however, it is certainly plausible that they can be, as it makes sense that family members' frustration with their diagnosed relative will increase if they feel that they are "beaten down" by associative stigma themselves.

A powerful illustration of how perceptions of associative stigma can lead to expressions of hostility was provided by physician and writer Siddhartha Mukherjee in *The Gene,* in which he discussed how his father was impacted by his family's history with severe mental illness. At one point, Mukherjee discusses how his father's embarrassment regarding his brother Jagu's public behavior led him to become enraged:

> His face is hot with embarrassment . . . Now the neighbors know of Jagu's madness, of his confabulations. My father has been shamed in their eyes: he is cheap, mean, hard-hearted, foolish, unable to control his brother. Or worse: defiled by a mental illness that runs in the family.

> He walks into Jagu's room and yanks him bodily off the bed . . . My father is livid, glowing with anger, dangerous.[51]

Although research on expressed emotion has fallen off dramatically in the past 20 years, there have recently been some suggestions that there may indeed be a connection between expressions such as the one just described and associative stigma. A study conducted in China with more than 900 family members of people with schizophrenia found that perceptions

---

[a] Degree of expressed emotion is usually assessed by rating an audiotaped interaction between the family caregiver and the diagnosed individual.

of community stigma among family members were strongly associated with the demonstration of "high" expressed emotion, even after statistically controlling for a number of other possible factors that could explain this association.[52] Another, smaller, study conducted in India revealed a similar association.[53] These studies suggest that it might be helpful to revisit the concept of expressed emotion, viewed through the lens of associative stigma.

Although expressions of criticism and anger can certainly be influenced by associative stigma, another behavioral expression in response to it might be the "flip-side": emotional distancing from the affected relative. In the book *Divided Minds*, written by identical twin sisters Pamela (who developed schizophrenia) and Carolyn (who did not and instead became a psychiatrist), Pamela discussed how their father essentially cut off all contact with her after her first episode of mental illness while at college. Describing their last meeting for approximately 30 years, in which he abruptly started crying, she stated: "I believe his tears are not for me; they're for him. They are tears not of sadness but of outrage, humiliation, and selfish rage … He leaves abruptly, without saying good-bye."[54]

Perhaps understandably, researchers are reluctant to ask family members who devote their time to helping an affected relative about the extent to which they have engaged in behaviors such as shunning or verbally criticizing their family members. However, research with people with mental illnesses indicates that instances of what could be called verbal abuse might occur with some frequency. Specifically, researchers at Temple University asked people with mental illnesses about instances of verbal harassment such as being yelled at, insulted, or teased, and found that of the 82% of participants who endorsed one of these types of experiences, the most frequent perpetrators were "friends," "parents," and "siblings."[55] Although more research is needed on this issue, this study suggests that it is possible that people with mental illnesses may often encounter verbal abuse from family members and other close associates.

There is also evidence that mental health professionals may demonstrate high "expressed emotion" in their interactions with clients with mental illnesses. A review of studies on this topic found that between 20–40% of professionals who work with people with psychotic disorders demonstrated "high" expressed emotion.[56] Although no research has examined if demonstrations of higher expressed emotion among professionals are impacted by associative stigma, it is certainly plausible that they would be. As indicated, it is also plausible that associative stigma may lead to a greater endorsement of negative stereotypes among professionals, and these may also be plausibly related to criticism and other indicators of expressed emotion.

Social Avoidance of Others. Another possible behavioral response to associative stigma among family members is social avoidance of other community members. This was reflected in the statements of many of Marian Yarrow's participants, who indicated that their reluctance to open up to others about their husbands' hospitalizations often led them to limit their social contacts. For example, one participant stated: "I haven't gotten too friendly with anyone at the office because I don't want people to know where my husband is. I figure if I get too friendly with them, then they would start asking questions."[57] More recent studies have also suggested that efforts to avoid allowing others to know about a family member's mental illness diagnosis can lead to generalized social avoidance. For example, in the Hong Kong-based study previously discussed, more than half of the sample endorsed the statement: "Given that I have a family member with mental illness, I've cut down the contacts with my neighbors."[58] Other studies have been less clear with regard to whether family member's efforts to conceal a relative's mental illness lead to general social avoidance, but findings certainly support that such efforts are fairly common. For example, the study of relatives of parents and spouses of people experiencing psychotic disorders in the New York area found that half of the sample endorsed *some* efforts at "concealment," with a quarter of the sample endorsing that "only close friends and neighbors know."[59]

Among professionals, our research supports that avoidance can often take the form of not wanting to discuss one's work with people who work outside of mental health. In our qualitative study, approximately one-fourth of participants described a reluctance to discuss their work with others. For example, one participant stated: "Unfortunately, I largely avoid discussing my work with people outside of the profession," while another explained that "as soon as people hear that word [schizophrenia], they conjure up whatever stereotype they've been exposed to regarding schizophrenia's portrayal in the media and immediately think I'm working with dangerous, crazy individuals."[60] In our larger survey, we found that 40–50% of respondents endorsed at least "sometimes" being reluctant to discuss their work with friends and family members outside of the mental health field. Although avoidance of discussing one's work is not of the magnitude of what might be encountered by family members, it is plausible that it can heighten a sense of isolation that can increase the likelihood that one will experience "compassion fatigue."

Impact of Responses to Associative Stigma on People with Mental Illness

As stated at the beginning of the chapter, our ultimate reason for concern about associative stigma is the extent to which it impacts people with mental illnesses. Given that there is evidence that experiences of shame can lead to concealment, strain, and emotional detachment, it is plausible that these types of behaviors could transmit important messages to people with mental illnesses that could subsequently impact their likelihood of developing stigma concern or self-stigma. Although there has not been very much research examining the relationship between experiences of associative stigma among family members and professionals and client outcomes, the research that has been conducted to date suggests that it can be an important factor.

Regarding family member interactions, findings from one study indicate that family members' response to their relative's having a mental illness may have an important impact on the likelihood that they will internalize stigma. This study, conducted by Tally Moses, examined adolescent children who had recently been hospitalized for a mental illness and their parents, and explored whether parents' attitudes and behaviors predicted the extent to which adolescents endorsed the internalization of stigma. Interestingly, although Moses did not find compelling evidence for an association between parents' expectations about mental illness and self-stigma, she found that there was a significant association between parental "inclination to conceal" their child's mental illness and the adolescent's degree of self-stigma.[61] This suggests that adolescents' interpretations of the extent to which their having a mental illness is shameful may be influenced by parental behaviors suggesting that it is something that needs to be hidden.

There is also evidence from one study with professionals that associative stigma might lead to more self-stigma. Specifically, a study conducted in Belgium found that people with mental illnesses who received services from professionals that endorsed more associative stigma experiences were also more likely to endorse more self-stigma.[62] Although it is not possible to infer whether there was a causal relationship between associative stigma among professionals and self-stigma among clients (it is certainly possible that both were impacted by some outside factor, such as the degree of stigma in their local communities), this finding is provocative in that it suggests that it is possible that professionals may communicate subtle messages of shame toward their clients, which can potentially impact their likelihood of internalizing stigma.

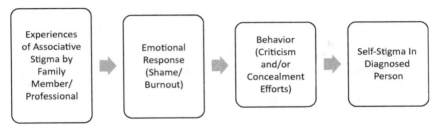

Figure 14   Hypothesized process by which associative stigma impacts self-stigma

Conclusion: From Associative Stigma to Internalized Stigma

In conclusion, although research evidence is not sufficient to draw firm conclusions, there is emerging evidence suggesting that experiences of associative stigma among family members and professionals impact emotional responses (such as shame and burnout), which in turn impact behavioral responses (including efforts to conceal or expressions of criticism). These behavioral responses, in turn have an impact on the likelihood that people diagnosed with mental illness perceive that their disorders are shameful and therefore develop self-stigma. The hypothesized chain of events is diagramed in Figure 14.

This theoretical process suggests that dealing with stigma is not just a problem for people diagnosed with mental illness, but is also a problem for family members and professionals. We will now turn to the subject of how the effects of the stigma process can be managed and possibly overcome in community-based and clinical interventions.

References

1 Liew, J. (2008). In my voice: Speaking out about mental health and stigma. In S. Hinshaw (Ed.), *Breaking the Silence: Mental Health Professionals Disclose Their Personal and Family Experiences of Mental Illness* (pp. 122–151). New York: Oxford University Press.

2 Felton, B. J. (2014). Family history. *Psychiatric Services, 65,* 716–717.

3 Vayshenker, B., Deluca, J., Bustle, T., & Yanos, P. T. (Under Review). "As soon as people hear that word …": Associative stigma among clinicians working with people with serious mental illness.

4 Goffman, E. (1963). *Stigma: Notes on the management of a spoiled identity.* New York: Prentice Hall.

5 Yarrow, M., Clausen, J. A., & Robins, P. R. (1955). The social meaning of mental illness. *Journal of Social Issues, 11,* 33–48.

6 Struening, E. L., Perlick, D. A., Link, B. G., Hellman, F., Herman, D., & Sirey, J. A. (2001). The extent to which caregivers believe most people devalue consumers and their families. *Psychiatric Services, 52*, 1633–1638.

7 Phelan, J. C., Bromet, E. J., & Link, B. G. (1998). Psychiatric illness and family stigma. *Schizophrenia Bulletin, 24*, 115–126.

8 Ostman, M., & Kjellin, L. (2002). Stigma by association: Psychological factors in relatives of people with mental illness. *British Journal of Psychiatry, 181*, 494–498.

9 Mak, W. W. S., & Cheung, R. Y. M. (2008). Affiliate stigma among caregivers of people with intellectual disability or mental illness. *Journal of Applied Research in Intellectual Disabilities, 21*, 532–545.

10 Krupchanka, D., Kruk, N., Murray, J., Davey, S., Bezborodovs, N., Winkler, P., Bukelskis, L., & Sartorius, N. (2016). Experience of stigma in private life of relatives of people diagnosed with schizophrenia in the Republic of Belarus. *Social Psychiatry and Psychiatric Epidemiology, 51*, 757–765.

11 Mehta, S. I., & Farina, A. (1988). Associative stigma: Perceptions of the difficulties of college-aged children of stigmatized fathers. *Journal of Social and Clinical Psychology, 7*, 192–202.

12 Koschade, J. E., & Lynd-Stevenson, R. M. (2011). The stigma of having a parent with mental illness: Genetic attributions and associative stigma. *Australian Journal of Psychology, 63*, 93–99.

13 Stuart, H., Sartorius, N., & Liinamaa, T. (2015). Images of psychiatry and psychiatrists. *Acta Psychiatrica Scandinavica, 131*, 21–28.

14 Gaebel, W., et al. (2015). Stigmatization of psychiatrists and general practitioners: Results of an international survey. *European Archives of Psychiatry and Clinical Neuroscience, 265*, 189–197.

15 Vayshenker, B., Deluca, J., Bustle, T., & Yanos, P. T. (Under Review). "As soon as people hear that word …": Associative stigma among clinicians working with people with serious mental illness.

16 Yanos, P. T., Vayshenker, B., DeLuca, J., & O'Connor, L. (2017). Development and validation of a scale of mental health clinicians' experiences of associative stigma. *Psychiatric Services, 68*, 1053–1060.

17 Corrigan, P. W., & Miller, F. E. (2004). Shame, blame and contamination: A review of the impact of mental illness stigma on family members. *Journal of Mental Health, 13*, 537–548.

18 Corrigan, P. W., Watson, A. C., & Miller, F. E. (2006). Blame, shame and contamination: The impact of mental illness and drug dependence stigma on family members. *Journal of Family Psychology, 20*, 239–246.

19 Vayshenker, B., Deluca, J., Bustle, T., & Yanos, P. T. (Under Review). "As soon as people hear that word …": Associative stigma among clinicians working with people with serious mental illness.

20 Stuart, H., Sartorius, N., & Liinamaa, T. (2015). Images of psychiatry and psychiatrists. *Acta Psychiatrica Scandinavica, 131*, 21–28.

21 Ebsworth, S. J., & Foster, J. L. H. (In Press). Public perceptions of mental health professionals: Stigma by association? *Journal of Mental Health.*

22 Accessed online August 23, 2017: http://mediamatters.org/blog/2015/01/30/fox-host-tells-caller-her-bipolar-disorder-is-m/202349.

23 Gallup Inc. (September, 2013). *Americans Fault Mental Health System Most for Gun Violence.* Accessed online August 23, 2017: www.gallup.com/poll/164507/americans-fault-mental-health-system-gun-violence.aspx.

24 Lefley, H. P. (1987). Impact of mental illness in families of mental health professionals. *Journal of Nervous and Mental Disease, 175,* 613–619.

25 Angermeyer, M. C., Schulze, B., & Dietrich, S. (2003). Courtesy stigma: A focus group study of relatives of schizophrenia patients. *Social Psychiatry and Psychiatric Epidemiology, 38,* 593–602.

26 Krupchanka, D. Kruk, N., Murray, J., Davey, S., Bezborodovs, N., Winkler, P., Bukelskis, L., & Sartorius, N. (2016). Experience of stigma in private life of relatives of people diagnosed with schizophrenia in the Republic of Belarus. *Social Psychiatry and Psychiatric Epidemiology, 51,* 757–765.

27 Verhaeghe, M., & Bracke, P. (2012). Associative stigma among mental health professionals: Implications for professional and service user well-being. *Journal of Health and Social Behavior, 53,* 17–32.

28 Yarrow, M., Clausen, J. A., & Robins, P. R. (1955). The social meaning of mental illness. *Journal of Social Issues, 11,* 33–48.

29 Phelan, J. C., Bromet, E. J., & Link, B. G. (1998). Psychiatric illness and family stigma. *Schizophrenia Bulletin, 24,* 115–126.

30 Ostman, M., & Kjellin, L. (2002). Stigma by association: Psychological factors in relatives of people with mental illness. *British Journal of Psychiatry, 181,* 494–498.

31 Moses, T. (2011). Adolescent mental health consumers' self-stigma: Association with parents' and adolescents' illness perceptions and parental stigma. *Journal of Community Psychology, 38,* 781–798.

32 Mak, W. W. S., & Cheung, R. Y. M. (2008). Affiliate stigma among caregivers of people with intellectual disability or mental illness. *Journal of Applied Research in Intellectual Disabilities, 21,* 532–545.

33 Corrigan, P. W., Watson, A. C., & Miller, F. E. (2006). Blame, shame and contamination: The impact of mental illness and drug dependence stigma on family members. *Journal of Family Psychology, 20,* 239–246.

34 Jones, D. W. (2004). Families and serious mental illness: Working with loss and ambivalence. *British Journal of Social Work, 34,* 961–979.

35 Torrey, E. F. (2013). *American psychosis.* New York: Oxford University Press.

36 Zisman-Ilani, Y., Levy-Frank, I., Hasson-Ohayon, I., Kravetz, S., Maschiach-Eisenberg, M., & Roe, D. (2013). Measuring the internalized stigma of parents of persons with a serious mental illness. *Journal of Nervous and Mental Disease, 201,* 183–187.

37 Moses, T. (2011). Adolescent mental health consumers' self-stigma: Association with parents' and adolescents' illness perceptions and parental stigma. *Journal of Community Psychology, 38,* 781–798.

38 Wong, C., Davidson, L., Anglin, D., Link, B., Gerson, R, Malaspina, D., et al. (2009). Stigma in families of individuals in early stages of psychotic

illness: Family stigma and early psychosis. *Early Intervention in Psychiatry*, *3*, 108–115.

39 Krupchanka, D., Kruk, N., Murray, J., Davey, S., Bezborodovs, N., Winkler, P., Bukelskis, L., & Sartorius, N. (2016). Experience of stigma in private life of relatives of people diagnosed with schizophrenia in the Republic of Belarus. *Social Psychiatry and Psychiatric Epidemiology*, *51*, 757–765.

40 Mak, W. W. S., & Cheung, R. Y. M. (2008). Affiliate stigma among caregivers of people with intellectual disability or mental illness. *Journal of Applied Research in Intellectual Disabilities*, *21*, 532–545.

41 Mak, W. W. S., & Cheung, R. Y. M. (2012). Psychological distress and subjective burden of caregivers of people with mental illness: The role of affiliate stigma and face concern. *Community Mental Health Journal*, *48*, 270–274.

42 Ostman, M., & Kjellin, L. (2002). Stigma by association: Psychological factors in relatives of people with mental illness. *British Journal of Psychiatry*, *181*, 494–498.

43 Mak, W. W. S., & Cheung, R. Y. M. (2012). Psychological distress and subjective burden of caregivers of people with mental illness: The role of affiliate stigma and face concern. *Community Mental Health Journal*, *48*, 270–274.

44 Hasson-Ohayon, I., Levy I., Kravetz, S., Vollanski-Narkis, A., & Roe, D. (2011). Insight into mental illness, self-stigma, and the family burden of parents of persons with severe mental illness. *Comprehensive Psychiatry*, *52*, 75–80.

45 van der Sanden, R. L. M., Pryor, J. B., Stutterheim, S. E., Kok, G., & Bos, A. E. R. (In Press). Stigma by association and family burden among family members of people with mental illness: the mediating role of coping. *Social Psychiatry and Psychiatric Epidemiology*.

46 Verhaeghe, M., & Bracke, P. (2012). Associative stigma among mental health professionals: Implications for professional and service user well-being. *Journal of Health and Social Behavior*, *53*, 17–32.

47 Yanos, P. T., Vayshenker, B., DeLuca, J., & O'Connor, L. (2017). Development and validation of a scale of mental health clinicians' experiences of associative stigma. *Psychiatric Services*, *68*, 1053–1060.

48 Wahl, O., & Aroesty-Cohen, E. (2010). Attitudes of mental health professionals about mental illness: A review of the recent literature. *Journal of Community Psychology*, *38*, 49–62.

49 Luhrmann, T. M. (2000). *Of two minds: An anthropologist looks at modern psychiatry*. New York: Vintage.

50 Hashemi, A. H., & Cochrane, R. (1999). Expressed emotion and schizophrenia: A review of studies across cultures. *International Review of Psychiatry*, *11*, 219–224.

51 Mukherjee, S. (2016). *The gene: An intimate history*. New York: Scribner.

52 Phillips, M. R., Pearson, V., Li, F., Xu, M., & Yang, L. (2002). Stigma and expressed emotion: a study of people Stigma and expressed emotion: A study

of people with schizophrenia and their family members with schizophrenia and their family members in China. *British Journal of Psychiatry, 181,* 488–493.

53 Gupta, N., & Mohanty, S. (2016). Stigma and expressed emotion in spouses of schizophrenic patients. *Indian Journal of Community Psychology, 12,* 98–106.

54 Spiro Wagner, P., & Spiro, C. S. (2005). *Divided minds: Twin sisters and their journey through schizophrenia.* New York: St. Marten's Press.

55 Karni-Vizer, N., & Salzer, M. S. (2016). Verbal violence experiences of adults with serious mental illness. *Psychiatric Rehabilitation Journal, 39,* 299–304.

56 Berry, K., Barrowclough, C., & Haddock., G. (2011). The role of expressed emotion in relationships between psychiatric staff and people with a diagnosis of psychosis: A review of the literature. *Schizophrenia Bulletin, 37,* 958–972.

57 Yarrow, M., Clausen, J. A., & Robins, P. R. (1955). The social meaning of mental illness. *Journal of Social Issues, 11,* 33–48.

58 Mak, W. W. S., & Cheung, R. Y. M. (2008). Affiliate stigma among caregivers of people with intellectual disability or mental illness. *Journal of Applied Research in Intellectual Disabilities, 21,* 532–545.

59 Phelan, J. C., Bromet, E. J., & Link, B. G. (1998). Psychiatric illness and family stigma. *Schizophrenia Bulletin, 24,* 115–126.

60 Vayshenker, B., Deluca, J., Bustle, T., & Yanos, P. T. (Under Review). "As soon as people hear that word . . .": Associative stigma among clinicians working with people with serious mental illness.

61 Moses, T. (2011). Adolescent mental health consumers' self-stigma: Association with parents' and adolescents' illness perceptions and parental stigma. *Journal of Community Psychology, 38,* 781–798.

62 Verhaeghe, M., & Bracke, P. (2012). Associative stigma among mental health professionals: Implications for professional and service user well-being. *Journal of Health and Social Behavior, 53,* 17–32.

CHAPTER 8

The Possibility of Change
Peer-Led Options

In the 1990s, Sascha Altman DuBrul was a young man with a large circle of friends who took part in a number of activities related to "alternative" culture – playing bass in the punk rock band *Choking Victim*, participating in political activism, writing for counter-cultural publications known as "zines," travelling by freight rail throughout the United States and Mexico, and engaging in urban organic farming. He also experienced a number of episodes where he developed the belief that the radio was talking to and about him, and his behavior became volatile and frightening to others; these episodes led to several psychiatric hospitalizations, as well as diagnoses of bipolar and schizoaffective disorder. At age 24, DuBrul recalls a therapist telling him "it's time for you to grow up," indicating that he should give up on his dreams of doing exciting things and changing the world.[1] However, DuBrul instead decided to open up publicly about his psychiatric experiences in an article called "Bipolar World" that was published in *SF Bay Guardian*. The outpouring of positive responses that he received inspired him to form a way for people to share their experiences and support one another online and in-person that he called the *Icarus Project*. In the mission statement for the project, DuBrul and his collaborators used the term "dangerous gifts" to characterize his view of what professionals had called mental illness, stating: "we see our condition as a dangerous gift to be cultivated and taken care of rather than as a disease or disorder needing to be 'cured' or 'eliminated.'"[2] Although acknowledging that medication and other forms of professional treatment have a role to play in reducing the "danger" associated with "dangerous gifts," the *Icarus Project* emphasized that they wished to help people "overcome alienation related to the actions of a mental health system determined to label, categorize, and sort human behavior."[3] Later, DuBrul used the term "Mad Pride" to describe his vision for how people diagnosed with mental illnesses could feel positive about their experiences and labels.

Figure 15   Artwork associated with the Icarus Project, created by artist and graphic designer Kevin Caplicki

Although the *Icarus Project* and similar organizations do not always explicitly state that their mission is to help people overcome the effects of stigma (including self-stigma), their effort to redefine the meaning of mental illness is a direct attack on the effects of stigma articulated in Chapters 5 and 6. Specifically, "peer support" organizations (which are also known by a variety of other terms, as will be explained in this chapter), created by and for people diagnosed with mental illnesses, seek to counteract commonly held stereotypes that having a mental illness means that one is dangerous, incompetent, and unable to recover, and replace them with the view that being diagnosed with a mental illness can be something that is "okay" or even a "gift" that one can be proud of.

The potentially transformative effect of participating in peer support on one's identity and life was described by Ekhaya, a young woman from New York City who had been diagnosed with a psychotic disorder after having visions of her deceased father. In an interview for a documentary film, Ekhaya stated that before she started attending a peer support program, "you kind of lose hope, you kind of think that this is what I'm going to be doing with the rest of my life, I might collect disability or a social security check, and I really didn't see anything beyond that." However, after chancing upon a drop-in program run by the peer support agency Baltic Street AEH, "she was shown that her own crisis had given her potential as a healer, which gave her life meaning and a role in her community."[4]

The *Icarus Project* and Baltic Street AEH[5, a] are only two recent examples of organized efforts by people with histories of psychiatric treatment to support others. In fact, peer support programs for people with mental illnesses have existed at least since 1970, and grew dramatically in the 1980s and 1990s. In this chapter, we will learn about the history and current status of mental health peer support services and will discuss the extent to which research supports the notion that peer support can serve as an effective antidote to the effects of stigma that have been detailed in the earlier chapters of this book.

The History of the Peer Support Movement and "Identity Politics"

Most historians agree that the modern self-help movement started in 1935 with the founding of Alcoholics Anonymous (AA) by William Wilson and Robert Smith (Bill W. and Dr. Bob) in Akron, Ohio.[6] The two men were both struggling to overcome their habitual alcohol use, and found that the mutual support that they provided to each other helped them to remain abstinent. They then decided to extend this support to other people dealing with alcohol abuse, and AA was born. AA did not concern itself with the types of mental disorders we have been discussing in this book, but an essential idea that it gave rise to was the notion of "self-help" or "mutual-aid": that people without any professional training, but with personal experience in dealing with a specific problem, could play a valuable role in helping others with the same problem to manage it. Although this principle does not explicitly address stigma, in a sense the idea of "self-help" is inherently destigmatizing, as it contradicts the view that someone with a particular problem (alcoholism, in the case of AA) is incompetent and incapable of helping oneself and others.

Inspired by AA, Cornelius Keogh, a Roman Catholic priest who had experienced psychiatric problems, formed an organization called GROW in 1957 in Sydney, Australia. Seeking a way for people with mental illnesses to support each other, just as people with alcohol problems were able to in AA, Keogh developed a set of procedures which closely followed those developed by Bill W. and Dr. Bob in AA (e.g., the use of 12-steps and procedures for conducting meetings).[7] GROW spread throughout Australia but did not become known in other countries until the 1980s.

---

[a] See the book *Madness: Heroes Returning from the Front Lines* for more accounts of how involvement in Baltic St. AEH facilitated recovery from mental illness.

Despite the precedent of AA and GROW, the initial impetus for the formation of many mental health peer support organizations was not specifically mutual aid, but a desire to join together to protest injustices and abuses of rights that participants believed were being perpetrated by society and the mental health system.[b, 8] As described by Judi Chamberlain, the first "ex-patients" organizations were founded in Portland, Oregon, New York City, Boston, and San Francisco between 1970 and 1972, were inspired by the Civil Rights and Women's Rights movements, and had provocative names such as the Insane Liberation Front, the Mental Patient's Liberation Project, and the Network Against Psychiatric Assault.[9] In the process of organizing to protest injustice, however, the early "ex-patient" organizers also engaged in an activity called "consciousness-raising," which explicitly challenged the stigmatizing assumptions about "mental patients" that many people diagnosed with mental illnesses had come to hold. As described by Chamberlain:

> group members began to recognize a pattern they referred to as 'mentalism' and 'sane chauvinism,' a set of assumptions which most people seemed to hold about mental patients; that they were incompetent, unable to do things for themselves, constantly in need of supervision and assistance, unpredictable, likely to be violent and irrational, and so forth. Not only did the general public express mentalist ideas; so did ex-patients themselves. These crippling stereotypes became recognized as a form of internalized oppression.

Thus, although the term self-stigma was not used, consciousness-raising clearly identified, and sought to counteract, the process of internalizing negative stereotypes that we discussed in Chapters 5 and 6. This was accomplished, in part, by actions that sought to redefine how people diagnosed with mental illnesses were perceived by others. For example, by leading a protest, letter-writing campaign, or organizing a meeting, people who had been diagnosed with mental illnesses were demonstrating to others, and themselves, that they were not, in fact, "incompetent." A study of these early organizations described such action as "resistance rituals," and noted the potentially transformative power of participating in political action. As one early participant stated: "If I had to tell it to you in

---

[b] Recovery, Inc. (now Recovery International), which became a peer-run program in 1952, was started by psychiatrist Abraham Low in 1937 in Illinois. Although peer-run Recovery, Inc. meetings predated 1970, they are not being considered here since the organization was not founded by mental health service recipients.

Figure 16   Cover of "Madness Network News," newspaper of the 1970s
"Ex-Patients" movement. Source: Madness Network News Redux,
www.madnessnetworknews.com.

a nutshell, activism means that we're no longer willing to be pushed around, exploited, treated like the scum of the earth."[10]

At other times, direct statements were made (and shared in meetings) indicating that the behaviors that psychiatry had characterized as mental illness could be alternately conceptualized as expectable responses to traumatic events, "human difference" that society was not tolerant of, or even evidence of special gifts or abilities. For example, one early conference of ex-patients stated: "our basic philosophy is that 'breakdown' or extreme emotional crisis, with suitable conditions of emotional and physical support, can be a constructive and growth-producing experience."[11] Outsiders who observed the movement characterized these actions as a form of "identity politics."[12] That is, they were attempts to redefine the *meaning* of the behaviors and experiences that had led to psychiatric treatment, and recast them as experiences that one could make sense of in light of traumatic experiences, or even be seen as "gifts."[c, 13]

---

[c] In a related manner, the Hearing Voices Movement, which started in the Netherlands and UK in the 1980s and has grown considerably since then, has stressed that hearing voices can be a pleasant or mystical experience that need not be seen as pathological.

In the 1980s and early 1990s, the "ex-patients" movement grew and became less confrontational and much more willing to collaborate with the professional mental health services system. In the process, organizations of people who had been diagnosed with mental illnesses mostly stopped using the term "ex-patient" and "survivor" and instead began to call themselves "consumer," "service recipient," and "peer" organizations (note that the term "user" has been favored in Europe). Historical analyses[14] explain that the change in tone was influenced in part by the availability of federal and state funding in the 1980s that incentivized a more collaborative approach. However, it is also likely true that this approach grew from a desire to expand the base of those who could benefit from the support of peers, as well as take on the more practical task of providing specific "services" that could help people who were dealing with the life disruptions that often accompany mental health crises and treatment.[15] In the process, the primary emphasis of the organizations moved away from political activism and an antagonistic stance toward the professional system, and toward "peer support," which was envisioned as existing alongside (rather than replacing) traditional mental health services.

The dominant form of setting for "peer support" services came to be an agency with a storefront or other "brick-and-mortar" presence that housed a "drop-in center" offering a variety of support groups, as well as practical assistance with issues like obtaining housing and employment. Most settings received funding from state or county mental health departments and had funds to designate at least some participants as "staff." Support groups also increasingly placed a focus on teaching practical skills for managing "emotional crisis" and preventing relapse, with the *Wellness Recovery Action Plan* program, developed by consumer/mental health professional Mary Ellen Copeland, becoming a staple within peer support programs.[16] (There was also a growth during this period of the hiring of people with psychiatric histories in specific "peer specialist" roles within professionally run service systems, which we will discuss to some extent in the next chapter.)

Despite the diversification of the tasks of peer support programs, there is evidence that the reclamation of a valued identity remains central to their purpose. Sherry Meade, a mental health service recipient who became a social worker and formed the center for Intentional Peer Support in New Hampshire, has done much of the work of defining what peer support is and should ideally do.[17] In the process, she has made it clear that challenging self-stigma is at the heart of peer support. As Meade and her coauthors stated: "Peer support can offer a culture of health and ability as opposed to a culture of 'illness' and disability . . . The primary goal is to responsibly challenge the assumptions about mental illnesses and at the same time to validate the individual for whom they really are and where they have come from."[18]

It should be evident to the reader that one of the ways that peer support programs seek to help people overcome self-stigma is by facilitating the development of a "righteous anger" perspective. As the reader will recall from Chapter 6, righteous anger requires both identification with the target group (people diagnosed with mental illnesses) *and* rejection of the stereotypes held about that group. Thus, peer support programs aim to help people to "claim" the identity of having a mental illness label (even if they disagree with its validity), but at the same time alter the meaning of that label by asserting that the negative stereotypes that are attached to it are reflective of societal oppression. People are encouraged to move from being passive recipients of services and feeling that they are helpless in the face of their psychiatric symptoms to becoming actively engaged in their treatment and lives. This change process is typically called "empowerment" in peer support circles. Although the term is now so widely used that some believe that it has lost all meaning, writers within the peer support movement have clarified that empowerment includes "increasing one's positive self-image and overcoming stigma" as one of its key features.[19] Empowerment is not expected to occur instantaneously, but rather gradually over time. Sociologist Steven Onken described this process as one of "identity formation" that would occur in stages, ranging from "preawareness conformity or denial" to "introspection and synthesis."[20]

I first became aware of the peer support movement in the mid-1990s when I was a clinical psychology doctoral student, and subsequently have spent a good deal of time talking to people within peer support agencies at professional discussions and meetings, collaborating with them on research projects, and "hanging out" at peer-run programs. I can attest to the profound impact that interacting with people involved in the peer support movement has on one's expectations about the potential for people diagnosed with mental illnesses to direct their own lives and achieve their goals. When I started working with these individuals, recovery and self-determination changed from being abstract concepts to real things that I could link a name and personal story to. I consider some of the people that I've met through this process, like Ed Knight (formerly of New York State's Mental Health Empowerment Project) and Isaac Brown (of Baltic Street AEH), to be professional friends. If I was affected in this way as a professional, I can only imagine how big an impact coming into a setting like this could have on a person who had been treated in the mental health system and had absorbed the message that they could only be a passive recipient of treatment.

But Does It Work? Research on Peer Support Programs

Personal testimony aside, in this book we have been concerned with research evidence and assessing whether peer support programs work should be no different. Many readers will undoubtedly be suspicious of the extent to which people with mental illnesses can run organizations and provide support to each other without professional oversight. There are certainly legitimate reasons to question how well-equipped these organizations might be to handle psychiatric crises when they occur among their members (or even leaders).[d] So, the question is, does research support the idea that attending peer support services actually works to turn around the effects of stigma and facilitate "empowerment," potentially overturning many of the negative consequences of the self-stigma process discussed in Chapter 6?

Answering this question is complicated by the fact that most research studies on peer support programs have not specifically looked at their effects on self-stigma (although most have looked at the related concept of empowerment). Furthermore, research on peer support has been muddied by a number of factors, such as the inclusion of different types of programs in the same research studies, and the fact that the dominant paradigm for assessing the effectiveness of clinical interventions (random assignment, meaning that people's ability to decide which treatment they will receive is taken away and put in the hands of chance) is inherently at odds with the philosophy of "personal choice" that peer support programs define themselves by. To try to give us the best understanding of whether participation in peer support programs actually facilitates empowerment, I will discuss two types of studies that have been conducted – "naturalistic" studies that examined the impact of participation over time among people who self-select into such programs, and "experimental" studies that randomly assigned people to either be referred or not to peer support services. It should be emphasized that all of this research considers peer support services to be an addition to, rather than a replacement of, professional

---

[d] Sascha Altman Dubrul spoke openly about the irony of this in his book *Maps to the Other Side*, describing how he was hospitalized for a psychotic episode at New York's Bellevue hospital only a few weeks after conducting training with hospital staff based on his work with the *Icarus Project*.

services, so participants in these studies are presumed to continue to receive medication and other services. Note also that I am focusing on the effects of participation in peer-run programs, rather than the effects of the inclusion of peer providers in professionally run programs.

Naturalistic Studies of Peer Support Programs. Initial studies of the relationship between participation in peer support and empowerment were cross-sectional, and assessed whether people who were voluntarily participating in peer support services demonstrated different outcomes from people who did not. A large study of this type was conducted by Patrick Corrigan, who reported on the relationship between self-reported participation in peer-run services in the previous four months and a variety of outcomes, including "empowerment."[21] He found that there was a small but significant association between self-reported attendance of peer support services and a number of components of empowerment, including "self-esteem/self-efficacy," "righteous anger," and "optimism." The problem with this type of study design, however, is that it does not tell us whether these factors are the result of peer support involvement, of if greater empowerment led the individuals to become involved in peer support in the first place. For this reason, naturalistic studies that examine changes over time are more informative.

The first major study of peer support program participants that looked at change over time was conducted by Steven Segal and Carol Silverman from UC-Berkeley. Segal and Silverman interviewed 255 "long-term" users of four self-help agencies in the San Francisco Bay-area and assessed empowerment initially and six-months later.[22] They found that self-reported empowerment significantly improved over the six-month period, but that the frequency with which participants attended self-help services per week did not predict the likelihood that empowerment would improve. Nevertheless, it is clear that all individuals included in the study had been attending self-help services for some time and were regular attenders of the services, so it is likely that they all reached a threshold of "regular service use." A shortcoming of this study is that it did not include a comparison group of people who were not attending peer support services, so it is unclear if changes in empowerment were related to attending the service or to the effects of time. Furthermore, all participants were already "long-term" users, so it is plausible that the greatest changes in empowerment would have already occurred by the time they were recruited for the study.

A more thorough naturalistic study was conducted by Geoffrey Nelson and colleagues at Wilfrid Laurier University in Ontario, Canada. Nelson studied 118 new members of four organizations in Ontario and followed them up over 18 months.[23] To address the problem of lack of a comparison group, based on self-reported attendance, Nelson divided the sample into "active" and "non-active" participants, and administered measures of social support, quality of life, as well as self-esteem (which he questionably considered to be a measure of empowerment). Nelson found that by 18 months the active participants had demonstrated significant improvement in social support and an increase in daily activities in contrast with the nonparticipants (and spent less time in the hospital), but there was no evidence of significant improvement in self-esteem. Although this study represented a major step forward over previous naturalistic studies, findings are limited by the use of a measure of self-esteem to represent empowerment. In addition, the use of self-reports to assess attendance is problematic because many individuals may not be able to reliably recall how often they have attended a particular service.

To address some of the problems of the above studies, I and colleagues conducted a naturalistic study of 50 "new" participants (defined as people who had only started attending within the previous month) in a peer-support drop-in program operated by Baltic Street AEH in New York City over a period of six months.[24] To address problems with attendance recall, we obtained permission to review program records to determine how many times participants had attended services over the course of the six months. We also specifically examined changes in self-stigma as well as empowerment over the course of the study. We found that roughly half of the participants did not continue attending the program after coming one or two times, but the other half became "moderate or high attenders," attending an average of 32 times over the six-month period. We also found that while participants who did and did not regularly attend did not substantially differ from each other at baseline, moderate or high attenders showed statistically significant improvements over time in internalized stigma and two aspects of empowerment (self-esteem–self-efficacy, and community activism–autonomy), in contrast with low attenders, who did not change in these areas. Findings from this study suggest that attending peer support services, at least for those who do so consistently, is indeed associated with reductions in self-stigma and related improvements in empowerment, although it is not possible to rule out the possibility that changes are related to some particular characteristics of those individuals that led them to decide to stay.

Experimental Studies of Peer Support Programs. Although the findings from the above naturalistic studies suggest that participation in peer support services can increase empowerment and reduce self-stigma, they fall short of the highest standard of methodological rigor for a clinical intervention – the "randomized controlled trial" (or RCT), which enrolls people who are willing to agree to being randomly assigned to a treatment or a control condition. As mentioned previously, although the idea of an RCT might seem to be inherently at odds with the principle of "choice" that is intrinsic to the philosophy of peer-support services, a compromise design that has been identified is the idea of assignment to a "referral" to peer support services, which individuals can then choose to follow up on or ignore. Two RCT's have been conducted assessing the effects of peer support services on empowerment and self-stigma.

The most ambitious study of peer support services was the multi-site "Consumer-Operated Service Program" (COSP) study conducted in the early 2000s. This study randomly assigned over 1,800 persons involved in mental health services in the United States to either remain in mental health "treatment as usual," or receive a referral for secondary services at one of eight different peer support service settings (both "drop-in" and "advocacy" service settings were included in the study). Participants were followed up four times over 12 months, and the main outcome variable for the study was "empowerment," which was divided into "personal empowerment" and "making-decisions empowerment."[25] Ultimately, the study did not find an overall difference over time in empowerment between people who were or were not assigned to peer support services, but the authors found that this was mainly attributable to a "site effect," whereby participants in one site did not improve (and may have actually gotten worse); when this site was removed from analyses, there was evidence that participants in the peer-run services at the other seven sites improved significantly in both personal and "making-decisions" empowerment. There was also evidence that findings were strongly affected by lack of attendance of the peer support programs. Of those "assigned" to the programs, only 15% ended up being classified as "high users" of the services. Analyses comparing the "high users" to "low" and "no" users found that the high users improved significantly more in empowerment over time than others, but this finding is essentially no different than what we have learned from the naturalistic studies described previously.

The COSP study left the field with a number of frustrating questions. For example, what were the characteristics of the program that did not show any positive effects? (The authors of the report of study findings did not identify it, but a description of events occurring during the course of the study offered in the book *On Our Own, Together* indicates that one site experienced substantial turmoil during the course of the project, which might plausibly have negatively impacted the service environment.[26]) Why did so many people assigned to peer support services drop out of them over time, and what were the characteristics of those who did and did not decide to stay? The COSP study report did not provide information on this.

Fortunately, another RCT study was conducted by Steven Segal and colleagues at UC-Berkeley that provided some clarification on these issues. This study employed random assignment to either peer support or "treatment as usual," but also looked at the impact of referral to two different types of peer-run agencies: "self-help agencies" (defined as agencies run as "participatory democracies") and "hierarchically organized agencies" (defined as agencies that are run by people with mental health histories but that mirror professional organizations in their hierarchical organization). This study also employed measures of self-stigma and empowerment. Segal and colleagues found that *only* participants in the "self-help agencies" showed superior improvement in self-stigma and empowerment over people in treatment as usual, and that participants in the "hierarchical" programs did not show any advantage over treatment as usual.[27] In addition, participants in the "self-help agencies" who attended services more frequently showed *more* improvement in self-stigma and empowerment. These findings indicate that only peer support programs that attempt to create an atmosphere that provides a true alternative to professional services can be reasonably expected to impact self-stigma.

Conclusion: Yes, But...

Based on the findings from the above research, it is difficult to give a clear answer to the question "do peer support services facilitate a reduction in self-stigma?" Based on the limited amount of research that has been done so far, the best answer that can be offered is a qualified "yes," with the main qualification being: "1) *if* it's a program that follows the principles of joint decision-making and 2) *if* the person referred to the peer support program actually attends with some regularity."

The second qualification also points to a major issue that all the research that has thus far been conducted on peer-run services has identified: Many, if not the majority, of people who initially attend peer support services do not continue to attend them. This was evident in both my own study and Geoffrey Nelson's study, which found that roughly half of new participants continued participating in services regularly, and the COSP study, which found that only 30% of participants randomized to a peer-support referral demonstrated either "low use" or "high use" (with only 15% demonstrating "high use"). Other research that I and colleagues conducted with administrative data from Baltic Street AEH (including 1,700 individuals) found that the average "length of stay" for people in peer-support services was roughly four months.[28] Thus, even among those who do attend services, most individuals are not likely to become long-term participants. These findings suggest that there may be particular types of people who are drawn to attend peer support services, but that most mental health service recipients are apparently not interested in regularly attending these services. An early examination of the factors associated with dropping out of peer support services found that people who were younger, less educated, and currently or previously married were most likely to drop out early.[29] While not examining the factors associated with early drop-out, our research compared the characteristics of people using peer support program services to the characteristics of public mental health clients in New York City, and found that peer support program users were more likely to be male and diagnosed with a mood disorder (such as bipolar disorder or major depression) and less likely to be Latino, than public mental health clients in New York City in general.

Although these findings do not in any way negate the potential contribution that peer support programs can make to helping people overcome the effects of self-stigma, they do indicate that they are not likely to work for everyone. For this reason, there is an evident need to develop other ways of addressing self-stigma, possibly within the professional mental health system. In Chapter 9, we will discuss approaches that have been developed to address self-stigma within the context of the professional mental health service system.

References

1 DuBrul, S. A. (2013). *Maps to the other sides: The adventures of a bipolar cartographer*. Portland, OR: Microcosm Publishing.
2 Accessed online November 15, 2016: www.theicarusproject.net/icarus-organizational/origins-and-purpose.
3 Accessed online November 15, 2016: www.theicarusproject.net/about-us/icarus-project-mission-statement.
4 Accessed online August 23, 2017: http://crazywisefilm.com/2014/10/27/ekhaya-wounded-healer/.
5 Forbes, J. L. (2015). *Madness: Heroes returning from the front lines*. New York: Lulu.

6 Accessed online August 23, 2017: www.aa.org/pages/en_US/historical-data-the-birth-of-aa-and-its-growth-in-the-uscanada.

7 Keck, L., & Mussey, C. (2005). GROW in Illinois. In S. Clay (Ed.). *On our own, together: Peer programs for people with mental illness.* Nashville, TN: Vanderbilt University Press.

8 Murray, P. (1996). Recovery, Inc., as an adjunct to treatment in the era of managed care. *Psychiatric Services, 47,* 1378–1381.

9 Chamberlain, J. (1990). The ex-patients' movement: Where we've been and where we're going. *Journal of Mind and Behavior, 11,* 323–336.

10 Herman, N. J., & Musolf, G. R. (1998). Resistance among ex-psychiatric patients: Expressive and instrumental rituals. *Journal of Contemporary Ethnography, 26,* 426–449.

11 Quoted in: Anspach, R. (1979). Political activism among the physically disabled and former mental patients. *Social Science and Medicine, 13,* 765–773.

12 Anspach, R. (1979). Political activism among the physically disabled and former mental patients. *Social Science and Medicine, 13,* 765–773.

13 Corstens, D., Longden, E., McCarthey-Jones, S., Waddingham, R., & Thomas, N. (2014). Emerging perspectives from the Hearing Voices Movement: Implications for research and practice. *Schizophrenia Bulletin, 40,* S285–S294.

14 Jacobson, N. (2004). *In recovery: The making of mental health policy.* Nashville, TN: Vanderbilt University Press.

15 Campbell, J. (2005). The historical and philosophical development of peer-run support programs. In S. Clay (Ed.). *On our own, together: Peer programs for people with mental illness.* Nashville, TN: Vanderbilt University Press.

16 Copeland, M. E. (1997). *Wellness recovery action plan.* Dummerston, VT: Peach Press.

17 Accessed online August 23, 2017: www.intentionalpeersupport.org/.

18 Mead, S., Hilton, D., & Curtis, L. (2001). Peer support: A theoretical perspective. *Psychiatric Rehabilitation Journal, 25,* 134–141.

19 Chamberlain, J. (2013). A working definition of empowerment. National Empowerment Center. Accessed online August 23, 2017: www.power2u.org/articles/empower/working_def.html.

20 Onken, S. J., & Slaten, E. (2000). Disability identity formation and affirmation: The experiences of persons with severe mental illness. *Sociological Practice: A Journal of Clinical and Applied Sociology, 2,* 99–111.

21 Corrigan, P. W. (2006). Impact of consumer-operated services on empowerment and recovery of people with psychiatric disabilities. *Psychiatric Services, 57,* 1493–1496.

22 Segal, S. P., & Silverman, C. (2002). Determinants of client outcomes in self-help agencies. *Psychiatric Services, 53,* 304–309.

23 Nelson, G., Ochocka, J., Janzen, R., & Trainor, J. (2006). A longitudinal study of mental health consumer/survivor initiatives: Part 2- a quantitative study of impacts of participation on new members. *Journal of Community Psychology, 34,* 261–272.

24 Vayshenker, B., Mulay, A. L., Gonzales, L., West, M. L., Brown, I., & Yanos, P. T. (2016). Participation in peer support services and outcomes related to recovery. *Psychiatric Rehabilitation Journal*, *39*, 274–281.

25 Rogers, E. S., Teague, G. B., Lichtenstein, C., Campbell, J., Lyass, A., Chen, R., & Banks, S. (2007). Effects of participation in consumer-operated service programs on both personal and organizationally mediated empowerment: Results of a multi-site study. *Journal of Rehabilitation Research and Development*, *44*, 785–800.

26 Clay, S. (2005). With us: Where are we going? In S. Clay (Ed.). *On our own, together: Peer programs for people with mental illness*. Nashville, TN: Vanderbilt University Press.

27 Segal, S. P., Silverman, C. J., & Tempkin, T. L. (2013). Self-stigma and empowerment in combined-CMHA and consumer-run services: Two controlled trials. *Psychiatric Services*, *64*, 990–996; Segal, S. P., Silverman, C. J., & Tempkin, T. L. (2010). Self-help and community mental health agency outcomes: A recovery-focused randomized controlled trial. *Psychiatric Services*, *61*, 905–910.

28 Chan, G., Vayshenker, B., Gonzales, L., Mulay, A. L., Brown, I., & Yanos, P. T. (2014). Characteristics and service use of participants in a large consumer-operated service agency. *Psychiatric Rehabilitation Journal*, *37*, 58–61.

29 Luke, D. A., Roberts, L., & Rappaport, J. (1993). Individual, group context, and individual-group fit predictors of self-help group attendance. *Journal of Applied Behavioral Science*, *29*, 216–238.

CHAPTER 9

The Possibility of Change and Interventions
Professional Options

In 2007, David Roe, Paul Lysaker, and I had begun conducting some of our first studies on the "Illness Identity" model and were finding compelling evidence confirming many of our concerns about the detrimental effects of self-stigma (as reviewed in Chapter 6). So, we had identified that self-stigma was a major problem, but what were we going to do about it? At the time, the only professional approaches that we were aware of that attempted to alter the experience of stigma among people receiving mental health services were "psychoeducational" groups. These groups discussed the inaccuracy of negative stereotypes about mental illnesses and often presented information about famous persons with mental illness as a way of inspiring hope. There was almost no research on the effectiveness of these approaches (which we didn't think did nearly enough), but one intervention that focused on stigma (developed by a researcher that we knew and greatly admired – Bruce Link) had been studied and had not been able to find *any* effect on perceptions of stigma or other relevant outcomes.[1] Maybe there was a reason why most others had not developed interventions in this area: Perhaps "identity" was something that was too intractable to be changed through professional treatment. Who were we to think that we could do better?

Despite these discouraging signs, my colleagues and I decided that we needed to try to develop a professionally led intervention that specifically aimed to help people diagnosed with mental illnesses develop new ways of viewing themselves that were less affected by self-stigma. We did this with full recognition of, and respect for, the peer support movement's emphasis on changing identity, but with an understanding that not everyone served by the mental health system has access to, or is interested in attending, peer-run services. Therefore, developing something that could also be offered in the professional sector might increase the number of people who could be helped. In addition, as has been discussed in previous chapters, there have been many suggestions that the professional system's emphasis on the need for acceptance of one's diagnosis and need for treatment at all costs can potentially increase self-stigma. Psychiatrist John Strauss summarized the standard psychiatric "line" about schizophrenia as something like this: "You have an illness called schizophrenia; you will have it all your life; it is like diabetes. You will have to take medication all your life, and there will be many things you will never be able to do."[2] Though well-intentioned, these types of statements essentially convey the message that one needs to give up on one's dreams and aspirations. For this reason, it seemed to us that it might be particularly appropriate and compelling to offer an intervention approach that counteracts many of the implicitly disempowering messages of the professional service system *within that system*.

David, Paul, and I therefore began to talk regularly to "brainstorm" ways that we thought might be effective at combatting self-stigma, based on our prior experience with providing individual and group treatment (David and I already had a good deal of experience with developing "psychoeducational" groups). We developed an outline for a group-based intervention (which we eventually decided to call "Narrative Enhancement and Cognitive Therapy," or NECT) that would include education about stigma and the inaccuracy of negative stereotypes, and would teach "cognitive-restructuring" strategies for examining and reconsidering negative thoughts related to stigma. In addition, the treatment that we outlined would also include a significant component focused on altering the stories, or "narratives," that people tell about themselves. This would be accomplished through exercises prompting participants to write and read stories about their lives to other group members, and to consider how different perspectives on the stories might change the form of the narrative.

Why focus on narrative? Based on our clinical experience, we believed that negative stereotypes might "take hold" of individuals' self-definitions by becoming embedded in the types of stories they tell about themselves. In some cases, this could be what an individual considers to be "the story of my life," which demonstrates a recurring theme that is reflected in multiple accounts (in the case of people with prominent self-stigma, the recurring theme would usually be one of failure or unmet promise). This theme could be deeply rooted and reflected in beliefs like "I used to do things, but I can't anymore," or "I can't do anything by myself." Although, in full honesty, the inspiration for including a focus on narrative in our intervention came from clinical experience rather than a knowledge of others' research, there is in fact a wealth of basic psychological research evidence that supports the idea that narrative is a (if not *the*) fundamental way by which humans make sense of themselves and the world,[3] and that the types of narratives people tell about themselves have a substantial impact on their well-being.[4] Furthermore, interventions that attempt to provide college students from negatively stereotyped racial/ethnic backgrounds with "affirming narratives" have been found to be effective at improving academic achievement, suggesting that narrative-based interventions have promise for overturning the effects of stigma.[5]

As the title (*Written Off*) of this book implies, a big part of the way that stigma impacts people with severe mental illnesses is by negating or dismissing the contribution of their stories. We believed that self-stigma ultimately impacts people by leading them to incorporate this negation into the stories that they tell about themselves; thus, if we wanted to have deep impact on self-stigma, we would need to address it at the level of personal narrative. This was powerfully expressed by a parent who recently emailed me about her adult son's struggle with the effects of self-stigma, stating that she cries every time she recalls him once saying "I do not have a story." Conversely, the potentially helpful effects of developing a positive narrative was expressed by recently deceased actress and author Carrie Fisher (who spoke openly later in her life about having bipolar disorder and her resulting experience of hospitalization) who recommended to another person with bipolar disorder that "we have been given a challenging illness, and there is no other option than to meet those challenges. Think of it as an opportunity to be heroic – not 'I survived living in Mosul during an attack' heroic, but an emotional survival."[6]

In 2008, my colleagues and I received federal research funding to develop a manual for NECT and to study its effectiveness, and our journey toward exploring whether it can have its intended impact began. At the same time, as sometimes occurs, interest in self-stigma was "in the air," so (although we were not initially aware of them) others also independently came up with the idea to develop professional interventions addressing self-stigma. As a result, there are now several intervention models that show promise for helping people diagnosed with severe mental illnesses to overcome the effects of self-stigma. In this chapter, I will describe and review evidence for, and consider the relative strengths and weaknesses of, four approaches: NECT, Ending Self-Stigma, the Anti-Stigma Photovoice intervention, and Coming Out Proud (also known as Honest, Open, and Proud). Table 9.1 summarizes general information on these interventions.

As Table 9.1 shows, there are a number of common elements to the interventions that have been developed so far. All are group-based, and three out of four (NECT, ESS, and Anti-Stigma Photovoice) include some

Table 9.1 *Major professionally developed interventions targeting self-stigma*

Intervention name	Format	# of sessions	Available languages	Mechanism of action
Narrative Enhancement and Cognitive Therapy (NECT)	Group	20	English, Spanish, Hebrew, Russian, Swedish, Danish	Psychoeducation; cognitive restructuring; storytelling exercises
Ending Self-Stigma (ESS)	Group	9	English	Psychoeducation; cognitive restructuring
Anti-Stigma Photovoice	Group	10	English	Psychoeducation; taking and sharing photographs, writing narratives related to photographs
Coming Out Proud	Group	3	English, German	Discussion of pros and cons of disclosure; telling one's story

component of "psychoeducation" about negative stereotypes and stigma. Furthermore, two interventions (NECT and ESS) teach people cognitive restructuring techniques, and three out of four (NECT, Anti-Stigma Photovoice, and Coming Out Proud) also contain an element that involves the elicitation of a "narrative" in some manner (although, as we'll see, the specific types of narratives elicited differ between them). However, a major difference concerns the length of the interventions, with NECT being considerably longer (lasting 20 sessions) and the other interventions being no longer than ten sessions long. In addition, NECT has been the most widely translated, with the other interventions mostly limited to English. In this chapter, I will discuss key features and the current evidence-base for each of these intervention approaches in greater detail.

Narrative Enhancement and Cognitive Therapy (NECT)

As previously discussed, NECT developed out of my collaboration with David Roe and Paul Lysaker, and our mutual interest in addressing what we believed to be a gap in the professional service sector. Specifically, as discussed in Chapter 6, we were concerned that many of the people that we saw presenting for treatment in professional service settings had achieved symptom "stability," but seemed to have given up on the possibility that they could do other things in life. As we saw it, the professional system was not offering any way to help to inspire these individuals to pursue their full potential as human beings, and may have actually facilitated the process of them giving up by communicating the message that the most important thing for them to do was to develop "insight" into the seriousness of their disorders and be "compliant" with recommended treatment.

On the surface, there is little that is radical about NECT. It is a group-based intervention that is designed to be offered in traditional mental health treatment programs, such as outpatient and day treatment settings, where many people diagnosed with severe mental illnesses receive services. It is also designed to be offered by people with mental health training, although there is no reason why groups cannot be facilitated by people with personal experience of mental illness working in "peer specialist" roles (groups offered in some locations have in fact been facilitated by peer specialists). NECT is highly structured, in that group leaders and participants are given a "workbook" that includes many educational passages and writing exercises, and the workbook is supposed to be moved through progressively (meaning that group leaders are not supposed to skip around to different topics) over the 20 sessions of the group (these sessions usually occur once per week, but can be more frequent if preferred). Group leaders are trained to follow the workbook, but to use their clinical skills to encourage participants to explore how the issues discussed in it relate to their own experiences, and to encourage participants to discuss their experiences with each other in a supportive environment.

Despite its conventionality, however, perhaps what is most "different" about NECT is that it encourages participants to consider that they are active participants in the process of defining themselves, and understanding how mental illness has affected them. NECT groups are envisioned as a type of "journey" of self-exploration and discovery that the participants and group leaders take with each other. NECT starts with an orientation section in which participants write introductory descriptions of themselves and consider how having a mental illness diagnosis affects their view of themselves. Groups then progress to the psychoeducational section, lasting roughly three sessions, which focuses on providing participants with information on what stigma is, what the negative stereotypes about mental illness are, how they are not supported by research evidence, and what self-stigma is and how it affects people. The manual then shifts to the "cognitive restructuring" section (lasting roughly seven sessions), where participants learn how thoughts (and thoughts related to stigma in particular) affect feelings and behavior, how to examine the validity of thoughts, and ways to replace unhelpful thoughts with less biased thoughts. Finally, the group enters the "narrative enhancement" phase, where group members write and share stories about themselves and obtain feedback on them from other group members (this also lasts roughly seven sessions). The last session of the group consists of a review and summary of the different components of the intervention and how they fit together.

Before presenting current research evidence for NECT, it might be helpful to relate a story that illustrates some of the transformative potential of the approach. In early 2015, I was preparing to attend the biannual conference of the International Society for the Psychological and Social Approaches to Psychosis (ISPS) in New York City. The conference brings together an internationally diverse group of professionals and service users with an interest in the use of psychological and social approaches to improving the lives of people diagnosed with psychotic disorders. Although I had already planned to attend, prior to the event I was contacted by email by Annika, a psychiatric nurse from Gothenburg, Sweden, who informed me that she would be attending and presenting at the conference; she specifically indicated that she would like to meet me and introduce me to someone. Although I did not know her, Annika was familiar with me because she had attended a training event in NECT that I had conducted in Gothenburg the previous Spring. It turned out that Annika wanted me to meet a young woman who had been one of the clients in the NECT groups at her clinic, who would be presenting with her at the ISPS conference on an anti-stigma effort they were leading in the Gothenburg community. I eventually met with both of them for lunch during one of the conference days, where they both talked about NECT and how important it had been to them. The young woman, who I'll call Frida, indicated that being a participant in the group had facilitated a major turnaround for her, and had precipitated her becoming much more involved in her community, including the anti-stigma effort that they were presenting about at the conference. She stated that she particularly bene-fitted from the "Narrative Enhancement" section of the manual, and also gave me her candid opinion about some of the aspects of the manual that she did not like (some of which were related to translation changes that altered the meaning from the English original). I later met with Annika and Frida again in Gothenburg roughly six months later, and heard from Frida about her continued engagement in community activities. This indicated that the "awakening" she had experienced relating to her partici-pation in NECT was not just a short-lived one. Although Frida's story is not necessarily typical, it demonstrates some of the potential for identity transformation that can accompany participation in NECT.

From the beginning, my colleagues and I have been focused on documenting the effectiveness of NECT through research, and to date, there have been a number of studies that provide evidence that NECT is likely to indeed be an effective approach to helping people overcome the effects of self-stigma. First, supportive findings emerged from two nonexperimental studies. In a nonexperimental study with a comparison group (meaning that participants were not randomly assigned to the treatment or comparison group, but were similar individuals in different locations, some of whom received NECT and some of whom did not) conducted in Israel, we found that individuals who participated in NECT showed significant reductions in self-stigma and improvements in self-esteem and subjective life satisfaction, in comparison with participants who remained in "treatment as usual."[7] Similarly, a study conducted in Sweden without a comparison group found that participants in NECT improved substantially over time in self-stigma, self-esteem, and subjective life satisfaction.[8]

While the findings from these studies are encouraging, they fall short of the "gold standard" of rigor for the assessment of interventions: the randomized controlled trial (RCT). To date, two RCTs have been completed comparing people assigned to NECT with people who were assigned to remain in "treatment as usual." The first one, conducted by me and my colleagues in New York and Indiana, had a very small number of participants (39) and as a result did not observe statistically significant findings, but noted "trends" for improvement in self-stigma and insight among participants in NECT.[9] The second RCT, a larger study with over 100 participants conducted in Gothenburg by Swedish researcher Lars Hansson, found that participants in NECT improved significantly in self-stigma and self-esteem (but not in subjective life satisfaction) in comparison with those assigned to remain in "treatment as usual," and that these improvements persisted for six months after the completion of treatment.[10] In fact, participants in NECT continued to improve in self-stigma and self-esteem during the 6 months after completing treatment. These findings indicate that there is evidence that NECT does indeed show effectiveness when subjected to the RCT standard with an adequate sample size, and that improvements are lasting and not just present immediately after persons have attended groups.

Despite the evidence from the Swedish RCT, additional questions remain about the potential impact of NECT. For example, do improvements in self-stigma lead to more generalized improvements in social functioning, as the "Illness Identity" model would predict? Currently, I (along with my colleagues Paul Lysaker and Steve Silverstein) am conducting a study funded by the National Institute for Mental Health that is addressing these questions. The study, which is being conducted in New Jersey and Indianapolis, Indiana, aims to randomly assign over 175 persons to NECT or supportive group therapy, and assesses "object-ive" outcomes such as social functioning, in addition to "subjective" outcomes such as self-stigma and self-esteem. Although the study has not yet been completed, preliminary analyses from the first 100 participants assigned to NECT or the control group indicated that those assigned to NECT showed improvements in both self-stigma and social functioning, especially for a subscale indicating the extent to which the person shows "engagement and motivation" to do things in the community. We are hopeful that this pattern of findings will hold after the full sample has been recruited and will persist over the six-month follow-up period of the study.

In conclusion, while not all questions have yet been answered regarding the impact of NECT, there is compelling evidence that participation in it can reduce self-stigma and increase self-esteem among people with severe mental illnesses. Despite these positive findings, a possible disadvantage of NECT is that it is relatively long (lasting roughly five months, if groups meet weekly) and therefore requires a fairly clear commitment from participants to engage in the collaborative "journey." While the rationale for having the group last so long was to allow adequate time for more deep-seated change, this may reduce the number of people who can benefit from the intervention, especially if they have other commitments that may interfere with their ability to remain in the group. For this reason, it is important to consider some of the other treatment approaches that have been developed to address self-stigma, all of which are of shorter duration.

Ending Self-Stigma

Ending Self-Stigma (ESS) was developed by Alicia Lucksted and Amy Drapalski from the University of Maryland-Baltimore Campus School of Medicine.[11] Like NECT, ESS is a manualized group-based intervention that follows a structured schedule, but it is intended to last for nine weekly sessions. As described by its creators, ESS sessions "combine information, reflection and experience sharing, mutual support and discussion, skill/strategy practice, interactive exercises, and home-based practice."[12] Group sessions cover a sequence of information that starts with psychoeducation and also includes training in cognitive-restructuring. Session foci include: "telling myth and stereotype from fact" (Session 1), "using cognitive–behavioral principles to change one's self-stigmatizing thinking" (Sessions 2 and 3), "strengthening positive aspects/views of one's self" (Session 4), "increasing belongingness and reducing alienation in the community" (Session 5) and with family/friends (Session 6), and "responding to societal prejudice and discrimination" (Session 7). Sessions 8 and 9 focus on reviewing and practicing strategies and making plans for the future following the conclusion of the intervention.

To date, two studies have been conducted which provide evidence that ESS can be a helpful way to combat self-stigma in professional service settings. The first was a study without a comparison group that included 34 participants. This study found that individuals who participated in ESS showed significant improvements over time in self-stigma and related outcomes such as "empowerment."[13] More recently, a large RCT of over 200 persons with severe mental illnesses randomized to ESS or "treatment as usual" was completed.[14] This study found that participants assigned to ESS improved significantly in comparison with those in treatment as usual in self-stigma as well as "recovery orientation" (a concept similar to the concept of empowerment discussed in Chapter 8). However, these changes did not persist when participants were followed-up six months later. These findings indicate that participation in ESS is likely to be of short-term benefit to people who participate in it, but that it is possible that the positive effects of the intervention may dissipate over time, and require "booster" sessions or other strategies to allow gains to be maintained.

Anti-Stigma Photovoice

The Anti-Stigma Photovoice program was developed by Zlatka Russinova and colleagues at the Boston University Center for Psychiatric Rehabilitation.[15] Like NECT and ESS, it is a group-based intervention (designed to be conducted over 10 weekly sessions), but it incorporates the unique element of having participants take pictures and record narratives that relate to what they have photographed. Another distinguishing feature of this intervention is that sessions are intended to be led by trained peer facilitators (that is, people with personal experience with mental illness). Thus, although it is designed to be conducted in professional service settings, this intervention incorporates some aspects of "peer support" that might potentially enhance its effectiveness.

The anti-stigma photovoice intervention starts with a number of sessions that focus on "psychoeducation about stigma" (an element that it has in common with both NECT and ESS). Psychoeducation sessions largely

Figure 17   Photo generated by photovoice group participant.
Source: Boston University Center for Psychiatric Rehabilitation.

focus on confronting stereotypes about mental illness and teaching "proactive" coping strategies for dealing with perceived stigma and self-stigma. After two initial psychoeducation sessions, participants are then taught to use the photovoice method, which involves the use of cameras to photograph "objects or events in their daily lives that concern them" (psychoeducational work also continues after the initiation of the photovoice component). The photovoice method used in this intervention was adapted from a research approach initially developed as a way to help participants reflect on personal and community issues.[16] Participants are instructed to take photos documenting "everyday health and/or work realities of concern" outside of the group, and to bring the photos to the group, where they are encouraged to generate brief narratives about themselves that relate to the photos. Participants are taught to generate narratives using a technique that asks: "a) What do you see here? b) What is really happening here? c) How does this relate to our lives? d) Why does this problem, concern, or strength exist? e) How could this image educate others? and f) What can we do about it?"[17] As should be evident from this description, the "narratives" that are elicited in the photovoice intervention differ from those elicited in NECT, as they are specifically focused on the content of the photograph. The photovoice intervention usually ends with a "gallery" demonstration, where participants are able to display some of their photos and narratives to others at the settings where they receive clinical services. Figure 17 presents an example of an image generated by a photovoice participant, with the following narrative:

> This is a picture of an 1800's textile factory that is now boarded up and vandalized. This building has not been used in a long time.
>
> The factory has been forgotten.

People with mental illness are sometimes forgotten or ignored. Sometimes buildings and people look rough on the outside but with a little TLC, and effort, the beauty can be seen.

With some effort this building could be useful; it could house the elderly or low income people. People with mental illness need society to see the beauty in them. You may be surprised how productive and beautiful members of society they can be.

What is the evidence that the anti-stigma photovoice intervention can help people to overcome the effects of self-stigma? To date, one study has been conducted on it, but this study found compelling support for its effectiveness. In the study, 82 people with severe mental illnesses were randomly assigned to either the photovoice intervention or a wait-list control group (meaning that they didn't receive any specialized treatment during the course of the intervention, but would at the conclusion of the study). People assigned to the photovoice intervention showed significant improvement, in contrast with those assigned to the wait-list, in self-stigma, a measure assessing how they cope with stigma, and a measure of "personal growth and recovery."[18] These changes were maintained when participants were assessed three months after the conclusion of the inter-vention, suggesting that gains were not fleeting and could be maintained. Notably, however, the study investigators did not include any measures of "objective" functioning, such as community participation or involvement in work or school, so it is unknown if the photovoice intervention impacted any of these areas. Currently, Russinova and colleagues are conducting a larger RCT of the anti-stigma photovoice intervention that will include measures of community participation outcomes.

Coming Out Proud

Coming Out Proud (now also called Honest, Open, and Proud)[19] is an intervention developed by Patrick Corrigan and colleagues at the Illinois Institute of Technology.[20] Like all the other approaches discussed, Coming Out Proud is manualized and group-based, and, like the Anti-Stigma Photovoice intervention, it is designed to be delivered by trained peer-facilitators. However, it is distinguished from the other interventions we've discussed so far by its brevity (only three sessions, lasting two hours each), and in its focus on encouraging participants to explore and consider disclosing their mental illness as a way of overcoming self-stigma. This focus was based on findings with other stigmatized groups, such as members of the LGBT community, supporting that the ability to disclose that one is a member of a stigmatized community ("coming out") facilitates reductions in the internalization of negative stereotypes, as well as other positive outcomes.

How does Coming Out Proud aim to help people to consider, and possibly increase, the extent to which they are willing to disclose their mental illness? As described by Corrigan, the intervention includes some methods that are derived from a therapeutic approach called motivational interviewing, which aims to help people decide if they would like to change a target behavior (motivational interviewing has a large evidence-base in the area of helping people to reduce their use of addictive substances). Specifically, Coming Out Proud participants engage in a weighing of the pros and cons of disclosure, and consider whether and how they might want to disclose facets of their lives related to having a mental illness. They are then taught about types of disclosure (ranging from complete secrecy to "public broadcasting") and consider the advantages and disadvantages of each type in various life contexts. The third and final session of Coming Out Proud focuses on "Telling Your Story," which facilitates the development of a narrative about one's mental illness, but also provides participants with the opportunity to "practice" telling their story to others in a way that can facilitate future disclosure experiences. Although the use of storytelling in Coming Out Proud bears some resemblance to the storytelling exercises used in NECT, Coming Out Proud participants don't have the opportunity to repeat different stories and gain feedback from others on them, so the way in which storytelling is engaged in differs between the two interventions.

What evidence supports the use of Coming Out Proud as an intervention for reducing the effects of self-stigma? To date, two research studies, both RCT's, have been conducted assessing its effects. The first, conducted in the German-speaking part of Switzerland, recruited 100 people with a variety of psychiatric issues (the majority self-identified as having depression) and randomly assigned them to Coming Out Proud or "Treatment as Usual."[21] This study found that Coming Out Proud had no impact on self-stigma (the primary outcome measure), but significantly reduced "stigma stress" (or people's perception that they could manage stigma) and increased their perception of the benefits of disclosure. Another study, conducted in California, randomly assigned over 100 people to Coming Out Proud or a wait-list control group (no diagnostic information on the participants was offered, although participants were recruited from community mental health centers and peer support agencies).[22] This study found that participants in Coming Out Proud did significantly improve, in contrast with the control group, in the extent to which they endorsed negative stereotypes and applied them to themselves (a component of self-stigma), and also showed improvements in "stigma stress," paralleling the findings from the first study.

Based on the two studies that have been conducted on it, it is unclear if Coming Out Proud is able to accomplish its intended goal of reducing self-stigma, although evidence is fairly compelling that it is able to help people reduce the extent to which they experience "stigma stress," and to increase their comfort with the disclosure process. There is also no indication that the intervention impacts community participation more broadly, although these outcomes were not assessed in either study. Patrick Corrigan and colleagues are currently planning to conduct a larger study of the intervention (now being called Honest, Open, and Proud) that will more rigorously assess its effects on self-stigma and related outcomes.

Conclusion: Promise and Limitations of Existing Interventions

Based on the findings reported in this chapter, it is evident that NECT, ESS, Anti-Stigma Photovoice, and Coming Out Proud show promise as ways of diminishing the impact of self-stigma. However, findings have, in some respects, been inconsistent, and none has yet reached the status of an "evidence-based practice" (standards in science require that an intervention be supported by at least two randomized controlled trials conducted by independent research groups to be considered "evidence-based"). NECT has been the most widely disseminated internationally, and is now offered in multiple locations in Israel, Denmark, and Sweden, as well as several locations in the United States (including an upcoming study using the Spanish translation of the manual with Spanish speakers in El Paso, Texas).

A criticism of the existing approaches that have been developed is that they are all group-based, and that this limits their generalizability to persons receiving mental health services who do not like to participate in groups. It also limits their availability to people who (because of factors related to stigma) do not venture into clinical settings where groups can be conducted, but prefer to be seen in the community near their homes. This is an important criticism, because it is in fact true that many people with severe mental illnesses are uncomfortable with participating in groups. I also am well familiar with the subset of people who receive services in the community from my work with Assertive Community Treatment teams in New York City. These teams meet with people in the general community (including their homes), and many clients almost never travel to the team's office.

Why, then, have the intervention models chosen to be group-based? The truth is that the group format offers many advantages. It is arguably an ideal setting for presenting participants with information that might be more threatening if presented in an individual setting; specifically, presenting information to a group provides an opportunity for people to be exposed to information without feeling personally targeted. Furthermore, groups provide great opportunities for people to get support from peers in a way that can facilitate the process of learning and developing skills. For NECT, at least, we could not imagine doing the storytelling component of the intervention without the "audience" of the other group members being present.

Nevertheless, the "groupness" of the existing professional interventions for targeting self-stigma is a factor that can potentially limit their ability to reach all individuals who might benefit from such service. For this reason, Anthony Morrison and colleagues in the United Kingdom have developed a new individual cognitive therapy approach to treating internalized stigma.[23] Initial research with the model did not show any significant effects on self-stigma, but more research will be conducted that will examine the potential effects of this individual treatment approach.

A further criticism of the interventions targeting self-stigma is that they do nothing to change the fundamental cause of stigma – community stigma, and its real-life consequences such as discrimination and social rejection. This is undoubtedly true, and researchers who have developed interventions targeting self-stigma have been united in their insistence that targeting self-stigma does not eliminate the need for efforts targeting community stigma.[24] In the final chapter of this book, we will discuss some of the efforts that are being conducted to address stigma on a societal level and how the refinement of these efforts might lead to a future where mental health stigma is no longer a major problem for society. We will also consider how efforts at addressing community stigma can potentially integrate a focus on self-stigma into their agendas to increase their overall impact.

References

1 Link, B. G., Struening, E. L., Neese-Todd, S., Asmussen, S., & Phelan, J. C. (2002). On describing and seeking to change the experience of stigma. *Psychiatric Rehabilitation Skills, 6*, 201–231.

2 Davidson, L., Rakfeldt, J., & Strauss, J. (2010). *The roots of the recovery movement in psychiatry: Lessons learned*. Chichester, West Sussex, UK: Wiley-Blackwell.

3 Bruner, J. (1986). *Actual minds, possible worlds*. Cambridge, MA: Harvard University Press; Gottschall, J. (2013). *The storytelling animal: How stories make us human*. New York: Mariner Books; McAdams, D. P., Josselson, R., & Lieblich, A. (2006). *Identity and story: Creating self in narrative*. Washington, DC: American Psychological Association.

4 Adler, J. M., Lodi-Smith, J., Philippe, F. L., & Houle, I. (2016). The incremental validity of narrative identity in predicting well-being: A review of the field and recommendations for the future. *Personality and Social Psychology Review, 20*, 142–175.

5 Sherman, D. K., et al. (2013). Deflecting the trajectory and changing the narrative: How self-affirmation affects academic performance and motivation under identity threat. *Journal of Personality and Social Psychology, 104*, 591–618.

6 Fisher, C. (2016). Ask Carrie Fisher: I'm bipolar- How do you feel at peace with mental illness? *The Guardian*. Accessed online August 23, 2017: www.theguardian.com/lifeandstyle/2016/nov/30/carrie-fisher-advice-column-mental-illness-bipolar-disorder.

7 Roe, D., Hasson-Ohayon, Mashiach–Eizenberg, M., Derhy, O., Lysaker, P. H., & Yanos, P. T. (2014). Narrative Enhancement and Cognitive Therapy (NECT) effectiveness: A quasi-experimental study. *Journal of Clinical Psychology, 70*, 303–312.

8 Hansson, L., & Yanos, P. T. (2016). Narrative Enhancement and Cognitive Therapy. A pilot study of outcomes of a self-stigma intervention in a Swedish clinical context. *Stigma and Health, 1*, 280–286.

9 Yanos, P. T., Roe, D., West, M. L., Smith, S. M., & Lysaker, P. H. (2012). Group-based treatment for internalized stigma among persons with severe mental illness: Findings from a randomized controlled trial. *Psychological Services, 9*, 248–258.

10 Hansson, L., Lexen, A., & Holmen, J. (In Press). The effectiveness of narrative enhancement and cognitive therapy: A randomized controlled study of a self-stigma intervention. *Social Psychiatry and Psychiatric Epidemiology*.

11 Lucksted, A., Drapalski, A., Calmes, C., Forbes, C., DeForge, B., & Boyd, J. (2011). Ending self-stigma: Pilot evaluation of a new intervention to reduce internalized stigma among people with mental illnesses. *Psychiatric Rehabilitation Journal, 35*, 51–54.

12 Lucksted, A., Drapalski, A., Calmes, C., Forbes, C., DeForge, B., & Boyd, J. (2011). Ending self-stigma: Pilot evaluation of a new intervention to reduce internalized stigma among people with mental illnesses. *Psychiatric Rehabilitation Journal, 35*, 51–54.

13 Lucksted, A., Drapalski, A., Calmes, C., Forbes, C., DeForge, B., & Boyd, J. (2011). Ending self-stigma: Pilot evaluation of a new intervention to reduce internalized stigma among people with mental illnesses. *Psychiatric Rehabilitation Journal, 35*, 51–54.

14 Lucksted, A., Drapalski, A., Brown, C. H., Wilson, C., Charlotte, M., Mullane, A., & Fang, L. J. (In Press). Outcomes of a psychoeducational

intervention to reduce internalized stigma among psychosocial rehabilitation clients. *Psychiatric Services*.

15 Russinova, Z., Rogers, E. S., Gagne, C., Bloch, P., Drake, K. M., & Mueser, K. T. (2014). A randomized controlled trial of a peer-run antistigma photovoice intervention. *Psychiatric Services, 65*, 242–246.

16 Catalani, C., & Minkler, M. (2010). Photovoice: A review of the literature in health and public health. *Health Education & Behavior, 37*, 424–451.

17 Russinova et al. (2014). A randomized controlled trial of a peer-run antistigma photovoice intervention. *Psychiatric Services, 65*, 242–246.

18 Russinova, Z., Rogers, E. S., Gagne, C., Bloch, P., Drake, K. M., & Mueser, K. T. (2014). A randomized controlled trial of a peer-run antistigma photovoice intervention. *Psychiatric Services, 65*, 242–246.

19 Accessed online August 23, 2017: http://comingoutproudprogram.org/.

20 Corrigan, P.W., Kosyluk, K.A., & Rüsch, N. (2013).Reducing self-stigma by coming out proud. *American Journal of Public Health, 103*, 794–800.

21 Rüsch, N., Abbruzzese, E., Hagedorn, E., Hartenhauer, D., Kaufmann, I., Curschellas, J., & Corrigan, P. W. (2014). Efficacy of Coming Out Proud to reduce stigma's impact among people with mental illness: Pilot randomised controlled trial. *The British Journal of Psychiatry, 204*, 391–397.

22 Corrigan, P. W., Larson, J. E., Michaels, P. J., Buchholz, B. A., DelRossi, R., Fontecchio, M. J., & Rüsch, N. (2015). Diminishing the self-stigma of mental illness by coming out proud. *Psychiatry Research, 229*, 48–154.

23 Morrison, A. P., Burke, E., Murphy, E., Pyle, M., Bowe, S., Varese, F., & Wood, L. J. (2016). Cognitive therapy for internalised stigma in people experiencing psychosis: A pilot randomised controlled trial. *Psychiatry Research, 240*, 96–102.

24 Yanos, P. T., Lucksted, A., Drapalski, A., Roe, D., & Lysaker, P. (2015). Interventions targeting mental health self-stigma: A review and comparison. *Psychiatric Rehabilitation Journal, 38*, 171–178.

CHAPTER 10

Where Do We Go from Here?

"You used to laugh about everyone that was hanging out. Now you don't talk so loud. Now you don't act so proud. How does it feel?"
                                                                              – Bob Dylan

In this book, we have learned about many facets of the mental health stigma process that are now fairly well understood after more than 50 years of research. As we have seen, stigma affects people diagnosed with mental illnesses in multiple ways, including:

- by leading community members who agree with negative stereotypes to discriminate against and socially reject or avoid people with mental illnesses; such discrimination limits the opportunities for employment, housing, and social relationships of people with mental illnesses;
- by leading governments to enact legal restrictions that impact fundamental rights of people with mental illnesses such as the right to parent and vote;
- by leading people with mental illnesses to be concerned about others' stigma, thereby restricting much of their social contact;
- most insidiously, by leading people with mental illnesses to incorporate negative stereotypes into their identity, resulting in a diminishment of self-esteem and sense of hope for the future.

The end result of these combined processes is that a challenging life circumstance (the experience of periodic psychotic or major mood symptoms) is made much worse, and the community participation of people with mental health problems is significantly more restricted than it would be if they had to contend with the symptoms alone.

In addition to the general conclusions I have just indicated, there are a number of themes, or "take-home messages," from the previous nine chapters that I also think should be highlighted, specifically because they have often been left out of others' discussions about stigma.

- Although some degree of stigma affects all mental disorders, severe mental disorders, which typically include psychotic symptoms (particularly schizophrenia-spectrum disorders and bipolar disorder), are the most stigmatized.
- There is compelling evidence that psychotic experiences are part of the human experience, and that psychotic and major mood disorders often appear later in life among persons who have been previously asymptomatic. By stigmatizing mental illness, we are denying the reality that the tables can be turned, and any of us can be affected by mental illness at some point in life (as alluded to by the Bob Dylan quote at the beginning of this chapter).
- Stigma involves the process of assigning discrediting labels to *people*, not just behaviors. This is often lost in discussions that claim that stigma arises only in response to symptoms, a view that ignores clear evidence that the effects of labels persist even when people are not demonstrating any symptoms.
- Stigma toward people with mental illness is *not* the result of the public being accurately concerned about the dangerousness of people with psychotic disorders. Despite evidence that psychotic disorders are associated with increased risk of violence, the public's perception of the risk is substantially disproportionate to the reality of increased risk, and there are other groups (such as young men) who are *more* dangerous than people with mental illness but who are not similarly stigmatized.
- There is evidence that justifications for stigma have changed over time; in the early 20th century, stigma existed just as strongly, but with the justification that people with mental illness ("the insane") were a "drain" on society's resources and a detriment to its genetic integrity. This led to mass sterilization programs in many countries (including the United States) and the Nazi genocide against people with mental illnesses.
- Although many in the mental health field believed (and some still believe) that emphasizing the biological and genetic aspects of mental illness would lead to a decrease in the endorsement of stigma, there is compelling evidence that emphasizing these characteristics *increases* stigma.
- Although the focus of researchers has tended to be on more overt expressions of discrimination or social rejection related to stigma, much of the behavior that affects people with mental illnesses consists of more subtle discriminatory actions, or "microaggressions," that communicate exclusion and discredit.

- A great deal of stigma is legally codified, even in pluralistic democracies such as the United States and the United Kingdom, but especially so in autocratic countries such as Russia, where a diagnosis of mental illness can lead to a complete loss of citizenship rights.
- The endorsement of negative stereotypes is more prevalent among some subgroups of society, including people with less education, people who hold authoritarian political views, and ethnic groups that have strong culturally sanctioned ideas about the discrediting nature of mental illness.
- Perceived or anticipated stigma is not just a problem because it interferes with help-seeking. It is true that many people do avoid seeking help because of concern about stigma, but the effects of stigma frequently persist among people actively involved in treatment, so just engaging people in treatment does not eliminate the problem of stigma.
- We will not eliminate the negative effects of stigma by emphasizing that people with mental illnesses need to have "insight," or by coercing them into treatment. The "illness identity model" indicates that imposing professional views about mental illness on people in a way that amplifies self-stigma leads to a chain of damaging effects.
- Stigma also impacts family members and mental health professionals, leading them to become overwhelmed and burned out, and there is evidence that the way family members and professionals handle "associative stigma" increases the likelihood that stigma will be internalized by their diagnosed family members or clients.

Many of these take-home messages diverge from what is often stated about stigma by those calling themselves experts and advocates. Examples of these influential views can be seen in a recently published textbook geared toward graduate students in psychology, which states that "stigma is a process not of diagnostic labels, but rather of disturbed and sometimes disturbing behavior that precedes labeling,"[1] and in the recent assertions of an "advocacy" organization claiming that stigma is mainly caused by the violent behavior of people with mental illness.[2] While these represent more extreme examples of the denial of the relevance of stigma, the core messages of this book also diverge from those of many who acknowledge stigma's relevance, but see it as something that can dissipate once "word gets out" about the effectiveness of mental health treatment. For example, in his recent book *Shrinks: The Untold Story of Psychiatry*, psychiatrist Jeffrey Lieberman (chair of the psychiatry department at New York's prominent Columbia University Medical School and former president of the American Psychiatric Association) stresses the importance of stigma but suggests that it will end once the general public becomes aware of the effectiveness of treatment: "[O]ur first real opportunity to eliminate stigma shrouding mental illness has finally arrived because most mental illness can be diagnosed and treated very effectively. Yet the stigma has persisted because the public has not become aware of psychiatry's advances."[3] Based on what we have learned from this book, it should be evident that this is a great oversimplification of the challenge that we have ahead of us if we are to bring an end to mental health stigma.

The Promise of Anti-Stigma Campaigns

If just informing people about the effectiveness of professional treatment is not going to be enough, is there any realistic way that we can end, or at least significantly decrease, the impact of stigma? We have already learned about interventions that attempt to address the internalization of stigma among people with mental illnesses, but these negative stereotypes originate in the attitudes of general community members. This suggests that a more direct solution to the problem might be to "cut it off at the source" and change the attitudes of community members. In fact, this is what has been attempted in several local and national "anti-stigma" campaigns, many of which are still ongoing. At the time of this writing, the "Global Anti-Stigma Alliance" lists 14 campaigns in 9 countries (some countries, such as the United Kingdom and Spain, have multiple campaigns in different regions) focused on addressing stigma through a variety of means.[4]

The most ambitious, comprehensive, and well researched of the national anti-stigma programs is the still-ongoing *Time to Change* intervention in England. *Time to Change* began in 2007 and includes multiple strategies to combat community stigma, including a "social marketing" campaign aimed at the general public (e.g., video clips that can be viewed on television or the internet), and targeted interventions aimed at specific groups including medical students, teachers, employers, and members of the media.[5] A particularly effective video clip created by the campaign is called "Schizo: The Movie" and starts off as a pseudo-trailer for a horror film, with ominous music that, along with the title, evokes clichés of insane axe murderers. The viewer is then led down a hallway where a door opens, and we meet a gentle man in his kitchen making coffee, who explains that he has been diagnosed with schizophrenia and receives the support needed to live a full life.[6]

Rigorous evaluations of the first few years of *Time to Change* found that its implementation was related to modest but meaningful changes in the English public's endorsement of willingness to interact with people with mental illnesses (specifically, 8% more people indicated such a willingness in the years after the implementation of the intervention). Furthermore, there was a significant decrease in the proportion of people diagnosed with mental illnesses reporting that they had experienced discrimination after six years of *Time to Change* implementation.[7] However, despite the decrease in *experienced* discrimination among mental health service recipients, there was no difference in *anticipated* discrimination over time, and more than 70% of participants consistently endorsed that they concealed their diagnosis over the time frame studied. This indicates that, although community attitudes and behavior can potentially be impacted by large and well-run anti-stigma campaigns, changes among community members may not "trickle down" to impact perceptions of stigma (and, presumably, self-stigma) among mental health service users.

Anti-stigma campaigns, large and small, when properly thought out, have demonstrated the ability to "move the needle" on public stigma, at least in the short term. Beyond evidence from population-based interventions, meta-analytic reviews of smaller controlled investigations support that interventions using both education[8] and contact-based[9] strategies are moderately effective in altering public stigma. Nevertheless, there is presently *no* evidence that these interventions can impact either "stigma concern" or "self-stigma," which account for so much of stigma's impact on the community participation of people with mental illnesses, as I hope that I've demonstrated in this book.

Where Do We Take What We've Learned? Future Directions

Writers summarizing the effects of anti-stigma campaigns have begun to acknowledge that the omission of perceived and self-stigma is a notable problem, and have recommended that they be incorporated as targets in the future efforts of anti-stigma campaigns.[10] An example of a campaign that has already taken this step is the *One of Us* campaign in Denmark.[11] Based on data indicating that a major concern among Danish mental health service recipients is lack of attention to stigma concern and self-stigma, this campaign explored the literature on self-stigma interventions, and decided to adapt NECT for implementation as part of its campaign. In late 2015, I was honored to be invited to Denmark to speak to service users, clinicians, and family members about how NECT could be adapted

Figure 18   English and Danish Logos for "One of Us" – Denmark's National Anti-Stigma Campaign. Source: en-af-os.dk.

for use in the Danish context. Efforts are now under way to implement NECT in a variety of settings with peer facilitators throughout Denmark. Although data has yet to be collected on the effects of this effort to incorporate a self-stigma intervention into an anti-stigma campaign, I believe that it is a positive development given the historic exclusion of this aspect of self-stigma in such efforts.

The United States has been notably absent from the group of countries engaged in major anti-stigma efforts (although there have been some local and state-wide campaigns). However, there is evidence that federal agencies may be considering initiating an anti-stigma effort in this large and influential nation (although the election of Donald J. Trump – who to date has shown little interest in mental health issues, with the exception of uninformed comments about the need to build institutions for "sickos"[12] – casts doubt on whether this will remain a priority). In 2015, the US Department of Health and Human Services asked the National Academies of Sciences, Engineering, and Medicine to conduct a study of the science of stigma change and to issue recommendations that could potentially guide future interventions. The resulting report[13] gave a series of recommendations for how the United States could add itself to the list of nations with a national anti-stigma campaign. Consistent with what was discussed earlier in this chapter, the report highlighted the need to use "contact-based" interventions and not just rely on education emphasizing the biomedical origins of mental illness. In addition, and most relevant to our discussion here, the report emphasized the need to address self-stigma as well as public stigma. Furthermore, the report specifically stressed the need to increase funding of peer-led interventions targeting self-stigma. This was a positive step, which I wholeheartedly support; however, given evidence that a limited number of mental health service recipients engage in peer-led services, it would have been helpful if the report would have also recommended the incorporation of self-stigma interventions in the professional sector.

Anti-stigma campaigns also need to be sensitive to the need to target messaging to groups where we have compelling evidence that mental health stigma is particularly prevalent (as we learned in Chapter 4). In the United States, this might consist of politically conservative white and African American communities and immigrant groups, such as the Chinese, South Asian, and Eastern European communities. We have good evidence that contact-based interventions work in all contexts, but contact needs to be from individuals that members of the target groups can identify with. For this reason, a successful anti-stigma campaign in the United States would need to consider how to incorporate contact with persons representing these communities, as well as targeted educational messages, into their presentations. For example, as I've already indicated, despite the strong association between political conservativism and the endorsement of negative stereotypes about people with mental illness, we have evidence that this association does not hold when political conservatives have had close-contact experiences with mental illness (as illustrated by the examples of conservative standard-bearers like Glenn Beck and Sarah Palin, who have been open with their personal and family experiences with mental illness). A good example of how "culturally tailored" messages can be incorporated into a broad anti-stigma campaign is provided by New Zealand's campaign, *Like Minds, Like Mine.*[14] From the beginning, this campaign has been committed to developing messages that would resonate with New Zealand's Maori community, in addition to its larger population of persons of European heritage. The campaign has attempted to engage the Maori community by working through community hubs such as churches and radio networks that specifically reach a Maori audience. I can imagine an anti-stigma campaign targeting the US conservative community that conveys its message through houses of worship, as well as a media campaign focusing on networks such as Fox News, incorporating testimonials from leaders like Sarah Palin, as well as other individuals that Fox News watchers would be more likely to see as credible.

Another important lesson that can be learned from anti-stigma campaigns in other locations is that a broad targeting of "mental illness," or a specific targeting of less stigmatized disorders such as depression, is not

Figure 19   Logo for "Like Minds, Like Mine" – New Zealand's
National Anti-Stigma Campaign. Source: likeminds.org.nz.

likely to impact stigma toward psychotic disorders, which are most affected
by stigma. As summarized by British human rights activist Liz Sayce,[15] some
campaigns (including *Like Minds, Like Mine*) initially focused their efforts
on depression, based on the assumption that a reduction of stigma toward
depression would "generalize" to psychotic disorders. However, there was
no evidence for a "generalization" effect, and *Like Minds, Like Mine* eventually switched its focus to more stigmatized disorders such as schizophrenia. Sayce speculated that focusing on less stigmatized disorders might
actually make matters worse for people with psychotic disorders because it
might send the message that some disorders are more normal while others
are not and "inadvertently reinforce the 'otherness' of the 'really mad.'"
I agree, and believe that an effective US-based anti-stigma campaign would
need to place a large part of its focus on destigmatizing psychotic disorders
rather than just depression, anxiety, or "mental illness" more generally.

An anti-stigma campaign in the United States would also do well to
target some of the types of "structural stigma" discussed in Chapter 3.
Although each state is responsible for most of its own laws, an anti-stigma
campaign could take the lead in galvanizing efforts to overturn local laws
that clearly discriminate against people with mental illness (like New York
State's Social Services Law Sec. 384-b, which states that parental rights can
be terminated solely on the basis of "mental illness or mental retardation").
Educating media outlets on how the way they report about mental illness
impacts public perceptions would also be an important aspect of "structural stigma" to be addressed. Currently, media outlets almost always
report if an individual who has engaged in an act of violence has a
psychiatric history, whether or not it bears any relation to the actual crime.
Experimental research, conducted by my colleague Ginny Chan and
myself, found that individuals were roughly 10 times more likely to infer
that mental illness is the *cause* of a violent crime when randomly assigned

to read an account of an incident where a history of mental illness was mentioned than when they were randomly assigned to read a description of the same incident without such a mention. Most alarmingly, participants often developed specific "false memories" about how symptoms were stated to have led to the crime, when nothing of the kind was mentioned in the actual description (e.g., based on the simple statement that a man suspected of an attack had a history of schizophrenia, a participant stated that "delusions stemming from schizophrenia appear to have caused this attack," while others mentioned hallucinations and other symptoms that were not discussed).[16] Thus, the media may inadvertently reinforce assumptions that mental illness frequently leads to violence when they report the psychiatric history of the alleged perpetrators of violence. Interventions targeting media outlets, incorporated as a component of a national anti-stigma campaign, could educate members of the media about this process and hopefully lead to a change in these reporting practices that reinforce public stigma. Canada's anti-stigma campaign *Opening Minds* has focused on educating media outlets, and there are indications that it is having a positive effect on media behavior. Specifically, an analysis of Canadian television coverage of mental illness between 2013 and 2015 found that the proportion of news stories linking mental illness to violence declined from 72% to 57% over the course of the three years, suggesting that the campaign was successful in influencing the behavior of the media outlets (although much more work remains to be done).[17]

A sensitivity to the existence of "microaggressions" in relation to mental illness can also be incorporated into future anti-stigma campaigns. As previously indicated, in our research on microaggression behavior among community members, more than 60% agreed that if someone they were close to developed a mental illness, they would "frequently remind them to take their medication" or "talk to them more slowly." These behaviors might be engaged in by relatively well-meaning friends and family members who do not realize that people diagnosed with mental illnesses find them to be insulting and demeaning. Anti-stigma campaigns could include testimonials from people with mental illness that explain the concept of microaggressions and educate friends and family members about ways to interact that do not convey disrespect.

We have also discussed the reality of associative stigma among family members and clinicians, and the plausible connection between associative stigma, burnout, and strain, and the development of self-stigma among people with mental illness. So far, anti-stigma campaigns have not included a formal component that considers the way family members and professionals manage associative stigma. Based on the research reviewed in this book, there is ample evidence that professionals and family members' management of associative stigma would be a worthwhile additional intervention target in anti-stigma campaigns.

Another emerging area that should be considered in future anti-stigma campaigns is interventions that aim to prevent the *development* of stigma. Adolescents who are developing their attitudes toward mental illness in themselves and their peers represent an obvious target. If one is able to prevent the development of stigma in this group, people who go on to develop mental illness might never see their social networks diminish after the experience of symptoms, and may never feel the need to conceal their mental illness or internalize beliefs that it is shameful. Patrick Corrigan and colleagues conducted a review of 19 controlled studies examining the impact of interventions targeting stigma among adolescents, and found that in-person, contact-based interventions (usually featuring a presentation by a person diagnosed with mental illness) had a significant and meaningful impact on the attitudes and intended behavior among adolescents.[18] There are promising models that have been established for use with middle and high school students, but they are not being widely offered in most schools. For example, my colleague Joseph DeLuca and I are currently involved in an effort to conduct an RCT to study the effectiveness of an intervention approach called *Ending the Silence,* developed by the National Alliance on Mental Illness.[19] Perhaps, in the future, such interventions will be as much a part of the standard curriculum among high school students as sex education. Although this will not mean that stigma will completely disappear (any more than teen pregnancy has), there is clear evidence that the implementation of such widespread initiatives has a substantial impact, over time (in the case of teenaged pregnancy, it has declined dramatically from almost 60 per 1,000 in 1990 to 24 per 1,000 in 2014[20]).

Another area of early intervention that holds promise is the prevention of *self-stigma*. Currently, there is a growing emphasis on the implementation of targeted interventions for people who are experiencing their first episode of psychosis. A widely implemented approach to this type of treatment is the "Coordinated Specialty Care" (CSC) model, which aims to engage people who have experienced a first psychotic episode in treatment by following the principles of "shared-decision making."[21] Findings from a large, multi-site randomized controlled trial supported the efficacy of this model in contrast with "usual care" services.[22] However, the model does not have an extensive focus on preventing the development of self-stigma, so it might make sense to add such a focus in future variations on the model. My colleagues and I are currently engaged in an effort to develop a version of NECT that is modified for use with persons receiving treatment in early psychosis programs. It is our hope that, if implemented at this crucial juncture, NECT or similar programs may be able to prevent the development of stigmatized identities among people who have recently experienced a first psychotic episode.

Interventions that use online social media, which are heavily used by young people, might present another avenue for the prevention of self-stigma.[23] Although a downside of broad-based social media use is that these platforms may also be used by bullies or "trolls," whose actions can exacerbate feelings of alienation, there is also evidence that engagement in social media outlets that have a specific focus on bringing people from marginalized groups together may have positive effects.[24] To be effective in helping young people with mental illness to feel less alienated and to combat the development of self-stigma, I believe that social media sites will need to be actively moderated, with clearly delineated behavioral ground rules, and closed to the general public. I am currently exploring the effectiveness of an online social media platform called "Technology Enhanced Peer Support" that includes the elements described earlier.

Conclusion: We're All in This Together

Returning to the contention made in Chapter 1, I again emphasize that the need to combat mental health stigma is a social justice issue. The experiences that we call "mental illness" can affect any of us at any time, as they can any of our friends, family members, or neighbors. Pretending that mental illness is something that only happens to "them" might make people feel better, but it doesn't help society in general, and it leaves one particularly vulnerable to the damaging effects of stigma when it happens to "us." Realizing that mental illness is a concern for "all of us" makes it evident that it is imperative for mental illness to not be something that leads one to be "written off" by society and/or oneself. People with mental illness have considerable gifts and talents to offer society, and we are substantially diminished as a community when we lead their contributions to be excluded. Anything worth accomplishing as a society requires a commitment and concerted effort, and the commitment to overcome mental health stigma will be no different, but I believe that the research-based information I have explained in this book points a way to how it could be done.

In this book I have largely avoided talking about my own experiences, but it is hard to resist talking about them here at the conclusion. In my own adolescence I was somewhat troubled, had few friends, and experienced quite a bit of social anxiety and depression. There were times when I felt that things would never get better and I would never be able live life like a "normal" person. I never developed psychotic symptoms or attempted suicide, but I know that my parents were pretty worried about me for a few years, and I believe that things could have gone that route had I not met the right people. Partly as a result of my decision to learn how to play guitar and connect with people through music, I had a series of positive experiences that helped me to eventually become one of the "mentally well."[a] Sometimes, when I feel myself getting too self-satisfied, I think about the lyrics of a song called "Freaks" by the band *Soul Asylum* that I used to listen to (from their 1986 album *While You Were Out*). I realize that the term "freak" may be offensive to some, but many embrace the term as a badge of honor. The punk rock band *The Ramones* seems to have felt this way when they saw the movie *Freaks*, which inspired them to write their anthem of inclusion, "Pinhead" (which includes the refrain, largely lifted from the film: "Gabba gabba we accept you/gabba gabba one of us"). My favorite part of the song "Freaks" is its conclusion, when the song's target is reminded that he or she needs to remember who they are, as they think about moving on to the mainstream world:

> Have you forgotten?
> Did they spoil you rotten?
> Have you forgotten?
> Have you forgotten?
> You're just another freak
> A beautiful freak
> We are freaks.

The true alternative to stigmatizing is not just tolerating, but accepting and embracing difference. If we can all accept and embrace the beauty of our own "freakness," and recognize it as such, we will be much more likely to accept and embrace the "freakness" of others. Indeed, sometimes the active presentation of the symptoms of mental illness can make this a challenging proposition, but when we learn to embrace one another as complete persons, we will be much less likely to allow negative stereotypes to lead us to completely discredit people and deny their humanity.

---

[a] Of course, I say this in full recognition of the reality that things can change in the future given the many biological and environmental vicissitudes of life.

References

1 Lillienfield, S. O., Smith, S. F., & Watts, A. L. (2013). Issues in diagnosis: Conceptual issues and controversies. In W. E. Craighead, D. J. Miklowitz & L. W. Craighead (Eds.), *Psychopathology* (2nd Ed., p. 10). Hoboken, NJ: Wiley.

2 Treatment Advocacy Center (2014). What is the main cause of stigma against people with serious mental illness? Accessed online August 16, 2017: www .treatmentadvocacycenter.org/storage/documents/backgrounders/what%20is% 20the%20main%20cause%20of%20stigma%20against%20individuals%20with %20serious%20mental%20illness%20final.pdf.

3 Lieberman, J., & Ogas, O. (2015). *Shrinks: The untold story of psychiatry.* New York: Little Brown & Co.

4 Global Anti-Stigma Alliance. Accessed online August 16, 2017: www.time-to-change.org.uk/globalalliance.

5 Henderson, C., Evans-Lacko, S., & Thornicroft, G. (2017). The Time to Change programme to reduce stigma and discrimination in England and its wider context. In W. Gaebel, W. Rossler & N. Sartorius (Eds.), *The stigma of mental illness – end of the story?* (pp. 339–356). Basel: Springer International.

6 Accessed online August 16, 2017: www.time-to-change.org.uk/resources-youth-professionals/video-resources.

7 Corker, E., Hamilton, S., Robinson, E., Cotney, J., Pinfold, V., Rose, D., Thornicroft, G., & Henderson, C. (2016). Viewpoint survey of mental health service users' experiences of discrimination in England 2008–2014. *Acta Psychiatrica Scandinavica, 134,* 6–13.

8 Mehta, N., Clement, S., Marcus, E., Stona, A.-C., Bezborodovs, N., Evans-Lacko, S., et al. (2015) Evidence for effective interventions to reduce mental health-related stigma and discrimination in the medium and long term: Systematic review. *British Journal of Psychiatry, 207,* 377–384.

9 Corrigan, P. W., Morris, S. B., Michaels, P. J., Rafacz J. E., & Rüsch, N. (2012). Challenging the public stigma of mental illness: A meta-analysis of outcome studies. *Psychiatric Services, 63,* 963–973.

10 Gaebel, W., Rossler, W., & Sartorius, N. (2017). Conclusion and recommendations for future action. In W. Gaebel, W. Rossler & N. Sartorius (Eds.), *The stigma of mental illness – end of the story?* (pp. 641–650). Basel: Springer International.

11 Bratbo, J., & Vedelsby, A. K. (2017). One of Us: The national campaign for anti-stigma in Denmark. In W. Gaebel, W. Rossler & N. Sartorius (Eds.), *The stigma of mental illness – end of the story?* (pp. 317–338). Basel: Springer International.

12 Jones, S. (2016). Trump: 'Build . . . institutions for people that are sickos. We have sickos all over the place.' *CNSNews.* Accessed online August 16, 2017: www.cnsnews.com/news/article/susan-jones/trump-buildinstitutions-people-are-sickos-we-have-sickos-all-over-place/.

13 Committee on the Science of Changing Behavioral Health Social Norms. (2016). *Ending discrimination against people with mental and substance use*

disorders: The evidence for stigma change. Washington, DC: National Academies Press.

14 Cunningham, R., Peterson, R., & Collings, S. (2017). Like Minds, Like Mine: 17 years of countering stigma and discrimination against people with experience of mental distress in New Zealand. In W. Gaebel, W. Rossler & N. Sartorius (Eds.), *The stigma of mental illness – end of the story?* (pp. 641–650). Basel: Springer International.

15 Sayce, K. (2016). *From psychiatric patient to citizen revisited.* London: Palgrave.

16 Chan, G., & Yanos, P. T. (In Press). Media depictions and the priming of mental illness stigma. *Stigma and Health.*

17 Whitely, R. & Wang, J. (In Press). Television coverage of mental illness in Canada: 2013–2015. *Social Psychiatry and Psychiatric Epidemiology.*

18 Corrigan, P. W., Morris, S. B., Michaels, P. J., Rafacz J. E., & Rüsch, N. (2012). Challenging the public stigma of mental illness: A meta-analysis of outcome studies. *Psychiatric Services, 63*, 963–973.

19 National Alliance on Mental Illness. Accessed online August 16, 2017: www.nami.org/Find-Support/NAMI-Programs/NAMI-Ending-the-Silence.

20 Martin, J. A., Hamilton, B. E., & Ventura, S. J. (2015). *Births: Final data for 2014.* Hyattsville, MD: National Center for Health Statistics.

21 Heinssen, R. K., Goldstein, A. B., & Azrin, S. T. (2014). *Evidence-based treatments for first episode psychosis: Components of coordinated specialty care.* National Institute for Mental Health. Accessed online August 16, 2017: www .nimh.nih.gov/health/topics/schizophrenia/raise/nimh-white-paper-csc-for-fep_ 147096.pdf.

22 Kane, J., Robinson, D. G., Schooler, N. R., Mueser, K. T., Penn, D. L., Rosenheck, R. A., et al. (2016). Comprehensive versus usual community care for first episode psychosis: 2-year outcomes from the NIMH RAISE early treatment program. *The American Journal of Psychiatry, 173*, 362–372.

23 Naslund, J. A., Aschbrenner, K. A., Marsch, L. A., & Bartels, S. J. (2016). The future of mental health care: Peer-to-peer support and social media. *Epidemiology and Psychiatry Services, 25*, 113–122.

24 Chong, E. K., Zhang, Y., Mak, W. S., & Pang, I. Y. (2015). Social media as social capital of LGB individuals in Hong Kong: Its relations with group membership, stigma, and mental well-being. *American Journal of Community Psychology, 55*, 228–238.

Index